> To Bob Hammel,
> Thank you for helping to make Jim's dream of leaving this written record become real.
> — Virginia

Jim McCartney:
My Life in Flight

by

James F. McCartney
and
Angela McCartney Miró

Copyright © 2012 James F. McCartney and Angela McCartney Miró
All rights reserved.

ISBN: 1470012936
ISBN 13: 9781470012939

Library of Congress Control Number: 2012902295
CreateSpace, North Charleston, SC

Dedications

James F. McCartney

Dedicated to my children and grandchildren, who always delighted me, and to all the pilots and others I met during my aviation career.

Angela McCartney Miró

Dedicated to my friend and sister-in-law, Virginia Balch Landrum McCartney, and to my family and friends.

Acknowledgments

Thanks to Bob Hammel for reading and editing a later draft. Thanks to John Swanson for reading an early draft and reading Bob's edited draft. Thanks to Bob and John for their compliments and encouragement. Thanks to Connie and Claire Carney for reading Bob's edited draft with the unedited "Final Chapter." Thanks to Phillissa Russell, Deborah Sutton and Kathy Connell for reading incomplete drafts and encouraging us to continue.

Table of Contents

Regular text by James F. McCartney
Italic text by Angela McCartney Miro

1. Introduction   1

Part One: Childhood

2. Growing Up   9
3. Return to Arkansas in 1941   15
4. Venture into Capitalism   25

Part Two: Becoming A Pilot

5. Off into the Wild Blue Yonder   31
6. Pursuit of an Airline Career   39
7. Seeking Flight Positions   43

Part Three: Pan American Sulphur

8. Pan American Sulphur   49
9. Mexico Adventures   53
10. Politics   57
11. Flying at Pan American Sulphur   59
12. Eastern Airlines   63
13. Return to Pan American Sulphur   67

Part Four: Airline Career

14. Trans Texas Airlines (TTA)   73
15. People and Events   81
16. Labor Relations and ALPA   99

17.	Based In Dallas	105
18.	Enter Frank Lorenzo	109
19.	Lorenzo Takes the Helm	113
20.	Operational Problems with Lorenzo	119
21.	Weight and Balance Issues	125
22.	Two-Man Crew Issue	133
23.	Flight Operations at TI	139
24.	In-Flight Emergencies	149
25.	Labor Relations at TTA, TI and Continental	161
26.	Contract Negotiations	165
27.	Purchase of Continental	175
28.	Lorenzo Makes a Run for Eastern	183
29.	Trans Star f/k/a Muse Air	185
30.	Evergreen Airlines	187
31.	America West Airlines	197
32.	The Captain Speaks	215

Part Five: Retirement Years

33.	Flight Instructor; Buying & Selling Airplanes	221
34.	Aviation Program at Arkansas State College, Newport, Arkansas	227
35.	Newport Airport Commission	235
36.	Taylor Made Ambulance, Corporate Pilot	239
37.	BMG Aviation; Flight Instructor; Charter Pilot	245
38.	My Final Chapter	249

Part Six: Pancreatic Cancer Prognosis And Treatment

39.	Diagnosis/Prognosis of Pancreatic Cancer	255
40.	Cancer Crisis	273
41.	Treatment with Theraspheres	279
42.	More Chemo	283
43.	Unrelated Hiccup	285
44.	Continuing Chemo and Problems	287
45.	Hospice	291
46.	Facts about Pancreatic Cancer	295
	Glossary	297

Appendix:

Appendix A	Chronology of Aviation Career	301
Appendix B	NTSB Report Number NTSB-AAR-74-4: First Two Pages Only	302
Appendix C	ALPA Code Of Ethics	304
Appendix D	The Straight Bull Newsletter	307
Appendix E	T-Pattern Instrument Panel	310
Appendix F	Jim McCartney Treatment for Pancreatic Cancer: Chemo And Diagnostic Tests; Lab Work; CA 19-9 Tumor Markers	311

CHAPTER 1

Introduction

The cockpit of an airplane is the most comfortable place I can be. It is where I feel most relaxed, at home and at peace with God, the universe and within. I've been blessed. I did the one thing I wanted to do, that I loved, during my whole life – fly airplanes. I have six logbooks covering some fifty years of flying. The logbooks are reminders of many events. Some of the stories I have told many times, others are new.

I was diagnosed with Stage IV pancreatic cancer with metastases to the liver in August 2010. It was shocking to realize that my time on earth was limited. Three oncologists gave me three months to live, but 18 months later, I'm still here. Because of that diagnosis, I decided to record some of the things that happened during my aviation career. It is a special blessing to have this time to put down my life experiences for my children and grandchildren.

In writing about my aviation experiences, I particularly want to pay tribute to the many pilots and others I encountered in the field of aviation to whom I owe a tremendous debt. They taught me about flying, negotiating and life in general. I learned many lessons that have served me well during my life and the aviation career I love.

I reviewed my six logbooks and the following is a shortlist of the incidents that occurred while flying [See Appendix A: Chronology of Aviation Career]:
There are 29,391 hours in my logbooks.
12 engines were lost when I was in the cockpit.
Two major flight control malfunctions occurred.
Two radio failures occurred.
I made one gear up landing.
I received one bomb threat.
Two airplanes were hit by lightning while I was in the cockpit.

I didn't know anything about the life of an airline pilot. I didn't know any airline pilots when I was growing up. I had no mentors other than my family. I did not anticipate the direction of my career in aviation. All I knew was that I wanted to fly airplanes. When I actually started flying for an airline, I became aware of the pilots union and its role in setting the pay scale for the pilots, addressing safety issues, gaining benefits for the pilots, and the interaction with other employee unions. At the same time, it seemed obvious to me that a pilot's pay is dependent upon the financial health of the airline, but many pilots do not understand that the airline's financial status directly affects the pilot's paycheck. I became interested in developing more efficient and cost-effective ways of operating an airline. The existing structure of an airline sets up an adversarial atmosphere between an airline's management and its pilots. The exception in the industry is the ever-profitable Southwest Airlines, which embraces its personnel with a fun workplace atmosphere. There are underlying issues that affect the entire structure: seniority system; pilots who take advantage of other pilots; and the fact that not all pilots are created equal but all pilots seem to move into the Captain's seat irrespective of any demonstrated technical or cockpit management expertise, or the lack thereof.

A pilot's neighbor may observe him mowing his yard in the middle of the afternoon and may think he only works part-time or is unemployed. The neighbor does not realize that the pilot may have been flying half the night. When I first started flying, my neighbors thought I didn't have a job because I was home so much. Some offered to help

INTRODUCTION

me find a job. When I was new to the airline, I was on reserve status and had to be home waiting for the call to fly. Often during that time, I flew from midnight until 6 a.m. ferrying military recruits from Houston to Fort Polk, Louisiana, for basic training.

A passenger boards a commercial aircraft with two pilots in the cockpit for a two-hour flight from Dallas to Indianapolis. Looks like an easy day and a cushy job. What the passenger may not realize is that the flight originated in Los Angeles, with stops in Dallas and Indianapolis, and terminates in New York, only to make a turnaround for the return to Los Angeles with the same Indianapolis and Dallas stops. That sometimes causes a 16-hour day, but the pilots are paid only for the time from the start of engines until the engines are stopped for each leg of the flight. Pilots are not paid for the wait time between flights. Pilots are not paid for any pre-flight work such as running the checklist or reviewing weather reports on destinations and alternates. Pilots are required to arrive at least one-hour prior to departure. Pilots can be scheduled for a 14-hour duty period. That duty period can be extended two hours if bad weather or maintenance is encountered. During those duty periods, a pilot may have to wait between two to four hours before the flight continues. Again, the pilot is only paid for actual flight time – from engine start to engine shut down.

I didn't know anything about unions, or how they changed the work place in America, but it was something I should have known. Mom and Dad both worked in the automobile factories in Detroit, and were active in the UAW local labor union there, alongside Dad's two brothers and three sisters. Strangely, my Dad never discussed his union membership with me, but he did talk about it to my sister.

Jamie, the name I have called my brother since childhood, always knew he wanted to be a pilot when he grew up. He is probably the only person I know who had a dream for his life from an early age, achieved that dream and thoroughly enjoyed his life. I didn't have a plan for my life, rather just did what had to be done until I finally stumbled into something that I loved – being a paralegal. I have always admired my brother and enjoyed watching him work to achieve his ambition. When he bought a PT-19 army trainer in the late 50s, I flew with him in the open cockpit as he worked to build his hours. Over the years I watched as he attained each goal on his path to becoming an airline pilot. After he became an airline pilot, he became a union negotiator to improve working conditions and safety practices in aviation. He also worked as a charter pilot, corporate pilot, check airman, and flight instructor. He has shared his enthusiasm for flight with everyone he met from grade school students, to doctors and lawyers, and to a reluctant Presbyterian minister.

Daddy and I both read the newspaper daily and usually discussed whatever was being written that was of the most interest – labor unions, politics and baseball. I once asked Daddy if he had ever belonged to a union and he said, "Yes." He said they went on strike mainly to improve working conditions. When Daddy first started working in the factory, the engine had to be lifted by several men and placed inside the chassis of the automobile. That was back breaking labor to say the least. The men on the assembly line decided it would be better to lift the engine by ropes attached to an overhead pulley that could be moved along a track to place the engine above the chassis then slowly lowered into the chassis. The idea was submitted to management but they declined to make the change. During a subsequent contract negotiation and strike, this became an issue and it was eventually implemented. When Mother was an auxiliary member of the union during one strike, she was appointed to a union committee to go to Lansing to speak to the Governor of Michigan in an effort to get him to intervene so the men could get back to work.

Many people live ordinary lives. My brother and I have lived such lives, and mostly the people we know are ordinary people like us. Everyone has challenges in life, rich or poor, ordinary or elite. People learn from their own mistakes and sometimes from the mistakes of others. Life is not easy for anyone. Everyone meets snags in life's flight plan.

I read a book in the 1960s about a young mother diagnosed with lymphoma. The book was <u>Walking Through the Fire</u> by Laurel Lee. Her cancer treatment was harsh and she was not expected to survive. Her condition was so dire that her husband sold her clothes. She divorced the husband, not because he sold her clothes, but because it was one more indication of his inability to cope with her illness. She recovered, got her life back, and wrote the book – a best-seller at the time. It impressed me because she had no discernible training or ability to

INTRODUCTION

do what she did, but she met the challenge. She studied medical books about lymphoma and actively participated in her treatment. She was an "ordinary" person. Many "ordinary" people face extraordinary circumstances and call upon an indefinable spirit inside to find their path to success. Success is not always defined by healing; sometimes success is acceptance of the inevitable.

At age 43, our Dad faced the diagnosis of terminal lung cancer with grace. Our Mother called M.D. Anderson to see if that cancer research hospital would be willing to treat Daddy with any experimental regimens they were investigating with the understanding that it would not benefit him, but might help in research that could benefit others in the future. The answer was no. Yet my Dad told me one morning at the breakfast table that he had lived a good life and he was glad that Jamie and I were grown, and he (our Dad) was at peace. That gave me a lot of comfort. Daddy died more peacefully than anyone I have known before or since.

People walk similar paths through life, choosing one path over another, or going where the wind blows. All of us face the unthinkable, the unexpected, and what we believe to be unbearable, yet we cope with adversity as well as our experiences and beliefs have made us capable. Jamie found his hidden reserve that made it possible for him to cope with his diagnosis of Stage IV pancreatic cancer. The second Friday after his diagnosis, he told me that he had been praying that God would help him and he had a sudden feeling of peace that all would be well and that finally he (Jamie) felt at peace with the situation no matter what the outcome may turn out to be. On Sunday, Jamie, Virginia (his wife), Tammy (his daughter) and I went to Jamie and Virginia's church, United Presbyterian Church in Bloomington, Indiana. The pastor told the congregation that he had special words in his sermon for Jim in light of his cancer diagnosis. At that moment, Jamie stood up and told the congregation about his prayer, and that it had been answered and he was at peace with whatever might come. I was proud.

Part One
Childhood

CHAPTER 2

Growing Up

I was born October 31, 1937, in Detroit, Michigan. Mom and Dad lived with my Dad's sister, her husband, and their four children, while awaiting the birth of their own first child – me. My cousins-to-be were out on Halloween night for trick or treating, but they would often stop by to see if I had been born yet. Eventually, I was born at 11:30 p.m. A few days later, Mom and Dad moved into a place of their own and lived in Michigan another four years.

When Jamie was born in Detroit, the doctor Mother expected to come out to deliver the baby was not on call. Instead, Dr. Brent arrived. He was young and good-looking. Mother was 18 and just about died of embarrassment to have her first baby delivered by a handsome young doctor that she had never seen before.

In August 1940, Mom and I went to visit her parents, Jim and Brooxie Kelley, in Balch, Arkansas to await the birth of my parents' second and last child. Mom wanted Dr. Harris for this birth because he promised he would help her with the pain of childbirth. *Dr. Harris was much older and looked like a grandfather; I think that was the main reason she wanted to go back to Arkansas for the birth of her second child.* Dad came later just in time to go get Dr. Harris in Newport. On August 15, 1940, I was sitting on the front porch swing at Grandpa Kelley's house and I heard my sister, Angela Broox McCartney, come into the world. She was born inside the house and all the windows were open on that hot and humid August day. As I sat in the front porch swing, I heard her start to cry.

Another reason Mother wanted to go to Arkansas for the birth of the second baby was that Grandma Kelley took the train to Detroit for the birth of Jamie. When Grandma Kelley arrived in Detroit, no one was there to meet her at the train station. She used her egg money for a taxi to go to the address for Mother and Daddy's new apartment. When she got there, the apartment was empty. Grandma Kelley got back in the taxi to go to the home of Daddy's sister. Needless to say, she was angry; and she never let anyone forget it! No one ever said how long she stayed in Detroit but it was probably a short visit. I'm pretty sure she made it clear she was not making the trip again.

Two weeks after I was born, the family was packed for the return automobile trip to Detroit with Grandma Kelley's pithy comment to Daddy ringing in Mother's ears: "I hope you have enough money to buy a casket because your wife is going to need one!"

I doubt that Daddy paid any attention to the comment but Mother never forgot it. Daddy didn't have to buy a casket for his wife. She bought one for him 20 years later in 1960. Daddy died at age 43 of lung cancer. Mother died in 2009 at age 90 of lymphoma.

While living in Detroit, Mother had her hands full keeping up with Jamie. He was always getting into mischief. He was not mean, sickly or troublesome, just adventurous. Once while living in an apartment building, Jamie, who was three or four at the time, was outside playing. He found a hammer and used it to tap on every ground-level basement window, and every window he tapped shattered. The landlord caught him and took him to Mother. She said she was sorry and the only thing she knew to do was to pay for the damage, even though they really didn't have the money. The landlord felt sorry for her and said if she would pay for the glass, he would install the windows. She was appreciative.

Jamie cried a lot as an infant. She thought he was spoiled because he was the only baby around in a large extended family. He was such a pretty baby with dark hair and blue eyes that everyone wanted to play with him, so he got used to being held and entertained. He never wanted to go to bed at night and had to be rocked to sleep every night. When Grandpa Kelley carried him around, he would walk the floor with him. Then he would walk a few steps and stop.

Grandpa Kelley would tell Jamie, "Kick, son. Kick if you want Grandpa to walk."

Quickly, Jamie learned to kick his foot so Grandpa Kelley would start walking again. That made Grandpa Kelley so proud! He told the story for years and years.

When the family settled into an apartment in Detroit after I was born, the first night Mother was so busy setting up her household and bathing the new baby that she forgot about Jamie. After I was asleep, she looked around and Jamie had fallen asleep by himself on the floor. She said he was as dirty as a little pig after playing all day, so she picked him up, gave him a sponge bath from head to toe, put pajamas on him, and put him to bed. He didn't wake up while she undressed, bathed and dressed him. Every night after that, he went to bed by himself and immediately went to sleep. He never needed to be rocked again. After her experience with Jamie, Mother didn't let anyone that came along pick me up. She didn't want me to be spoiled.

One day as Jamie was outside playing, Mother heard her Italian neighbor, Rose, call Jamie a "god damn hillbilly!" Mother went outside, grabbed Rose by the hair of her head, and started hitting her. She got Rose down on the ground and started pounding her head against the sidewalk. Someone pulled Mother off Rose, who was hysterical. Mother told Rose she'd better keep her mouth shut from now on. Mother grabbed Jamie and took him back to her apartment. The police came and talked to Rose. The policeman knocked on Mother's door and asked for her side of the story. She told him Rose's comment was the last straw in a long string of comments she had made about Jamie. And to emphasize, Mother told him that if Rose ever bothered her child again, she would do the same thing to her all over again. The policeman left and Mother was not arrested. From that day forward, when Mother walked down the sidewalk, Rose would cross the street to avoid meeting her.

Mother always ended the story with, "You better not bother one of my kids!"

We were in Detroit when the Japanese bombed Pearl Harbor. Daddy wanted to join the army, but was not accepted. He worked in the automobile industry and was considered a critical worker for the war effort. The automobile factories were converted to support the building of war material, munitions, guns and aircraft. No cars were built during World War II.

Mother was a stalwart Southern Baptist and did not intend to succumb to a degenerate and sinful life, as lived by Daddy's siblings. They

Snapshot of the authors as children in Detroit

all smoked (which was okay, but Mother never smoked), drank alcohol (not okay) and gambled (not okay). One day in Detroit she left me at home with Daddy when I was only a few months old while she took Jamie shopping. When she got home, Mother found Daddy and his brothers sitting at the kitchen table shooting dice and gambling. She picked up the dice and threw them out the window and told them,

"There will be no gambling in my house!"

Next, she turned to the female neighbor who was feeding me a bottle, and took me from her arms.

The woman authoritatively said, "I know how to take care of a baby, I had a baby."

Mother retorted, "And it died, too, didn't it?"

That cleared the room. Everyone went home. There was no alcohol or gambling in our home.

CHAPTER 3

Return to Arkansas in 1941

*C*aring for Grandpa McCartney: *Daddy was the youngest of seven children – two brothers, three sisters, and a brother who died as a child before Daddy was born. The McCartneys grew up in rural Arkansas where they farmed with their parents. Gradually all the McCartney sons and daughters moved to Detroit to work in the auto industry. In 1941, Grandpa McCartney developed what was then thought to be tuberculosis and required care. The McCartney sons and daughters determined that my father and his family would return to Arkansas to take care of Grandpa McCartney. He died in 1945.*

Our family moved to Balch, a small cotton farming community in Jackson County in Northeast Arkansas. I had a wonderful childhood filled with fun – for me. Dad took me with him everywhere – farming, fishing, hunting, the cotton gin and walking the fields. On Sunday afternoons, if Dad was not working in the fields, he drove the family around to look at his cotton fields and all neighboring cotton fields to compare crops. Dad always pointed out that the rows he plowed were straight as an arrow. He was proud of that precision. Dad would stop by each field and we would walk across the cotton rows to closely inspect the cotton plants, their health and growth. In the spring, the cotton was planted then weeds were chopped out of the rows with a hoe. In the fall, the cotton was picked, taken to the gin to be seeded and processed into bales and sold. That's when the money rolled in. After money was put aside for next year's cotton crop, Mom and Dad bought for the family's needs for the home – food and clothing. Many items were ordered from the Sears & Roebuck catalog.

Farming: Dad was progressive in his approach to farming. He went to Farm Bureau meetings, visited with other farmers and became acquainted with the County Extension Agents who were promoting the use of new and innovative farming practices. Even though our Dad had a limited education (through sixth grade, before he left school to work on the family farm), he was always interested in learning about everything. He read every page of the newspaper daily – from front to back. On Sunday afternoons after church, we all piled up on the bed and Dad read the comics to Angela and me. We learned early not to mess with the newspaper until he had finished reading it. That wasn't much of a problem since he was always the first one awake to get the paper. Dad had the first automatic cotton picker in that area of Arkansas. He was the first to experiment with herbicide control on cotton plants, the first to use anhydrous ammonia as fertilizer for his cotton crops. He applied anhydrous ammonia to his cotton field to the derisive comments of fellow farmers. All those derisive comments vanished when Dad's cotton yield outstripped those of his neighbors. Next spring, Dad developed a new income source by applying anhydrous ammonia to the crops of his neighbors eager to achieve the same yield Dad had demonstrated was possible. I had a great time growing up on the farm. Dad bought me a 10-horsepower tractor that made me feel like I owned the world. I was about 11 years old and I put a lawn mower on the back of the tractor so I could mow yards around the community to make a little money. One of my first purchases was a shiny Schwinn bicycle.

There was one thing we had on the farm that I was not too enthused about. Dad bought a horse, saddle and bridle. Riding away from the barn, I would really have to work to make that horse move: it only wanted to walk. But going back, when we got within a quarter-mile of the barn, that horse would break out running and I couldn't slow him down. One day

Mom was preparing lunch and needed a loaf of bread and some canned goods, so she sent me to the store on the horse to get what she needed. I was about nine. I saddled up the horse and rode to the store about a mile away. I had a loaf of bread and two or three cans in a paper sack and got on the horse to go home. The horse walked along until we got about a quarter–mile from the house, then it broke and ran. I was hanging on for dear life and the grocery sack broke open. The cans fell out of the sack onto the road and the bread tumbled out after the cans. The gates to the barn were usually open but when we got near the barn, the gates were closed. I thought the horse was going to run into the gates and I was trying to get off. But the horse stopped on all fours in front of the gate and I went over the horse's head, banged right into the gate, and broke the boards in the gate. I put the horse in the stable and removed the bridle and saddle. I walked back down the road and picked up the bread and cans. I really didn't enjoy that horse. That was the one thing on the farm that I really did not like.

Growing Okra: In the early 50's Bird's Eye Frozen Foods opened a processing plant in Searcy, Arkansas – about 35 miles away – to prepare and package frozen okra. Dad got wind of this and arranged not only to grow okra for the plant but also to pick up okra from other growers and deliver all the fresh picked okra to the processing plant in Searcy. I went on several of those trips with Dad.

Driving: Dad taught me how to drive all the farm equipment, including the truck. Once I was in the field with Dad, and he sent me to the house to get something he needed. I got in the truck, started it up, and started driving home. I had to cross a really narrow wooden bridge over the ditch near our house, but I made it without incident. Mother looked out the window and saw the truck coming. When the truck got closer, she couldn't see a driver in the truck. That gave her some pause. When I stopped at the house, she realized it was me driving the truck. I was about 9 years old and could just barely see through the windshield.

Before that, Mom was teaching me to drive a Chrysler coupe that we had, with me sitting on her lap. When we turned into the yard of the house, Mother pushed the brake pedal and it went to the floorboard – no brakes, and, of course, no seatbelts. We hit the front of the house. I was about 6; Angie was thrown into the windshield and got a bump on her head. That was the only injury. It was a treat to ride in the back of the pickup. When it was time to pick cotton, Dad put wooden sides on the back of the pickup to hold the cotton that was picked for transport to the gin. It was even more fun to ride on top of the cotton.

My Dog, Blackie: When I was about seven or eight, Dad bought me a dog that I named Blackie. I picked him from a litter of puppies. Dad tried to train Blackie to be a squirrel dog, but Blackie was not interested. Blackie had long black shiny hair with tan spots. He looked a bit like a hound and became my constant companion as I roamed across the fields, down by the ditches and under small wooden bridges. While Blackie wouldn't hunt squirrel, he loved killing snakes and we had lots of snakes – water moccasins one of the most deadly. Frequently Blackie would spot a snake before I did, and grab it before I stepped on it. One day, I was out with one of my friends, Terry Balch, who lived just down the road from us. There was another house and an old barn across the road and between our houses. Terry and I crossed over the road to the barn. It was a spooky place with old cow bones lying about. As we left the barn, Blackie found a snake. To kill a snake, Blackie would grab its middle with his mouth and shake it from side to side really hard, then turn it loose when the snake was dead. This time, when Blackie turned the snake loose, the snake flew through the air, hit Terry, and wrapped around his neck. Terry's voice reached a high pitch and he was in a panic. I would have died if it had happened to me! It was not a poisonous snake, but it was deader than a doornail when Blackie turned it loose. Blackie never let go of a snake until it was no longer able to slither away through the grass.

First House on the Farm: Our first house in Balch was known as the Dallas Johnson house, located near the Balch cemetery. There was a big tree in the back yard, a garden, a barn, and an apple orchard that separated the house from the cemetery. I don't remember being afraid of the cemetery because it was a place we frequently visited. Mom went there with Grandma Kelley from the time she was a child to tend the graves of relatives. Grandparents, great-grandparents, aunts, uncles, cousins and friends are buried there. Mom and Dad were both laid to rest there.

First Prank: Mom and Dad loved movies and often took us to double-feature movies in Detroit. Back in Balch there was no movie theater. However, one enterprising venture put up a tent near the Balch store (owned by Seth Overstreet) and ran movies on the weekends. He charged ten cents to see the feature film, Movietone news, and an adventure serial titled, "The Jungle Girl," and the main character was Nyoka. That jungle business so inspired me that I planned one of my first pranks. I tied string about my body and limbs and stuffed sage grass under the string to give myself an "apelike" appearance. I climbed up the tree in the backyard of the Dallas Johnson house and called my gullible little sister, Angela, age 4, to come out in the back yard. She came out and I jumped out of the tree in front of her in an apelike stance with apelike grunts and gestures. I can still hear her scream as she raced back into the house.

Angie Sees a Thing: Another time in the same house, Angela came in from outside and told Mom that there was a "thing" on the back of the barn.

Mom asked "What kind of thing?"

Angela said, "I don't know, just a big thing."

Mom armed herself with a kitchen knife and we trekked out to the barn. Slithering down the backside of the barn was a King snake. That was considered a good thing. King snakes are non-poisonous, and good for killing mice and rats. The King snake was normally a welcome guest in the barn, but Mom got the hoe and killed it.

Model Airplanes: Angela became the audience for my pranks, served as my co-pilot as we pretended to fly at the kitchen table, and if I overstepped, she would retaliate by poking her finger through the tissue paper of one of my model airplanes. I have wanted to fly airplanes since I started talking. My first four years were spent in Detroit with older cousins who were interested in flying. One went on to become a flight engineer during World War II and had a good flight career with various airlines after the War. After we moved back to Arkansas I spent many hours building model airplanes out of balsa wood, glue and tissue paper that came in model airplane kits. If one were to be destroyed, I greatly preferred to simulate a dogfight and have the plane go down in flames rather than having my little sister poke her finger into the tissue paper fuselage. Most of the time, I hung the models from the ceiling to keep them out of her reach.

Air Base in Newport: In Newport the Army Air Corps built an airbase for training pilots during World War II. There were several auxiliary fields used to shoot touch-and-go landings. Near our house was an area used for practice bombing. I loved watching the planes fly over. Whatever I was doing, I would stop and watch. Frequently they would buzz tractors in the field and obviously had lots of fun scaring the farmers. It was really a thrill to me. One time when the base was still in operation, everyone was invited to come out to the base for a tour, and to go swimming. We did that and had great fun swimming in the pool. After the War, the field stayed open for a couple of years. After it closed, my Dad and I went out to the abandoned base in the late 40s, probably 1949, when I was about 11 or 12. All the hangars were still there and many of the buildings were still standing. We drove out on the flight line. Next to one of the hangars was an old stripped down PT-19, the wings gone and the fuselage fabric missing. The tail was still there but the elevators were gone. I wanted my Dad to take the airplane home so I could play with it. He said, "No, it still belongs to the government." The government was long gone. Another thing that kept fueling my ambition to become a pilot was watching those guys flying during World War II in the air and on Movietone News reels in the theater. It was exciting and dramatic. One farmer was milking his cow in late-afternoon when a bomb came through the roof of his barn. It was a practice bomb with no explosives in it, but it scared the devil out of the farmer.

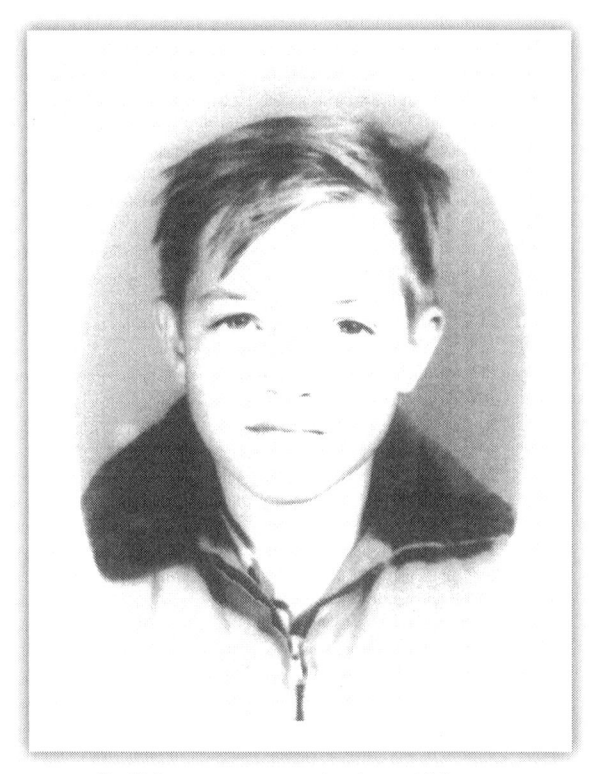

Jim McCartney as a young boy in rural Arkansas

Education in Balch: We went to grade school in Balch and it was bad – three rooms, three grades to a room– one for grades 1-3, one for grades 4-6, and one room for inside recess during bad weather. I never took a test until I went to the high school in Newport, the county seat of Jackson County (approximate population of 7,254). [As an aside, when I moved back to Newport a lifetime later after marrying my childhood sweetheart who lived there, the population was 7,811. The City of Newport had experienced minimal growth since I left in 1954.]

To get an improved education for the children in the Balch community, Dad and others in the Balch community prepared and carried a petition around for signatures to consolidate the Balch school with the Newport Independent School District, so we could go to school in Newport, on a big yellow school bus, and get a better education than had been available to our parents.

The summer before I was scheduled to go to Newport High School, Dad decided, after the poor education in Balch, I needed help to make it in high school. Dad sent me to summer school. I would not have made it in high school if he had not done that. One of the teachers I had that summer was Miss Irma Shoffner who was related to my Dad. She took me under her wing and taught me a lot.

One important lesson I learned at Newport High School was it was personally beneficial for me to take a mess of quail to Mrs. Getty, my Algebra teacher. In return, she gave me the special attention I needed to ensure that I learned Algebra and fully understood the concepts. Dad and I also took the Agriculture teacher to hunt quail. I was active in Future Farmers of America (FFA) and entered numerous cattle-judging contests to keep my Ag teacher happy. Another of my high school pursuits was public speaking.

First Tractor: When we were farming in Balch, we had the first tractor in the community — a green John Deere. Grandpa Kelley lived down the road from us when we first moved to the Dallas Johnson house in Balch. He and his son, Walker Kelley, had three teams of mules. Grandpa Kelley saw how well Daddy's tractor worked out so he bought a tractor the next year. In Balch, Dad rented land from Seth Overstreet, who owned many acres of land in the Balch Community. Seth owned the store in Balch and was the Postmaster. Seth built a four-room house for our family, but it was still close to Grandpa and Grandma Kelley.

Uncle Walker, Aunt Bonnie and their five children, Phillip, Carolyn, Walker Junior, Kay and Michael also lived near us. Phillip, the oldest in their family, was a year younger than Angela. They were fun playmates for Angela and me. We had some really good times with 4-H projects, trips and contests; Halloween hayrides, parties, etc.; picnics and trips to Memphis and Little Rock; fishing and swimming at Pickett Lake; Kelley family dinners at Grandma Kelley's house with Mom's four siblings, Mary, Dely, Mage and Walker, and their children, our cousins. Mom and Aunt Bonnie frequently loaded the kids into the back of the pickup and carted us all over Jackson County for various activities. Sometimes we went swimming in the irrigation pool of a rice farm – but not often, it was not safe.

Our House in Balch: *The house in Balch was a bare-bones minimum 4-room structure, no bathroom (an outhouse) and no running water. We had a hand pump on the back porch. That was a nice step-up in status because Grandma Kelley's pump was in the middle of her back yard next to the iron wash pot. The house was covered with "brick siding" – not brick, it was black tar paper coated with a grainy sand-like material in the shape of bricks with the black paper showing through as the "mortar" between the bricks. We did have electricity provided by the REA (Rural Electric Administration). I remember the house being very cozy and comfortable, but it certainly did not have the type of insulation used today. Mom filled the windows with lace curtains, and made crocheted doilies and embroidered scarves with crochet trim and covered all furniture surfaces with her handwork. To keep us entertained during cold weather, Mother kept Jamie and me occupied embroidering dishtowels. We had a radio and listened to "Baby Snooks," "Amos 'n Andy," "The Shadow," "Inner Sanctum" and many other radio programs of the day. We had an oblong tin tub on the back porch that we used for Saturday night baths – whether we needed them or not. We had an electric washing machine with a wringer on top and two round tin tubs for rinsing. Our clothes and bed linens were washed weekly and put through the wringer after the wash cycle and into the two tubs, the second laced with "bluing" to make the whites whiter, and* *again run through the wringer after each rinse. Then the laundry was hung outside on the clothesline to dry. The clothing had to be ironed. The lace curtains were put on stretchers outside to dry so they did not have to be ironed.*

With his increasing farming success, Dad was generous in providing for his family. He bought Mom one of the first electric stoves in the community to replace the oil cook stove. He also bought her an electric Singer sewing machine in a modern wooden cabinet with a padded stool covered with brown leather. I still have the cabinet but Mother traded the Singer for a Necchi machine in the 60s. I still have Grandma Kelley's treadle Singer sewing machine that she purchased in the 20s – she probably purchased it used. When he bought the electric sewing machine, Dad bought himself a new shotgun and one for Jamie. Jamie was 10 or 11, but he and Daddy needed those shotguns for their frequent quail hunting trips. We were in "high cotton."

CHAPTER 4

Venture into Capitalism

After a few years in Balch, my Dad bought a farm in Pennington, about two miles from Balch. I met Billy Tate in Pennington. We were about 14 or 15 and hit it off immediately. We both liked to hunt and fish. Both of our Dads were farmers so we had a lot of land to roam and hone our hunting and fishing skills. Soon we went into business together.

We moved into the house on the land in Pennington that Daddy bought. It was a wood frame house with an inside bathroom and three bedrooms. It was a nicer house than the one in Balch, but I missed the Balch community and all my cousins and friends!

Rabbit Business: Rabbits became one of our first sources of income. A store in Newport would buy the rabbits we killed – 25 cents each for the cotton tail rabbits, 35 cents each for the bigger swamp rabbits. Our profit margin was directly related to our ability to shoot accurately. With the price of the shotgun shells, if we shot over two shells to kill one rabbit, we lost money. We became pretty good shots. We liked the rabbit business because it was so much fun. One evening

I spent the night at Billy's house. Billy's Dad had planted a wheat field next to their house. At night, the rabbits would come to eat the wheat plants. Billy and I went out that night and shined the truck headlights on the field. The rabbits would freeze in place as the headlights blinded them, which made it easy to shoot them – they were not running. That was illegal, but we did it anyway. When we went out, I sat on the hood of the truck while Billy drove. The first time Billy stopped, I slid off the hood onto the ground because I didn't have anything to hold onto. So I got into the back of the truck. It was great shooting and we killed a lot of rabbits. We weren't paying too much attention to anything other than shooting the rabbits.

Suddenly, Billy's Dad came out on the porch about 10 o'clock that night and yelled, "You boys quit shooting! You're shooting up the house!"

That stopped the rabbit hunting in the wheat field.

We became good, lifelong friends. Billy was, and still is, a great guy.

Billy and I didn't have much money. We rode the school bus and worked in the school cafeteria to get 25 cent school lunches free, so we had our quarter to spend. It was not much money to finance our ambitions.

Selling Fudge: Next Billy and I started making fudge and selling it on the school bus. By the time we got to Newport, our fudge would be sold out for a nickel a bar. Of course, our Moms made the fudge. We bought the ingredients – cocoa and sugar. Mom and I cooked the fudge to the soft-boil stage, beat it to the right consistency, then poured it into aluminum ice trays without the cube separators. When the fudge was firm, Mom cut it into generous bars and wrapped them in waxed paper. One of the bus riders decided he would also go into the money-making fudge business. He started making bigger bars and sold them for a nickel. We sized up the competition on that first day. The next day Billy and I met him when he got on the bus and bought all his fudge. We sold our fudge on the bus and took the competition's fudge to school in Newport where we sold it for ten cents a bar. The town kids could afford the increase in price and didn't know we sold it for five cents a bar on the bus.

Publishing Newspaper: Our next venture into capitalism was a newspaper *(typed on Mom's Underwood manual typewriter with as* *many carbon copies as we could get into the typewriter).* Our "newspaper," which we sold on the school bus with the fudge, reported on various teachers and happenings at school. In the last issue, we reported that the bus driver drove 75 miles per hour on the way to school. School administrators, on a tip from the bus driver, shut down our newspaper, probably because of what we reported, but officially because it was written with such bad grammar and poor spelling, not to mention the many typos. We were home-schooled in typing. Billy and I saved our money from our various money-making ventures and we had about $40 to invest in our next adventure.

Investing: Once Billy and I skipped school to take our $40 to the Thursday cattle auction. We rode the bus to school and walked directly to the cattle auction. The only thing we could afford was an old goat for $16 and we decided we didn't want that. Our next idea was to visit Dr. Jabez Jackson to buy some land. Dr. Jackson owned about 200 acres of land on the Cash River bottoms. He humored us, but $40 was not enough for a down payment on the land. Billy Tate eventually wound up owning that piece of land. Billy and I had great adventures and high school was fun.

* * *

Life Long Best Friend: Billy now operates one of the largest farms in Jackson County. In addition to his farming operation, Billy operates a catfish farm and rents duck blinds. Billy and I visited in September 2011. Mike McDermott, one of my flying students, and Billy came to the motel in Newport where we were staying. Joe Taylor sent his MU-2 airplane from Newport to Bloomington to fly us to Newport for an overnight visit. Angie and I wanted to see the tombstone we had placed on Mom's gravesite in Balch. I was sick with pancreatic cancer. In the middle of our afternoon visit, Billy told us he had received a call from his daughter in Idaho that her 20-year-old son had been injured in an accident while driving a four-wheel ATV. The boy was just 20 years old with two children and a life full or promise ahead of him, but he suffered injuries so severe that it was doubtful he would live. A week later, Billy's only grandson died. In spite of good times, good fortune, we also experience tragedy. That's life.

Part Two
Becoming a Pilot

CHAPTER 5

Off Into the Wild Blue Yonder

I graduated from high school in 1954 when I was 16 years old. With no money to go to college, I decided to join the Air Force. I had always wanted to be a pilot. Mom said one of my first words was "airplane." I was headed to the Air Force. Cadet training started at 18 and a half years but I couldn't join the Air Force until I was 17, which was about five months away. The night before I turned 17, I got on a bus headed for Little Rock and on October 31, 1954, I joined the Air Force. The Air Force put me on a Trans Texas DC-3 that flew from Little Rock to Houston, with stops at Texarkana, Monroe and Lake Charles. Little did I know that 13 years later I would be flying that same Trans Texas DC-3.

Once we were in Houston we new recruits were transferred to another plane that took us to the San Antonio Airport. An Air Force bus took us to the Lackland AFB mess hall where we were served breakfast. Then we marched to our barracks. A sergeant came in and showed us how to make our beds. I knew I wouldn't be able to make my bed again with hospital corners and sheets pulled so tight you could bounce a quarter on the bed. That night I got in bed and didn't move a muscle all night so the bed would still be in good shape in the morning. To this day I cannot sleep with tight covers over my feet.

After three months in basic training, we were tested and placed at various skill levels that determined how we were assigned for additional training. I tested out at the highest technical skill level, and was assigned to the B-47 Aircraft & Engine Mechanics School (training to become an "A&E mechanic") at Amarillo, Texas. I spent three months in the A&E Mechanics training and graduated No. 1 in my class. Because of that ranking, I got to pick the base where I would be stationed. In the meantime, Dad had gotten out of the farming business and my family was living in Houston. I called Dad and gave him a list of my choices. Dad said the closest base was Lake Charles, Louisiana – about 150 miles from Houston. I picked Lake Charles. I was there as part of the 51st Bomb Squadron. Lake Charles Air Force Base had 60 B-47s and 60 KC-97s. I was assigned as a helper to a crew on a B47 with Pappy as crew chief and Barney as assistant crew chief. Lake Charles had been a B-29 operation but converted to jets except for the refueling tankers that were props (KC-97s). Soon, Pappy was discharged and Barney became crew chief and I became assistant crew chief. Six months later, Barney was discharged and I became crew chief. They didn't have any other mechanics to help so they assigned me an air policeman and a cook as my helpers on the B-47. **I was 17 years old and had responsibility for the maintenance of this B-47 airplane on my shoulders.**

In the Air Force it didn't really matter how well you maintained your airplane, if your boots were shined, your fatigues starched and ironed and you drank coffee with the line chief every day, then you were promoted. I didn't do that, didn't make staff sergeant, and was discharged out of the Air Force as airman first class.

When we arrived at Lake Charles, we met the squadron commander, Col. Paxton. He was a West Point graduate and a heck of a pilot. I came in with two other guys and Col. Paxton made the offer that if any of us wanted to go to cadet training, he would be glad to help us. I was interested in the program and sent off for some books to brush up my English and grammar skills. I quickly realized that I didn't have enough time after work to study. During one six-month period, I didn't have a single day off. Frequently they brought our lunches out to the flight line so we could keep working.

Jim McCartney, 18, in Air Force as Crew Chief on B-47 Bomber

Smoking: I did not smoke before I joined the Air Force in 1954. In 1955 when I was based in Lake Charles, I spent all my time working on the flight line where the airplanes were parked. Smoking was not permitted on the flight line. The only way to get off the flight line was to take a cigarette break. With a cigarette in hand, one could go through security and beyond the ramp area for a smoke break. I bought a pack of cigarettes so I could take a break every once in a while. Unfortunately, I couldn't put the cigarettes down as easily as I picked them up.

There was good reason for us to go away from the aircraft for smoking, but I didn't realize it until later. Military aircraft used JP4 fuel. Jet A fuel is the type used in civilian aircraft. JP4 had a lot of gasoline mixed in with it so it would not freeze at higher altitudes. There was no anti-icing capability for the fuel filters on military aircraft. There is anti-icing on civilian aircraft so if ice forms in the fuel there is a differential between the fuel filter going in one side and out the other. If it is more than 1.5 psi, heat is generated for the filter to melt the ice. Jet fuel basically absorbs water so there is always a little water in the fuel and that's why the military adds gasoline to its jet fuel. That is why smoking was not permitted on the ramp.

Two mechanics were working on a fuel cell in a B-47. They created a spark that caused an explosion and fire. It killed the two mechanics and the airplane caught fire. The ramp in Lake Charles was sloped toward the middle so all water would run off the ramp into drains. There were frequent rain showers in Lake Charles because it was close to the Gulf coast. When the airplane blew up, the fuel spilled out into the drainage system. Each airplane holds a little over 16,000 gallons of JP4 jet fuel. When the fuel from the burning aircraft went down the drains, it also caught fire. The fire came up from the drains under two other airplanes and a total of three airplanes were lost that day – burned to the ground. The next day, General Curtis Lemay, head of the Strategic Air Command (SAC), came to Lake Charles AFB and relieved the base Wing Commander from duty.

Advance Base: Our advance base, if we went to war, was Goose Bay, Labrador. We went up there quite often to keep combat-ready.

TDY: We had two temporary duty assignments (TDY) to England, one to Brize Norton AFB and the other to Cheltenham AFB. My first trip over was an adventure. I was a member of the advance party assigned to make sure the base was ready to handle the B-47s. I left Lake Charles AFB on a C-54 to Maguire AFB and had breakfast at Maguire AFB while the ground crew refueled the aircraft. On departure from Maguire, one engine could not make takeoff power. Four hours later, after changing to another aircraft, we were under way to our next fuel stop in Nova Scotia. The next stop was the Azores then on to Brize Norton AFB. The B-47s made the trip nonstop.

Strategic Air Command: SAC rotated B-47 squadrons in and out of Europe so the Air Force could gather intelligence. Before we went to England some of our airplanes were modified to accommodate an electronic counter measure (ECM) pod that was installed in the bomb bay. This ECM pod accommodated two airmen who were trained in electronic warfare. Their job with the ECM was to record the radar frequencies and location of sites used by the Russians. The B-47 would fly close enough to the Russian border to entice the Russians to activate their radar. Occasionally the flight would penetrate Russian airspace. This incursion into Russian airspace would sometimes be blamed on navigational error. The whole squadron would be on edge until these flights returned.

By this time, I was 18 and a half and I realized I didn't want a career in the Air Force. The second time we were in England the Russians launched Sputnik, the first satellite in outer space. From that time on, we were subject to strip alerts where we had to sleep on the flight line next to the airplane so we could launch within 15 minutes from the time the whistle blew. That convinced me I didn't want the Air Force as my career.

Also, I had a co-pilot, an ex-TWA pilot, who was assigned to fly the aircraft to which I was assigned as crew chief. He said, "Son, you don't want to fly in the Air Force; you want to get on with the airlines." That planted the seed for my career plan and solidified my decision on what I wanted to do with my life, and helped me make the decisions on how I was going to get there.

I got out of the Air Force in 1958 and had a plan of attack to get on with the airlines. They required two years of college plus 1,000 hours of multi-engine flying time. Of course, I didn't have any flying time except riding in a B-47. Crew Chiefs were on flying status; therefore, I was required to fly with my aircraft at least 4 hours a month. The flight pay doubled my income; I generally flew about 20 to 40 hours per month. There was not a space for the Crew Chief to fly on the B-47 but there was a jump seat on the steps used to climb into the co-pilot's seat. That was my spot on the B-47 when it was in flight.

Altitude Chamber: Prior to being assigned to flying status, I was required to go through the altitude chamber at Barksdale Air Force Base in Shreveport, Louisiana. They put about twelve trainees into the altitude chamber with two observers to make sure everyone was okay. The trainees put on oxygen masks attached to each trainee's helmet. With the oxygen masks in place, the air was pumped out of the altitude chamber until we reached an altitude of 35,000 feet.

The first of the twelve participants was instructed to remove his mask and he was given a deck of cards. Next he was instructed to place the cards into suits while breathing just the air in the chamber. Soon the trainee was putting clubs on diamonds and hearts on spades. If asked how he was feeling, the trainee would say he felt great. Oxygen deprivation makes a person feel drunk – or really high. The trainee was directed to put his oxygen mask back on and he immediately started putting the cards in the right stacks. All trainees repeated the same exercise; we all responded the same way as the first trainee.

The altitude chamber was brought back down to 8,000 feet and we could breathe normally. The oxygen masks were disconnected and hung from our helmets. Then the hatch was blown off and suddenly we went from 8,000 feet to 40,000 feet. The first thing that happens with rapid decompression is everything inside is sucked out. All the air comes out of the lungs; everything in one's nose comes out. It's a terrible mess and you must get the oxygen mask on in three to four seconds. If you don't, you're out of it. The guy next to me couldn't get his mask on. I got mine on and helped him get his on. It was excellent training on the importance of oxygen and the consequences of oxygen deprivation.

* * *

Discharge: When I was discharged from the Air Force on September 1, 1958, I moved to Houston and married Mary Jane Lewis. We had dated for several years while I was stationed in Lake Charles and making frequent weekend trips from Lake Charles to Houston with several Air Force buddies. The most frequent buddy who went to Houston with me was Ken Ealy from Yakima, Washington. Another frequent Houston visitor was James Loveless from Colorado. I would call ahead and ask Angela to line up dates for us for the weekend. I did not want Angela to be a date for one of my Air Force buddies. She got tired of scheduling dates for us and I started calling Carol Kelt (Angela's twirling friend). Carol got me a date with her friend, Mary Jane Lewis. After getting married, my major order of business was to break into the airlines, but I had to learn how to fly an airplane. While I pursued my ambition to be a pilot, Mary Jane and I had two children.

Family: Our first child, James Everett, was born April 12, 1960. I missed that because I was taking trigonometry night courses prior to entering college at the University of Houston. Our daughter, Tambra Kay, was born August 3, 1964. This time I took Mary Jane to the hospital and we sat in the parking lot trying to decide whether or not we should go in. We went in after about 30 minutes and Dr. McRoberts, a friend of Dr. Lewis, Mary Jane's father, was there for the delivery. Soon Dr. McRoberts came out and told me to come in the labor room. They put me in a gown to go in to see Mary Jane, and Dr. McRoberts told me that each time Mary Jane had a contraction, the baby's heart stopped beating. He then sent me back to the waiting room to make a decision on which one I wanted to save – my wife or the baby. I couldn't make such a decision but luckily didn't have to. Dr. McRoberts returned after 30 minutes to say it was okay, we had a baby girl. The umbilical cord was wrapped around her neck, she was skinny, almost skeletal, and long. But she was a good baby – all she wanted to do was eat for the first three months. She was making up for lost time.

James was studious; I never had to worry about his getting his lessons done. Tambra was a little bit the other way. She would do just enough to get by and have a good time. During the summers when they had time off from school, I would take them on trips with me. I would put James in the cockpit with me. When I took Tambra on a flight, I put her in the back with the flight attendants.

Tambra was always one to test the system. When James and Tambra started dating, I decided I didn't want to wait up for the curfew. That was before cell phones and beepers. I told them I would set the alarm clock by my bed for the curfew time and they were to turn off the alarm clock when they got home. I also told them if they realized they could not make it home in time, I didn't want them to drive 70 to 80 miles per hour to get home. In such an event, I told them to stop, give me a call, and say, "Hey, Dad, I'm running late." The system worked pretty well with James. But Tambra had to test the system. One night I was in bed and the alarm went off. One o'clock came, then two o'clock came. Finally, Tambra came dragging in. I asked her what happened.

Tambra said, "Well, Daddy, an 18-wheeler turned over on the Interstate and the traffic was backed up."

I got out of bed and started putting on my clothes.

Tambra said, "What are you going to do?"

I said, "We're going to go look at that 18-wheeler accident."

Tears started rolling down her cheeks and she admitted there wasn't any 18-wheeler accident to see.

When James and Tambra each reached 11th grade in school, I bought each of them a car. One day I came home, looked in the back of Tambra's car, and saw two beer cans.

I said, "Okay, Tambra, this is the deal. You're either going to straighten out or I'm going to take you up to Grandmother's house in Buffalo, Texas. You need to figure out what you're going to do the rest of your life."

She really did not want to be in Buffalo, Texas, population 1,034. At that time James was going to college at the University of Texas in Austin. I told her James was on track to make it out there in the world and that she needed to figure out what she was going to do.

Tambra said, "I want to be a pilot."

I said, "That's fine. I'm going to find you an instructor and you can start working toward getting your pilot license."

She straightened out in short order and started flying lessons.

Tambra pulled a funny stunt during her senior year in high school. She talked all the seniors into buying windup alarm clocks and put them in their lockers set to go off at ten o'clock one morning. The seniors were in classrooms when the alarms went off and the teachers didn't know what was going on. Again, Tambra tested the system.

James graduated with a computer science degree from the University of Texas in Austin. James went to work for one of the professors at UT on the Hubble spacecraft that was launched into space by NASA. James designed a program for the spacecraft to keep the telescope focused on the stars that NASA wanted to observe as the Hubble spacecraft orbited the earth. James is currently a Senior Engineer at Apple, Inc. where he works on the audio for Apple products.

After graduating from high school, Tambra found an aviation program that she liked at a college in Killeen, Texas. Tambra obtained her four-year degree in three years. She spent a number of years as Flight Instructor, teaching ground school and flying charters to build up her hours. She spent more years with commuter airlines until she finally landed at America West. Tambra is now Captain on an Airbus A-320 for US Airways f/k/a America West.

CHAPTER 6

Pursuit of an Airline Career

After discharge from the Air Force, I started taking night courses so I could register for college. Then I got a job at Southwestern Industrial Electronics working on transformers, mixing up chemicals. I worked there for a while, and when college registration came up, I quit and went to college – engineering school – with a plan to be a mechanical engineer. I thought that would help me get on with the airlines. Once more, when I got into college, I didn't know how to play the game. One chemistry class was a wash-out class for engineers - 800 students with a Chinese woman lecturer that you could barely hear beyond the first two rows. It was a terrible, terrible course to try to pass. I also had a calculus course in which I did pretty well on the math but the tests were graded on a curve. The fraternity boys finished the tests in 30 minutes and made 95s and 100s. It would take me two hours and I would make 70 to 85, torpedoed by the grading curve that was all the more irritating to me when I learned the Frat boys had all the tests in advance. This professor used the same tests every year. Again, I thought, this is not going my way.

At the same time I was taking flying lessons at Hull Field in Sugarland, Texas. It was not hard to decide I would rather be flying than trying to get through two years of college. I concentrated my time and effort on flying. The guy who taught me to fly, Mike Leveillard, was French and his English was difficult to understand through his heavy accent. He taught me with his hands, gesturing up or down to indicate what he wanted me to do with the airplane. Mike was a good guy and a great pilot. He had been the youngest pilot in France licensed to fly. Each year General Charles De Galle sent Mike a letter on his birthday. Mike and I got along great and I soloed in 1958 in a Cessna 172.

I needed 200 hours to get a commercial license. When I had about 60 to 70 hours I bought a PT 19, a World War II army trainer, like the one I saw at the abandoned air base in Newport. I paid $1,000 for the plane. It was a great airplane, open cockpit, plywood wings and fabric fuselage. It was manufactured with a 165 horsepower Ranger engine but the seller put in a 200 horsepower engine that made it a much better airplane. It was fully acrobatic and light on the controls. I flew it until I got close to getting my commercial requirements. I went to Doc Hull, who owned Hull Field in Sugarland, and asked how much flying time he would give me for my PT 19 because I was in a hurry to get my commercial license. Doc Hull and I worked out a deal: he credited me with $1,000 in flight time at $15 per hour, more than 60 hours of flight time. I traded the airplane to Doc Hull and flew as much as I could. In the meantime, I worked for a utility company in Bellaire, Texas, owned by my Dad's cousin. I worked digging ditches and flew every day that I could.

I took my private pilot check ride on August 10, 1959, and was issued my private pilot license. I met Leonard Warden, who was a designated FAA flight check inspector, and Leonard took a liking to me. On August 20, 1960, I called Leonard to ask if he was available to give a commercial check ride. He said he could do it that afternoon. He was complimentary and I received my commercial pilot license. I had achieved my first goal.

Jim McCartney's PT-19 World War II army trainer

My next step was to go to American Flyers in Fort Worth to get my multi-engine and instrument ratings. It was expensive – approximately $10,000, and of course, I didn't have the money. I went to see my father-in-law, Dr. Everett Lewis, to see if he would cosign a note at the bank for me. Dr. Lewis said he had a college fund for Mary Jane and since she was not going to college, he would give me the money from her college fund. I used part of Mary Jane's college fund and went to Fort Worth. On November 1, 1960, I received my instrument rating and on November 8, 1960, I passed my multi-engine check ride. Now with all my ratings and licenses, I was ready to get a job flying full time.

CHAPTER 7

Seeking Flight Positions

When I got back to Houston from Fort Worth, I started looking for a job and didn't fly for about a month. I had résumés out everywhere but couldn't find a job. Finally I went back to Leonard Warden at Andrau Airpark and told him I really needed to get a job.

He said, "Let me talk to a couple of people about this."

He called me back in a couple of days and said he had a job for me flying a trip in a Mooney and said, "I think they'll hire you full-time." George McAlpin had an oil company – Madrid Oil and Gas. George had been a roughneck for one of the big wildcatters in Houston, the legendary Glenn McCarthy. McAlpin bought the Mooney so he would have an advantage signing up oil leases; he could beat his competition by being the first to get to the people who had the land to lease. He had been a B29 gunner and he could fly, but he didn't have a license. McAlpin hired me and we flew that Mooney all over the country – Florida, Albuquerque, Mexico City, Acapulco, Zihuatanejo.

When flying for George McAlpin, I learned he had a mistress named Becky and his wife was named Betty. They looked alike. Becky was normally on board on overnight trips. I often wondered if this had anything to do with the purchase of the aircraft. On a trip back from Florida, Becky was not with us; Betty, the wife, was on board. I needed some maps from the backseat and I hollered "Becky, hand me the charts." Of course, it was Betty back there. That was a terrible mistake but nobody said a word; Betty handed me the charts. Probably wasn't the first time that had happened.

The problem with flying for George and his oil business was that on every payday, I might have to wait another two to three weeks to get paid and then would get just a portion of the pay due. After a few months, I couldn't make it on what George was willing to pay me, and he owed me about three months' pay. I had to leave.

Sometime after I quit working for George, he bought a Lockheed Lodestar (L18) that seated 12 to 20 passengers, according to how the seats were set up. He hired a former United Airlines pilot who had become disenchanted with the airlines. After a while, George's new pilot called me and said, "Hey, I'm having trouble getting my paycheck."

I said, "I know, I've been down that road with George."

The Lockheed Lodestar had a big rudder, elevator and ailerons. There were external control locks that you put on the elevator and rudders to keep them from flopping in the wind while on the ground. George and his pilot were departing from the Bahamas with 12 people on board. Unfortunately, they took off without removing the external control locks. This type of accident should never happen. It is difficult to enter the pilot seat or co-pilot seat with the controls installed because the control column is in the flight position not out of the way against the instrument panel. The checklist requires the flying pilot to check the flight controls for free and correct movement. With the locks installed the controls could not be moved. The plane crashed on takeoff killing the 12 people on board.

A few days after George McAlpin died in the crash in the Bahamas, Becky, his mistress, came out to the airport looking for me, and she said, "Jim, they came and took my townhouse and they took my Cadillac."

I said, "Becky, I don't really have any answers for you so I can't help you."

Becky had been featured in *Parade* magazine as a look-alike for Faye Dunaway. That was the last time I saw Becky and one of my last dealings with George's oil business.

Part Three
Pan American Sulphur – Corporate Pilot

CHAPTER 8

Pan American Sulphur

After I quit flying for George McAlpin, I visited Leonard Warden and told him the job with George McAlpin was not working out. Leonard understood. He said George wouldn't pay his hangar bill or his fuel bill and was in trouble all the time.

A few days later, Leonard called and asked if I had a good-looking suit. One, I said. Leonard told me to put it on and come out to Andrau Airpark. There, Leonard introduced me to Dick Barker, who was flying a Lockheed Lodestar for Pan American Sulphur. Dick told me he planned a trip to Mazatlan, Mexico. Dick said, "You should dress like you are now and I will pay you by the trip."

I was pleased because I didn't have much multi-engine time but what I did have was in a Lockheed 12 that had two 450 horsepower engines. The Pan American Sulphur Lockheed Lodestar L18 was powered by two 1200 horsepower engines and was the premier executive aircraft at the time. The Lockheed Lodestar L18 (along with many others) had been modernized by Bill Lear in San Antonio. His modifications put radar on board and improved the performance so the aircraft flew much faster. A modified Lodestar was often referred to as a "Learstar." Bill Lear, whose first accomplishment was the autopilot, is famous for building the Lear Jet line of executive aircraft.

On that first flight for Pan American Sulphur, we took off in a rainstorm on a Wednesday. It was about 7:30 in the morning when we got the airplane out, cranked it up, and I got our instrument flight plan (IFR) clearance. It was the first time I had been in that type of instrument weather. It was turbulent but we broke out on top at 9,000 feet and it was gloriously clear– just like we were in heaven. We cancelled the IFR flight plan and proceeded direct to Matamoros, south of Brownsville, to clear Mexico customs. From there we cut across the Gulf of Mexico to Mazatlan. Landing in Mazatlan was like landing in another world, on a primitive airport. There were no lights; they put out smudge pots at night for runway lights. A river ran close to the airport, and parrots and monkeys played in the trees. It was hot and humid. When we got back to Houston, Dick said, "I'll call you when I get another trip."

That was the beginning of a long and satisfying work relationship doing what I loved – flying – and building up the hours I needed to reach the Holy Grail: a position as pilot for one of the airlines.

A Bit of History: In 1939, German-owned Lufthansa was the only airline serving most countries in Central and South America. The United States government adopted a policy designed to force Lufthansa out of Central and South America. The USA plan was to help these countries set up their own national airlines. This policy created an urgent need for pilots. Dick Barker had a private pilot license from the U.S. with 40 well-padded hours. He went to Costa Rica and got a Costa Rica air transport rating in a Ford Tri-motor that he had never flown. He had one thing going for him: he had a co-pilot who had been a Captain at Eastern Airlines but couldn't pass the physical in the U.S. anymore so he was flying in Central America. Dick said the Eastern Captain taught him everything he needed to know. That's how Dick's career started in Mexico, Central and South America. He was a check airman and had flown DC-3s, DC-4s and the Ford Tri-motor. Now he was teaching me. And I was beginning a whole new life's experience, in a different land.

Pan American Sulphur Startup: The start-up of Pan American Sulphur was interesting to me. On the lowest part of the Gulf of Mexico is Coatzacoalcos, a free port. Prior to construction of the Panama Canal, a Trans-Isthmus Railroad was built from Coatzacoalcos to the Pacific side of Mexico. This port and the railroad were the main route for goods transported from the Gulf of Mexico to the Pacific side of Mexico. The terrain was unexplored jungle and swamp. When construction began, Shell Oil went ahead of the railroad construction and discovered a large deposit of sulphur. Shell was not interested in the sulphur deposit, only the oil production.

Guy Warren owned an oil company in Corpus Christi, Texas. Guy learned how to fly in World War I. He flew a Jenny out of Love Field when that airport was just one square mile of grass and a pilot took off whichever way the wind was blowing. He frequently flew from Dallas to Texarkana to see his girlfriend and had three forced landings on one trip. On that trip, the engine began to run rough and he landed in a farmer's field. The bolts that held the camshaft in place had broken. The farmer gave Guy some baling wire and Guy wired the contraption together so it would make the valves open and close. As he flew along, the wire stretched out and again the engine started running rough. He had to make two more emergency landings to tighten the baling wire.

Warren was from Arkansas and he went to Corpus Christi with 75 cents in his pocket. He went into a restaurant, spent 25 cents on a hamburger, and got a job working as a roughneck on an oil rig. He saved his money and bought the oil and mineral lease on a place called Turkey Creek. As he searched for capital to drill on the lease, he met a Vice President at Bank of the Southwest who put up the money. Warren drilled, hit oil, and the production out of that lease was fantastic. Some of the directors on the Board of Renoir Oil came from Bank of the Southwest because they put up the money for drilling. Renoir Oil was operated efficiently and made a lot of money. It accumulated a surplus of cash on which they had two choices: pay taxes on it or put the money into exploration. When the Mexican sulphur leases became available, Guy and his board decided it was a good opportunity to buy the undeveloped sulphur lease in Mexico, prove it up, and then sell it to Texas Gulf Sulphur, which at the time was the biggest producer of sulphur in the world. They got it with a stipulation that they had to have it producing sulphur by a certain date. As the date approached, it was clear that they could not meet the production date with the crew they had. Guy went to Texas Gulf Sulphur and hired Harry Webb. Harry had been a star baseball player at the University of Texas and was called "Pint" Webb because of his short stature. Webb went to Mexico and evaluated the situation. Warren thought they could break it up into small leases and sell it off in small chunks. Webb said that wouldn't fly and they would have to get the thing on line – producing. Webb got the plant up and running and turned into a money-making business as Pan American Sulphur.

CHAPTER 9

Mexico Adventures

T-Shirts for the Native Women: Virtually all the native women living around the plant, about 18 miles from Minatitlan in the jungles of Mexico, were topless. After the guesthouse was built, we took the Board of Directors and their wives to the plant in Mexico. The Directors and their wives were appalled at what they observed, i.e., the topless women. When we returned to the States, the order from the Board was to send T-shirts to the plant for the native women. On our next trip to the plant as we drove from the airport, all the women were wearing the T-shirts – with holes carefully cut out in the front. They said the fabric of the T-shirts made their nipples sore!

  Smuggling: As I mentioned, Coatzacoalcos is a free port, so anything shipped there was not subject to import duty (tax). From there, goods could be shipped from Mexico to any other country without issues of restrictions on U.S. goods. Once I saw at least 20 D-8 Caterpillars (earth movers) in a row awaiting shipment to Russia and Cuba. This came into play for our company.

The sulphur dome had tar over the top. Sulphur is mined by inserting super-heated steam into the ground to melt the sulphur so it can be pumped to the surface. The tar on top of the sulphur would melt, mix into the sulphur and turn it dark. It didn't degrade the sulphur but the buyers didn't want to buy the dark sulphur. To fix the problem, the workers devised a filtering system that required a stainless steel mesh in the line to catch the asphalt (tar). One of the restrictions for importing material into Mexico was if it was made in Mexico you couldn't import it into Mexico. The stainless steel mesh was called stainless steel wire "cloth." Mexico made cloth so we couldn't import the stainless steel wire "cloth." Pan American Sulphur smuggled the stainless steel wire "cloth" from Texas into Mexico on its airplane.

The Lodestar had three baggage bins, one in the nose and two in the belly. We put the baggage in the nose bin and the contraband in the two belly bins. Upon arrival in Mexico, only the nose bin was opened, everything was removed for inspection, returned to the nose bin that was closed after inspection, and we were on our way. After we landed at Minatitlan, Larry, one of the men at the plant, would go out late in the evening, slip the stuff out of the belly bins, and take it back to the mine. This went on for a couple of years without a hitch.

One night Larry went out to pick up the contraband stored in the belly bins. A soldier put a gun to Larry's head and said, "Hey, what are you doing?"

This occurred just before Christmas and there was a lot of stuff in the bins other than wire cloth, i.e., toys for the kids in Minatitlan and other Christmas contraband for the plant and employees. The soldier told Larry he would have to take him in. Larry countered with an offer of $400 if he would just walk away. The soldier said he couldn't do it because he had called the commandant at the port. The soldier kept the $400 and told Larry to take everything off the aircraft before the commandant arrived.

The commandant was a Major in the Mexican Army. He had a house in Mazatlan, another in Mexico City and one in Acapulco. He ran an under-the-table operation at the "free" port. When the commandant arrived, he opened up the main cabin door and looked through the cabin. There he found a bunch of toys hidden under the seats. Larry forgot to check the cabin. They took the lifeboat and had it spread out all over the place. They put out a warrant for the arrest of the crew of the Lodestar – Dick and me. Larry called and said to get the crew out of the mine area so the police couldn't find them. The commandant came, looked the situation over and said, "This is what I'm going to do. This has already gone to Mexico City, but I will get it set up so you can come directly here from Houston and you won't have to stop at Matamoros and clear customs. But you will have to pay to me 10 percent of the value of whatever you bring from the U.S."

Pan American Sulphur paid a $9,000 fine to satisfy the Mexico City officials. The commandant's plan was accepted. After that incident, we flew from Houston to Minatitlan with a bill of lading, paid the 10 percent to the commandant, and were happy to do so. The commandant really liked TVs and Smith & Wesson 38 pistols. I can't tell you how many TVs and pistols we gave him. Such is life in Mexico. That was the time we were caught smuggling, but we escaped the inside of a Mexican jail.

Trailing Antenna: New Orleans Over Seas controls the air traffic over the Gulf of Mexico. The navigation aid stations for flying across the Gulf were located at Galveston, Texas, Grand Island, Louisiana, Tampa, Florida and Merida, Mexico. These aids were low frequency. The aircraft had to have an Automatic Directional Finder (ADF) on board to use these navigation aids. The ADF was reliable if there were no thunderstorms, but the ADF would point out every thunderstorm but rarely pointed to the navigation aid stations. We would hold a heading and when we got about 150 to 200 miles from the coastline, we turned our radar on ground mode to see where we would cross land and make corrections to get back on course. When we flew across the Gulf, we used high frequency (HF) radio for communications because the very high frequency (VHF) was line of sight, but would not give us communication all the way across the Gulf.

The Lodestar had a trailing antenna rolled up in the belly and every time we were assigned a new frequency, we had to look up how many feet of trailing antenna had to be put out to get that frequency. Occasionally when we landed, the cable would not retract because it had flopped around and twisted until it had a knot in it. We landed many times with about 100 - 200 feet of copper wire trailing with a funnel on the end. It was embarrassing. After a couple of landings trailing

200 feet of copper wire, Dick said we had to figure out something to solve the problem. We went to a plumbing store and bought a toilet stopper. We took the funnel off and replaced it with the toilet stopper with a golf ball inside. That fixed the problem; we never again landed with copper wire trailing and a funnel flopping on the runway.

On the Menu: One weekend at the mine in Minatitlan, one of the engineers suggested we go out for lunch. Minatitlan was in a humid area of Mexico, about 25 miles from the Gulf Coast, in the lower part of the Gulf of Mexico. One of the guys suggested a restaurant on an extinct volcano. The restaurant was on a lake with a pier built out over the lake, about 50 miles south of Vera Cruz. We drove a little over 100 miles to the restaurant. We were in a Mercedes, and about halfway there the Freon was low and the air conditioner froze up. We had to drive the rest of the way with no air conditioning and with all the windows rolled down. It was really uncomfortable but as we started climbing up the side of the volcano, the lack of air conditioning was no longer a problem. The group included Dick Barker, Jack Lette, Bob Cimarod and me. Jack was in charge of drilling for the sulphur and Bob was in charge of production. Bob was an interesting guy. He frequently managed to outmaneuver Mr. Webb. Mr. Webb would say, "Bob, we need to pick up the tonnage next month. I need to lease another 15,000 tons of sulphur to be shipped." Bob would already have it on hand – in his stockpile. He stayed ahead of the production ordered and maintained a surplus to meet unexpected demands.

We had a good time sitting at tables on the pier over the volcanic lake, drinking beer and eating snacks indigenous to the Mexican tropics, while looking across the volcanic lake. I particularly recall little crushed fish that were fried whole and looked like potato chips. They were crispy and good. There were also little squares of dark meat on toothpicks, tasty and salty. I asked what the little meat things were and no one knew. I suggested we ask the waiter, and we found out it was monkey. I wished I hadn't asked. I felt like a cannibal and I couldn't eat any more.

CHAPTER 10

Politics

Marvin Sandlin, who was on the board of directors of Pan American Sulphur, was well connected with the Democratic Party. As a result we did a lot of flying for Marvin on his political junkets to LBJ's ranch and other places. In 1960, when he was running for Vice President with Jack Kennedy, LBJ hosted a barbeque at his Texas ranch in the hill country of Texas at $1,000 per plate. Marvin Sandlin took Dick and me to the barbeque. Many people were there; the airstrip was full of airplanes.

We went out to the house and through the receiving line. Marvin went first, then Dick and me. As Dick was shaking LBJ's hand, I was shaking Lady Bird's hand. Marvin said, "These two guys are my pilots." It was as if Lady Bird suddenly had a dead fish in her hand. Her hand went limp and she pulled it away.

I thought she could have pretended a little better than that.

After we went through the serving line, we found a place to sit under a mesquite tree out of the Texas hill country afternoon sun. Dan Blocker, the actor who played Hoss Cartwright on the television series

Bonanza, was seated at our table. Dan made an eloquent speech about his career teaching in Victoria, Texas, and then going on to star on television. I didn't realize how big Dan Blocker was, but when he stood up, he seemed as tall as the tree we were sitting under.

Marvin was *well* connected. Once we took him to Washington, D.C .to meet with some politico. Three times on the way up there he had us check to be sure the limo could come all the way out to the plane on the tarmac to pick him up. He *was* vain, but well connected.

Because of Sandlin's connections, after Kennedy was elected, an alliance with Latin America was established. Marvin volunteered our airplane for use by Senator Hubert Humphrey (D-Minn). We picked up Senator Humphrey in Houston for a tour of Mexico. We flew Senator Humphrey to the sulphur mine, Mexico City, Oxaca, Acapulco, and just about every major city in Mexico that he wanted to visit.

Senator Humphrey impressed me: he let Dick and me sit in with a reporter from U.S. News & World Report for an off-the-record interview. Senator Humphrey was talking about all the inventions that had come along. When the world is ready for something new, several people come out with it at the same time. Marconi invented the radio but at the same time several others came up with the same invention. With respect to the atom bomb, Senator Humphrey said that the Russians didn't get as much information from the Rosenberg spies as it was thought.

Senator Humphrey also said a politician's first and most important task is to get elected. Any good things to be accomplished would not happen unless you were elected. That hasn't lessened. Today politicians are so focused on getting elected and re-elected that they feel they must accommodate the lobbyists and special interest groups to stay in office. Could this be the reason we find the United States Government in such a mess now?

CHAPTER 11

Flying at Pan American Sulphur

In the Houston area, most executive pilot positions were for smaller operations without the opportunity for any substantial accumulation of flight time. Flights were usually limited to weekend trips to the ranch or occasional vacation trips. Pan American Sulphur had headquarters offices in Houston and Mexico City; the plant was located 18 miles from Minatitlan, Mexico; and there were operations in Coatzacoalcos, Mexico, Tampa, Florida and Nassau, Bahamas. We took customers to Mexico City and Acapulco, entertained them for four or five days and took them back to Houston. We made frequent trips to Cozumel, Mexico. At that time Cozumel had about 25 hotel rooms located on the beach, but no air conditioning. The aircraft was fueled out of 55-gallon drums.

When I first went to work as a corporate pilot flying the Lockheed Lodestar, what I had was still a Master/Apprentice type situation. The Captain was the Master and the co-pilot was the Apprentice. For most executive aircraft at that time, the co-pilot was also an A&E mechanic and his job was to work on the airplane between scheduled maintenance and make sure the aircraft was ready to go. Rarely did a co-pilot get to fly anything other than straight and level when the aircraft reached altitude. The Captain would take off, climb up to altitude and tell the co-pilot to hold the plane. When it was time to go down, the Captain would tell the First Officer, "I've got the controls." The Captain would make the approach and landing.

I was fortunate when I went to work for Pan American Sulphur. Dick Barker, the Captain, had been a Captain for the airlines. He allowed me to fly, and make takeoffs and landings. I can vividly remember the first time he put me in the left seat. We taxied out at Andrau Airpark, passed the maintenance hangar, and I was in the left seat. The mechanics were looking at me because they had never seen a co-pilot in the left – Captain's – seat of the Lodestar to take off. As we taxied on out, the mechanics jumped into a car and followed us out to the runway. I guess they thought I was stealing the airplane. They followed us to the run-up area. When we turned around, they saw Dick Barker in the right seat. That was my first takeoff from the left seat. Dick was very generous, taught me a lot, and I was very lucky to get on an operation in the corporate world where I got to do so much flying. It was good experience that helped me build a lot of flying hours.

There were many fun and interesting experiences outside of flying. Alan Shepherd, one of the original seven astronauts, kept his plane in Pan American Sulphur's hangar at Andrau Airpark. He was a nice guy and graciously signed our logbooks.

We went sail fishing in Acapulco and scuba diving and snorkeling in Cozumel. Once while sail fishing out of Acapulco, Mr. Webb saw a sea turtle that he wanted us to catch. We somehow reeled it into the boat. It was taken back to shore and Mr. Webb instructed the cook to prepare a meal using the sea turtle. I took a bite and the longer I chewed the turtle meat, the bigger the piece grew in my mouth. Finally, I used my napkin to spit out the bite and that was the end of my adventure in eating turtle.

For our first time scuba diving, Dick and I put on the oxygen tanks and jumped in with no prior training. Once near the bottom, I saw a manta ray approach and it scared me. At the same time Dick put his hand on my foot and I shot straight up. When I reached the surface, our boat appeared to be about two miles away. Still propelled by fear, I swam to the boat struggling with the oxygen tank on my back. When I reached the boat, the crew on deck told me to roll over on my back – I did and I was afloat.

While flying out of Andrau Airpark, we had quite a good time. Every day at lunch, we played ping pong. There were many hangars for all types of executive aircraft. One of the main hangars had a restaurant above it where customers could eat and watch the airplanes take off and land. This was quite an attraction for people to come out, have lunch and watch the airplanes. There was a special show one day. One of the mechanics, Ralph, told everybody what he was going to do to scare Rico, who fueled the planes and mowed the grass every Saturday. There was a concrete runway about 50 feet wide with a grassy area on each side of about 50 feet. Behind a barbed-wire fence was undeveloped land dotted with mesquite bushes and tumbleweeds. Ralph told everybody to be in the restaurant on Saturday morning when Rico started mowing, because he was going be wearing a gorilla suit and come at Rico out of the mesquite bushes. Ralph paid $200 to rent a gorilla suit and really did look like a gorilla when he put it on. Ralph invited a bunch of guys, including a reporter for the Houston *Chronicle*, to see his scare spectacle. As we sat watching, Rico made a pass mowing the grass near the runway. When Rico came by on his second pass, Ralph came out in the gorilla suit. Rico stopped the tractor, got off, and started running. He ran about 20 yards, then pulled out a pistol, turned around, and started shooting at the gorilla. Now it was Ralph who was scared. He tried to remove the gorilla head so Rico could see that it was him, a human, but he twisted the costume head, the head got stuck, and Ralph was really in trouble, he couldn't get it off and he couldn't see. Panicked, he ran through the barbed wire fence and out through the mesquite bushes, as everybody in the restaurant was rolling with laughter. Rico heard about the stunt Ralph planned and got himself a pistol with blanks in it. The stunt backfired on Ralph, and the incident was in the Houston *Chronicle* the next day.

The years I spent at Pan American Sulphur were educational, fun, and adventurous.

And never dull.

CHAPTER 12

Eastern Airlines

In 1963, I went to work for Eastern Airlines and took my flight training on the simulators in Miami. I also took "over-the-water" training, which was the best I ever had at any of the airlines where I worked. The Coast Guard took us out into the Atlantic – 23 pilots and several flight attendants. We were dumped into the water with instructions to inflate the life rafts and climb aboard. My previous over-the-water training was conducted in a swimming pool. Without waves, it was a snap to inflate the life rafts and climb aboard. But it was difficult to do the same thing in the ocean with the wave undulation. I finished simulator training in Miami and was based in Washington, D.C. We moved from Miami to Washington, D.C. and they told me the flight training would be in Newark.

I trained on a Lockheed Constellation, a four-engine aircraft with three rudders. Training started about midnight, when the airline shut down for the day. Captain Nickerson, my trainer, was a good pilot. My training partner had not had any multi-engine time to speak of so

Nickerson started with me. We took off out of Newark about midnight. We were over Philadelphia, Captain Nickerson was eating his box lunch, and he told me I had lost the No. 1 engine. I told the engineer to feather No. 1 and run a checklist.

A few minutes later, Nickerson said, "Okay, you've lost No. 2 engine."

I told the engineer to feather No. 2, run a checklist, and open the cross feed on the hydraulics. The way it was configured, Engine Nos. 1 and 2 had the hydraulic pumps that ran the flight control, Engine Nos. 3 and 4 had hydraulic pumps that ran the brakes and flaps.

When I asked the engineer to open the cross feed, Nickerson said, "No, you can't do that. You've lost all the fluid in 1 and 2 and you don't want to transfer the fluid out and lose it all."

As a result, the airplane was heavy on the controls with the boost on. To fly it with the boost off, I had to slow down to 160 knots and shift the elevators, rudder and ailerons manually, shift them down to have a mechanical advantage so it wouldn't be quite as hard, but it was still difficult.

We ran the checklist and Captain Nickerson said, "Okay, I want you to make a turn into the good engines."

Nickerson was still eating his box lunch and I rolled it into a 10 to 15 degree turn, it was coming around and I had both hands on the ailerons, and both feet on the rudders, holding it right. All of a sudden, the yoke jumped all the way over against the stop.

Nickerson threw his box lunch over his head and said, "God damn, boy. What did you do?"

I said, "I didn't do anything! I didn't do anything!"

We had the engineer open the hydraulic cross feed for hydraulic power to help move the flight controls. We unfeathered Engines 1 and 2. We ran the checklist and sent the engineer back to look. The engineer turned on the wing lights, looked the situation over, came back and said, "Both ailerons are in the full up position."

We had no roll control. The only way we could change headings was with the rudders and engine power. We worked our way back to Newark and turned on final about 10 miles out and landed. The next day Maintenance told us the main aileron cable had broken.

I finished my training in Newark, went back to D.C., and started flying the line. I was amazed that the first time I bid a regular flying line,

I got a bid, while most of my classmates were flying reserve. Many of the pilots that had been there several months or years were still flying reserve. My bid was flying with a Captain Shaw and I soon learned that he was a holy terror. He made the flight attendants cry. Captain Shaw thought any action by the crew was wrong. If his co-pilot made a good landing, Shaw would say the landing should have been 20 feet shorter. If his co-pilot flared the airplane on approach for any length of time, Shaw would grab the controls and shove the plane to the ground.

Captain Shaw wasn't just hard on his flight crew; he was hard on everyone. One of the trips we flew was just before Thanksgiving, out of Washington, DC to Louisville, KY. On the way back, we made a stop at Charleston. It was late in the evening when the trip left Louisville. When we stopped in Charleston, the passengers got off and new passengers were loaded. Late in the evening, we taxied out. The flight attendant reported there was a G.I. on board who slept through the landing in Charleston and missed getting off at his destination. I thought we could taxi back to the gate and let the guy off. It would make us about 10 minutes late, but once we landed at Washington National, our day was over. A ten-minute delay would not have been consequential, but Captain Shaw refused to taxi back and let the soldier off the plane. The soldier had to spend the night in Washington and probably had to pay for a hotel room before he could go back to Charleston. I thought Shaw handled the incident poorly, another example of his insensitivity toward others.

I flew with Captain Shaw for about two months. I was making about $485 a month and thought about my situation. I called Dick Barker, Chief Pilot at Pan American Sulphur, and said "Hey, Dick. I'm not happy up here. What's going on down there?" Dick said, "That's good. We're buying a new Gulfstream G1, state of the art turbo-prop airplane. If you want to come back, we'll make room for you, use you on the Gulfstream."

CHAPTER 13

Return to Pan American Sulphur

I returned to Pan American Sulphur where I made $685 per month. As it turned out, I flew the Lodestar for a couple of months before we took delivery on the Gulfstream. It was a nice airplane. I really enjoyed flying it.

Engine Failure: In the first fifty hours of flying on the Gulfstream, we took off from Houston's Hobby Airport to fly to Falfurrias for a hunting trip – the company had purchased a hunting lease near the King Ranch in South Texas. Upon takeoff, the right engine started spewing oil. We shut down the engine, feathered it, and returned to the airport. We learned that Grumman had changed one of the vent pipes on the engine and the new one was not properly installed. That was fixed.

Jet Fuel: Jet fuel is basically kerosene. Kerosene absorbs water and it's almost impossible to get all the water out. We used jet fuel in the Gulfstream and it was unbelievably cheap when we first started flying – around 9 or 10 cents a gallon in some places, and some places a little more. Overall it was cheap fuel. We were happy to be flying with it and didn't have any reservations about it until a flight engineer for Quantas Airways in Australia made a discovery. He was walking around his airplane, a Lockheed Electra, a four-engine turboprop, which burned jet fuel. He saw little drops of jet fuel coming off the wing. He reached up to wipe the fuel off to see where it was coming from. When he wiped it off, his hand went through the wing and fuel poured out.

The water in the kerosene contained little microbes – bugs. The bugs were not eating the aluminum, but the bug droppings were corroding the aluminum wherever the droppings touched it. That was the first indication of this phenomenon. There was an Airworthiness Directive Note to check all the aircraft. We checked the Gulfstream and found corrosion from the microbes. The corroded surfaces were ground down and a coating applied. About this time, the Learjets came out but without fuel heaters. Water didn't bother the Learjet engine. Of course, the Learjet didn't have access to JP4 fuel. The Learjet used a new fuel additive developed called Prist, which would keep ice from forming. Learjets used it all the time and when the Learjets were inspected for corrosion caused by the microbes, they found the Learjets didn't have any corrosion and didn't have the microbes. Apparently, the Prist additive killed the microbes. The bugs couldn't live in the fuel when Prist was added. After this discovery, we used the Prist additive in the Gulfstream to prevent the bugs and corrosion of the wings.

Stow-a-Way: When I was flying the Gulfstream, we were in Mexico City one morning to take our passengers back to Houston. I went out a little early and started the pre-flight on the airplane. On the first flight of the day on a Grumman, you first open up the wheel well doors that were normally closed after the gear was extended and, of course, after the gear was retracted. When I opened the wheel well doors, things started falling out. I looked in and saw a kid inside the wheel well hanging on; apparently, he was planning to ride with us in the wheel well to Houston. I called Security and they took him into custody. I think he was from Guatemala. He would have died on the flight to Houston. If he were not crushed to death in the wheel well when the gear retracted, he would have frozen when we reached cruising altitude where the temperature was 40 degrees below zero.

Hunting and the Rattlesnake: I really enjoyed hunting in South Texas – the company leased 16,000 acres with deer, quail, javalina, dove. Mr. Webb, the President of the company, would send some of his guests with me, and he would take the other guests so there would be kills for everyone for whatever game we were hunting. Mr. Webb and I were always the best shots among the Pan American group.

Dove-hunting in South Texas is excellent. The area is dry and there are few places for animals to get water. We would go to the watering holes late in the afternoon as the doves came in for water. The only problem was every kind of animal in the area would also be there, including rattlesnakes. If you did not pick up your bird as soon as you shot it, a rattlesnake would get it.

One afternoon I decided to go out alone to a place next to a maize field where I had spotted birds. I parked the jeep and walked out in the field near a mesquite tree. A few minutes passed and a bird flew over; I shot and the bird fell. The weeds were about knee-high. I watched where the bird fell and lined up a bush so I could walk a path that would take me to the spot. About halfway to where the bird fell, I felt something hit my leg just above my boot. A few steps later I realized a rattlesnake had bitten my leg. I looked around and the jeep was about a mile away. I began going into shock, feeling clammy, heart racing, and I could feel the poison flowing through my body. My theory of the situation was I was going to die from the rattlesnake bite if I did not take action to counteract the venom. Like any good pilot, I developed a plan of action. I cut my pants leg to use a strip from my pants for a tourniquet on my leg. As I cut open my pants leg, there it was: a big cactus needle was stuck in my leg. Obviously, my theory of the situation was wrong.

After the "rattlesnake" incident, our normal trips down to Minatitlan and Mexico City, Acapulco, Cozumel and the Bahamas continued. The Mexican government started making moves like they were going to take over the sulphur plant in Mexico. I decided that coming up on 30 years old, I needed to get on with the airlines. At that time, the airlines were not hiring people over 30 years old. In the corporate world, if a company starting cutting back, the first thing to go was the aviation department.

Part Four
Airline Career

CHAPTER 14

Trans Texas Airlines (TTA)

Being an airline pilot opened another whole new life for me. I never thought I would fly as a First Officer for such a long time during my career. I never envisioned myself involved in union activities. Growing up in Arkansas on a farm, I never heard anything about unions. Not until my my father's death did I even know he had been very active in the United Auto Workers local union when we lived in Detroit.

Pilots are more or less married to the airline where they are employed, because of the seniority system. If the airline goes under, or a pilot is furloughed or laid off, the pilot starts at the bottom all over again when he/she joins another airline. A pilot may be at one airline with thousands of hours, but with another airline, the pilot must start at the bottom of the list as a co-pilot for a captain that may not have as many hours flying. Airline management personnel go from one airline to another without penalty because there is no seniority system for airline management. Airline executives usually get a substantial raise when moving from one airline to another. That does not happen for airline pilots, regardless of their expertise and experience.

I could have gotten on at any of the major airlines, but I wanted to live in Houston. TTA acquired a route from Brownsville to Tampico then to Vera Cruz and needed six or seven pilots. I was part of a class of those six or seven pilots hired by TTA to handle the newly acquired route.

Training in DC-3: I started flying for TTA in January 1967 and trained on a DC-3. The man I was paired with for training was inexperienced. He had no multi-engine time and just barely enough single-engine hours to get hired. The check airman was Les Kagler. We met Les at Hobby Airport in Houston. Les asked what we had been flying. I had been flying the Lodestar and the Gulfstream and the other guy said he had been flying 150s and 172s.

Les put me in the right seat and said, "We'll start out with you."

We flew out toward Beaumont and did some air work, including turns and stalls. I did two or three landings and my time was up.

Kagler put the First Officer I was training with – Jay – in the right seat. First of all, he had never flown an airplane with a tail wheel. To explain, a problem of flying a plane with a tail wheel is that the center of gravity is behind the main wheels and the plane wants to turn around on you, so you really have to be careful. On the DC-3 and most large airplanes, when you get it going straight down the runway, the tail wheel lock helps keep the airplane going in a straight line. Jay taxied out and Les showed him how to use the tail wheel lock. Jay lined up the airplane on the runway, locked the tail wheel, and pushed the power up. The aircraft veered off toward the left side of the runway, almost off, then veered to the right side of the runway, almost off, again to the left side, almost off, then back to the center. Jay pulled it up and the aircraft had barely reached 60 knots. The airplane was just barely flying and shaking.

Les yelled, "Put the nose down! Put the nose down!"

Finally, Jay got the airplane up, went out, and did the air work. When we came back to land, Jay flared about hangar high and just held it there until the airplane stalled. That airplane hit the ground so hard that it shook dust out that had been in that plane for at least 30 years! I thought, my God, I'm going to die right here in training!

TRANS TEXAS AIRLINES (TTA)

Our training class went through ground school and advanced to the link trainer. The link trainer was a World War II simulator and was rickety. One of the guys had a real problem with the link trainer and as we sat for the final test, he got up in the classroom and said:

"Well, guys, either you know this stuff or you don't."

He went to lunch and never came back, so I guess he didn't know it.

Those of us who passed the test were released to fly online for a probationary period.

Pilot Fired: During probation, each new pilot had to get a letter of recommendation on how he performed from each Captain that he flew with during the month. One First Officer, the same Jay, had a difficult time during probation with the Captains. Jay's letters were minimal or unacceptable. Then Jay and I were furloughed for seven months. During the furlough, Jay got on with Allegheny Airlines flying Convairs with a nose wheel and he did okay at Allegheny. When Jay came back to TTA, he got back into the DC-3s and again experienced the same problems as before his furlough.

One morning on reserve Jay was called out early to fly. He had one car, a Volkswagen. He loaded up his wife and three kids who would drop Jay off at Hobby. On the Gulf Freeway to Hobby, Jay and his family were in an accident. One of the kids lost his leg. It was a horrific accident. When Jay's probation came up, everyone felt sorry for him and they didn't let him go in spite of his continuing poor performance in the cockpit. Jay checked out as a Captain the same time that I did. But he scared the co-pilots that flew with him. On one approach into Galveston, Jay flew under a power line on landing.

When TTA acquired jets, Jay was flying co-pilot. On the DC-9s, there was a hydraulic system (high 3000 psi, low 1500 psi) on takeoff and landing that was at 3,000 psi [psi means pounds per square inch]. After takeoff, the gear retracts, flaps up, gear handle in neutral, then the landing gear rests on the landing gear doors. If the gear doors were locked, the gear would stay retracted. The hydraulic pumps are turned on low so if a leak occurs, it would only be in the 1500 psi range.

Jay continued to have problems knowing when to let down, and how to line up his approaches. Jay was called in for a simulator check ride. When the Captain finished his check ride, it was Jay's turn to fly. Jay took off but performed the gear check too quickly. He didn't leave the gear handle down in the neutral position long enough to bleed off the 3000 psi to ensure that the gear would stay retracted. As Jay was flying along in the simulator, the gear came out and the airplane yawed all over.

The check airman said, "Jay, you busted the check ride."

Jay got so mad in the simulator that he went over to the office of the Vice President of Operations and called him an SOB for "setting him up" in the simulator check ride. Jay was fired.

* * *

Les Kagler, the Check Airman: Les and several Braniff pilots were involved in a scheme to avoid paying income tax. An old German, a former U-Boat Captain in Hawaii, set up the scheme and recruited pilots to participate. Les signed on. Each pilot would start his own "church" to qualify for exemption from income taxes. The pilots deposited their paychecks to their "church" bank account. Finally, the government started cracking down on the tax-evasion scheme. Criminal charges were filed against Les and the company decided to fire him. At that time I was a union representative and I told the company they couldn't fire him until he was convicted. The company put him on leave of absence until the court case was resolved. The court date arrived, and Les had a lawyer who hired a jury consultant. The lawyer negotiated it down so all Les owed was $5,000 for several years of back taxes assessed under the tax evasion scheme.

I said, "Les, just pay the $5,000."

Les said, "No, I'm not going to pay it. The jury consultant says we're going to win this case."

Les lost his court case and lost his job. Les, another pilot and that pilot's kid went together and bought a Cessna 210 and put all kinds of fuel tanks in it and started smuggling cocaine. The kid was coming out of Central America with 700 pounds of cocaine on board and Les was meeting him at a small airport in Tennessee. The father was also going to meet his kid at the Tennessee airport. As the kid's father was driving into the airport, he saw the Drug Enforcement Agency (DEA) cars so he turned around and left. Les didn't see the DEA cars. The plane landed and the DEA agents arrested Les and the kid and confiscated the

700 pounds of cocaine. Les got out on bail. Before the trial, Les' body was found floating in Tampa Bay. The murder was never solved. We think he was murdered because he lost the 700 pounds of cocaine and somebody was pissed.

* * *

Motorcycle Racing: One of the hobbies I started while flying for TTA was riding motorcycles. It's funny how you start a hobby. I was home on reserve riding a bicycle with one of the neighborhood kids on the handlebars. I couldn't see where I was going, so I hit the curb. The bike was going over, and I put out my foot to break the fall so I wouldn't dump the kid on the ground. That broke our fall, the kid was fine, but I broke my ankle. While home recuperating from that injury, I bought my first motorcycle.

There was a State Circuit in Texas of 16 enduro motorcycle races. Enduro races were generally 100 to 125 miles and they were like a road rally. We rode through all kinds of hazardous places – rivers, up and down hills, etc. It was challenging and fun. I rode that circuit for several years. I won my class once and always finished pretty high. I had one advantage. When I first started riding there were no computers on the bikes. That came later. I had an old aviation E6B circular slide rule used for flight, and I put it on the bike. I could calculate precisely with the circular slide rule so that I knew what time I was supposed to be at each checkpoint.

Motorcycle Parts for Sale: I found some other things I could do to improve my situation in the races. The chains became a real issue – chains had to be adjusted many times during a race or they would be ruined. For water crossings, I developed a chain oiler so that when I pulled a lever on the handlebar, the chain would be oiled prior to entering the water. Then the chain could be oiled again after the water crossing by again pulling the lever. Any time during the race that I felt the chain needed to be oiled, I could pull the lever and oil the chain. There were a lot of chain oilers on the market at the time that dripped oil continuously. When going through water, the oil would be washed off the chain and it would take a lot of time to re-lube the chain. That was one of the items Bill Baker and I developed and sold to other riders.

The brakes on a motorcycle are subject to failure due to mud and water on the trail getting into the brake drum. I developed a device to seal the hub. I was riding in a national race in Fort Hood, Texas, with a number of celebrities there. Actor Steve McQueen, an excellent rider, was entered in the race. I was riding Penton motorcycles at that time, which was a KTM imported into the United States by the Penton family who sold them under the Penton name in the U.S. In the Fort Hood race, four bikes started each minute. One of the Penton boys was in my start group. His father had a great deal of pull. The Penton boy was flying a helicopter in Vietnam and his father got him pulled out of Vietnam to ride in this national race because he had to qualify in six national races to be put on the team to go to the Isle of Man for a worldwide endurance race.

In the Fort Hood race, all the bikes were impounded before the race. Entrants arrived the day before the race. All bikes were inspected and a little red dot was put on every part of each bike – the tires, wheels and brakes, etc. If you wanted to take any parts, you had to take them in at that time. Fifteen minutes prior to the assigned start time, racers were allowed into the impound area to do whatever maintenance was required before getting in line to start. Racers were penalized for each minute they were late starting.

The Penton boy and I rode the first day and went through mud. The next day when we started out, the Penton boy was changing his brakes. I told him I didn't have to change my brakes. He asked why. I showed him my seals. After the race, I pulled the seals and showed him my brakes. He said he had to have some of those seals. I told him I just had a few that I made for myself. He said he and his Dad would be glad to buy some. In addition to selling the motorcycles, the Pentons also had a parts business that sold all kinds of motorcycle parts and gear under the name Highpoint. The Penton business was located in Lorraine, Ohio and the Penton boy asked me to come up, bring some of the seals, and talk to him and his Dad.

Bill Baker, my partner, and I flew to Cleveland, rented a car and drove over to Lorraine and met with the Penton boy and his Dad. They were interested in our brake seal and wanted to buy them from us. They gave us an order for 200 seals. Back in Texas we went to the place where these were built for us. We had only one mold, but we made a new mold so they could make four seals at a time. We started selling the seals and this little side business became profitable for us. It went a long way toward paying for our racing expenses. We also received a discount from Highpoint on equipment we bought from them. We bought from Highpoint direct and didn't go through dealers. That was an interesting adventure.

Motorcycle Accident: My wife at the time, Mary Jane, told me that riding motorcycles is like being pregnant; you will eventually go to the hospital. That was true. I dislocated a hip, a shoulder and had several other injuries during my motorcycle riding days. The hip dislocation was one of the major injuries.

I met Bill Baker when he and his wife moved to Houston. His wife, Wilma Bullington Baker, was my first cousin on my Mom's side of the family. Bill had grown up in Arkansas just a little north of where I lived – Bill in Walnut Ridge, I lived in Balch, Pennington and Newport. We did not know each other in Arkansas. When we met in Houston, we found we had a lot of things in common. We became friends after we met in Houston, but didn't get really close until we both started riding motorcycles. Bill and Wilma were divorced sometime after we met, but Bill and I have remained friends and, of course, Wilma will always be my cousin.

Bill and I bought motorcycles at about the same time. We drove out to the National forests and rode our bikes together. Then we got interested in doing the enduro races and became lifelong friends. Bill carried me a lot of times.

One time I dislocated my hip while racing just outside of San Antonio. I was going down a two-lane grassy road through a field. To pass another rider, I swerved out into the field. I hit an irrigation pipe hidden in tall grass. I went over the handlebars and landed in sand. I thought that wasn't too bad. About that time my motorcycle landed on top of me and hit me in the rear end. The motorcycle on top of me was still running, but I couldn't move to turn it off. Another rider came along and hit the same pipe. I thought he was going to run over me, but he got his bike shut down and wasn't hurt. He turned off my bike and moved it off me. I told him to go to the next checkpoint and tell Bill Baker I was down and needed him to come get me. Bill got a John Deere tractor and trailer, picked me up, and took me back to his car. I was in shock, shaking and freezing. Baker drove me to a hospital in San Antonio. I still had my leathers on. Hospital personnel came out to the car and gave me a shot for the pain. That eased the pain enough that they got me out of the car and inside the hospital. They started taking my leathers off.

I said, "Just go ahead and cut them off, it hurts too bad."

The doctor said, "No, I ride motorcycles and these things are expensive, I'm not going to cut them off."

My father-in-law, Dr. Lewis, was head of surgery at Hermann Hospital in Houston. I asked the surgeon to call Dr. Lewis before he did anything, tell him what he was going to do, and see if Dr. Lewis agreed with the plan. The surgeon called Dr. Lewis who agreed with the surgeon's plan. The surgeon set my dislocated hip. I spent the night in the hospital and went home the next day. I was on crutches for three months before I could get back to flying and the accident took me out for that racing season.

Baker and I rode in these races for a few more years. One of the next races was the Greenhorn in California. It started in Duarte, California, just a little outside of Los Angeles. We went over the mountains of the Angeles National Forest and rode out through the desert to Edwards AFB. We spent the night there and returned the next day. We were used to riding in the woods and mud. Our bikes were not equipped for desert racing. We had little skinny knobby tires and those accustomed to riding in the desert had big wide wheels. I guess we really were greenhorns. It was quite an adventure racing in the California desert, and I enjoyed the time I spent riding motorcycles.

CHAPTER 15

People and Events

Hit at Fort Polk: After the airline shut down each night about midnight, draftees were ferried from Houston to Fort Polk, Louisiana. These guys were going over for basic training prior to being sent to Vietnam. On one trip, one of the guys went to the back with a bunch of newspapers and set the bathroom on fire. He had been drafted and didn't want to go to Vietnam.

At Fort Polk, a fan marker called "Coco" activated a flashing light on the airplane's instrument panel. Incoming aircraft were not allowed to pass Coco without permission from the control tower. This procedure was established so the army base could shut down its firing range. One night, I was flying with Captain Ken Smith. Ken was a good pilot, check airman and later became Assistant Chief Pilot. Ken and I were headed in to land and it was foggy. I was flying and we were cleared to land. Just as we passed Coco we heard a big *BAWHAM!*

Ken Smith said, "Oh, shit. They shot us!"

The airplane was still flying. As we broke out of the clouds, Ken Smith said, "You got the runway?"

I said, "No, I can't see the runway."

Ken said, "It's straight ahead."

I told him I couldn't see the runway and he had to take it and make the landing. When we taxied in, we could see what had happened. A big goose hit the plane and blood was splattered all over my side of the windshield.

Portzline Hit: Our situation wasn't unique. Captain Gary Portzline's airplane hit a goose, just on the outer edge of the windshield next to the metal rim. The metal opened the windshield enough that the splatter squirted blood and feathers into the cockpit. The metal rim popped back into place but Gary and the co-pilot had blood and feathers all over them. Gary rang the bell for the Flight Attendant to come to the cockpit. She had heard the WHAM from the bird hitting the aircraft. When she opened the door, she saw that both pilots were bloody and she started screaming.

Gary said, "We're okay! We're okay! We just need some paper towels."

Superstar Flight Attendant: As stated above, we flew the troops over at night, returned to Houston without any passengers, picked up another load, and flew another group to Fort Polk, back and forth, and we would finish just about daybreak. One night we were making our shuttle of troops with our first black flight attendant. We were flying along late at night and the Captain was dozing. I was flying and didn't realize the flight attendant was in the cockpit. Her face was about three inches from mine. When I turned my head, all I saw were her eyes. I was so scared that I jumped and hit my head against the windshield. When I jumped, I scared her, too. When we recovered, we both laughed.

Later when we were flying jets, this same flight attendant was on board. We were on the ground in Albuquerque waiting for our passengers to board the airplane. As we were going through the checklist one of the guys said, "Hey, look! Here comes Jane Fonda!"

At the time Jane Fonda was married to Tom Hayden. She was coming up the stairs with a huge hatbox. Our flight attendant had been a Marine tech sergeant and she was really good. I always told the flight attendants not to take any guff from a passenger, just come and get me

PEOPLE AND EVENTS

to handle it. Jane Fonda came up the stairs and started to get on with her hatbox.

The flight attendant said, "Miss Fonda, you can't bring that hatbox on board, we'll have to put it down below."

Miss Fonda refused to relinquish the hatbox. The argument got louder, louder and louder and I started to get out of my seat.

Before I got up, I heard the flight attendant say, "Miss Fonda, I'm the only superstar on this airplane, and you're not getting on with that hatbox."

The hatbox was sent to the baggage bin and Miss Fonda took her seat.

18-Year-Old Flight Attendant: In one of its moves, TTA decided to hire younger flight attendants and dropped the age down to 18. That was a young age to put girls out into the real world. They weren't always worldly. The flight might land in New Orleans and a young flight attendant would ask what state we were in.

We had one of these youngsters on a flight scheduled to spend the night in Memphis. After reaching the hotel in Memphis, the crew decided to have dinner at Kip's Big Boy – a casual hamburger joint. We walked to Kip's, ordered our dinner, and as they were bringing the food to our table, the young flight attendant received an emergency phone call – at Kip's Big Boy. I don't how in the world they found her, but they did.

When she returned to the table, she was crying her eyes out! I asked if there was a death in the family. She said no. I said if you are this upset, you probably shouldn't fly tomorrow. I told her there was another jet due in Memphis tonight and we could get another flight attendant on it and she could be relieved from duty and go on back to Houston. She said, no, she would go ahead and fly.

The next morning we got ready for our morning departure to make our milk run back to Houston. The young flight attendant had obviously been crying all night. Her eyes were red. And she was still teary. The closer we got to Houston, the more uptight she became. Finally, she came into the cockpit and said she really had to tell us what was going on. She had been partying in Dallas, got drunk, and went to bed with a guy in Dallas. When she went home she started feeling guilty about it. She told her boyfriend just before she left on the Memphis trip that she had been raped in Dallas. She did not want her boyfriend to know that it was consensual. Her boyfriend went over to her Dad's house and told him that his daughter had been raped in Dallas. The emergency phone call she received at Kip's Big Boy was from her Daddy, who told her when she got to Houston, they were going to get on an airplane, fly to Dallas and get the guy who raped her. Sure enough, when we pulled up to the gate in Houston, her Daddy was there to meet her. She told us her Daddy had a gun with him. Apparently, she handled it because no one got shot. I don't know what she did, but every time I saw her over the next 15 years of flying, that was the first thing that popped into my mind.

Religious Flight Attendant: When I was called back to TTA from furlough, I went back to flying DC-3s and Convairs. One flight attendant's aim in life was to sleep with all the pilots. And she kept a list. I wasn't on that list. Then she got religion: she started calling the wives of all the pilots she had slept with to apologize and tell them how sorry she was. I can imagine how well that went over.

I had the religious flight attendant on board for a trip that stopped in Tyler, Texas. As we were taking off from Tyler that evening, the right engine fire warning came on the Convair's instrument panel. We feathered the engine and shot the fire bottle into it. I left the cockpit to go to the back of the cabin to see if the fire was out. When I stepped into the cabin, the flight attendant was standing outside the front galley reading the Bible to our passengers.

I grabbed her, pulled her over into the galley, and said, "Honey, we've already scared them to death and now you've just confirmed that they're all going to die!"

Sick Sacks on Board: One of the hazards of flying on a DC-3 was its really bumpy ride. "Sick sacks" for passengers who threw up were standard issue for each seat on the DC-3. When a passenger threw up in the "sick sacks," the filled sacks were stowed next to the exit door of the aircraft and were picked up by the ground crew agents at each stop. One co-pilot came up with what he thought was a clever prank to play on the flight attendant. He filled a "sick sack" with undiluted chicken noodle soup and stowed it in the filled "sick sack" location. After the flight landed, he walked out, picked up the "sick sack," opened it, sniffed it and told the flight attendant, "This smells pretty good." He grabbed a spoon and started eating the contents of the "sick sack." The flight attendant promptly tossed her cookies!

Smoking on Board: In 1960, when my Dad died of lung cancer at age 43, I thought I really should quit smoking. But Dad smoked Camels – unfiltered – and I smoked Larks that had a charcoal filter that took out all the bad stuff, or so they said. I continued smoking for another five years, for a total of ten years. In that last five-year period, I was always coughing and hacking and I thought this was not good for me. So I put the cigarettes down in 1965 and never smoked again.

Smoking became an issue in the cockpit. We had many pilots who were smokers and many who were non-smokers. When the two were in the cockpit together, there was always an argument over whether smoking would be permitted in the cockpit. Finally, ALPA, the pilot's union, passed a resolution prohibiting smoking in the cockpit.

When there was still a smoking section in the rear of the cabin, just walking to the back of the airplane, I could tell exactly what row started the smoking section. People sitting in that section looked "old and wrinkled," their age really showed on their faces. That was another good motivation for me to quit. One side effect discovered when smoking was banned on the aircraft was that maintenance on the aircraft decreased. The aircraft is pressurized from air bleeding off the engines. The air comes off the engines at about 105 degrees centigrade, then goes through a couple of heat exchangers and an air cycle machine to cool the air down. Part of the air is cooled down to 40 degrees, then it is mixed with the other air to be comfortable in the cabin. This keeps the cabin pressurized. Any time you pump air into the cabin, with a differential of about 8 psi more inside than outside, you have to keep letting some air out. The system maintains the differential of 8 psi by opening and closing the outflow valves. The outflow valves are on the aft side of the DC-9s and MD-80s. There is a big round hole on the outside, about 10-12 inches in diameter. When flying with smokers, frequently these valves would get stuck. When walking around the airplane during smoking days, you could see a yellow streak from the outflow valve all the way to the tail where the cigarette smoke and nicotine was coming out of the aircraft. When smoking was banned on airplanes, the outflow valve problems disappeared along with the yellow nicotine and smoke streak along the length of the fuselage.

Be Concise With Commands: When I first checked out as Captain, one of the things I learned was that you need to be careful how and what you say to your First Officer, especially if he is new to your cockpit. I was landing at an airport where it was raining hard on half of the runway with a medium shower on the other half of the runway. As I briefed the First Officer on the approach, I told him when I turned into approach I wanted him to turn the wipers on full when the rain turns heavy, to keep the windshield clear.

As I turned into final approach, the rain started picking up and I told him, "Give me Full…"

I never got to say "Windshield Wipers" – he put full flaps down. It pitched the airplane up and I couldn't imagine what had happened. Then I realized what he had done. From then on, prior to giving the command, I would say "Flaps full" or "Windshield Wipers full." It was a lesson I learned early on and one that has served me well.

First Fatal Flight: The company prided itself on never killing a passenger. That came to an end in Mena, Arkansas, on September 27, 1973.

In Dallas, I flew with a guy named Max Crossman. Max was a guy who – regardless of the subject – knew more about it than anyone within earshot. If the Bible was the subject, Max would say he had talked to God straight on and knew everything. He was domineering and opinionated. I wrote in my logbook that he would be troublesome some day because he never listened to anyone but himself.

Captain Crossman flew the west end of the company's route system because it was VFR (visual flight rules) ninety percent of the time. For some reason Crossman started to bid trips on the eastern end of the route system that had a lot of weather.

I was in bed and received a call about midnight from crew scheduling and they said, "We've got an airplane down."

I said, "How do you know you have an airplane down?"

"Well, it ran out of gas two hours ago and we've had no reports on it," was the reply.

I called the Captain's representative in Dallas and told him he needed to go over to Captain Crossman's home and get some people to hold his wife's hand and tell her what was going on. They got to her house but she was not home. They waited for her.

Flight 655 was a Convair 600 making a round trip flight from Dallas to Memphis, Tennessee, with intermediate stops at Texarkana, El Dorado and Pine Bluff, Arkansas. The accident occurred during the westbound flight from El Dorado to Texarkana with eight passengers and three crewmembers for a total of eleven on board. The crew of Flight 655 contacted the El Dorado Flight Services Station and requested an airport advisory. The controller on duty advised the crew of the prevailing wind, altimeter setting and traffic. He also told them that there were two pilots who had been briefed on the weather toward the west of El Dorado and they could supply Flight 655 with additional weather information. When Flight 655 landed in El Dorado, the crew conferred with the waiting pilots and used the Convair's weather radar to examine the weather echoes west of El Dorado. There was a cold front with associated thunderstorms and instrument meteorological conditions. Flight 655 departed El Dorado at 8:15 pm. As Flight 655 taxied to runway 22, the crew contacted the FSS (Flight Service Station) and stated that they were taxiing and would be proceeding under visual flight rules (VFR) to Texarkana. [See Appendix B: NTSB Report Number NTSB-AAR-74-4 – two pages only]

After takeoff, the crew was scud-running to skirt around clouds and thunderstorms in the cold front. The aircraft operated between altitudes of 1,500 feet and 3,000 feet until 8:49 pm. From that time until the time of impact at 8:54 pm the aircraft's altitude varied between 2,200 feet and 2,025 feet. Captain Crossman did not activate the computer-stored instrument flight plan. They were winding around to avoid the rainstorms, but were actually going around the mountainous terrain that was obscured by the clouds and rainstorms. They flew almost an hour on a 20-minute flight. The First Officer kept prodding the Captain, asking him where they were. The First Officer was flying and the Captain was watching the radar, but a lot of the echoes on the radar were mountains. The Cockpit Voice Recorder (CVR) and Flight Data Recorder (FDR) confirmed that the First Officer, who was flying the aircraft, was following the heading and altitude orders given by the Captain. Unfortunately, much of what the Captain saw on the radar were mountains.

Finally, the First Officer said, "Max, I need to know where we are."

The First Officer had Crossman hold the airplane while he looked at the chart.

The last thing on the CVR tape was the First Officer saying, "Minimum en route altitude is forty-four hund . . ."

Then KABOOM – the airplane crashed and killed the eleven people on board.

It was three days before the crash site was discovered. A Cessna pilot spotted the airplane's tail sticking up with the big star on it. The crash site was in the Ouachita Mountain Range near Mena, Arkansas. The crew had deviated approximately 100 nautical miles north of the direct course to their destination. It did not occur to anyone that the flight would be 100 miles off course. The NTSB report concluded that the crew attempted to operate the aircraft visually in instrument meteorological conditions. The report further stated the carrier did not monitor and control adequately the actions of the flight crew or the progress of the flight.

The site could not be reached by ground, so the company hired an Army helicopter and sent one of our pilots, a member of ALPA's Safety Committee. He was dropped on a rope from the helicopter to the crash site. The crash site was horrendous. The only item recognizable as an aircraft was the tail section spotted by the Cessna. All the pieces at the crash site were ten inches and smaller, including the engines, landing gears, wheels, and fuselage – everything. Body parts were all over the place. The aircraft crashed into the steep, heavily wooded, north slope of Black Fork Mountain in the Ouachita Mountain Range. Impact occurred at an elevation of 2,025 feet, 600 feet below the top of the ridge.

The pilot sent to the crash site was shook up after seeing the area where the only thing recognizable as an airplane was the tail. When he came back on line and started flying, he was having a tough time. His experience at the crash site affected his ability to fly. As he was shooting an approach into Los Angeles, it was 1,800 feet overcast, which is above minimums, yet he missed the approach. He came back in and landed. When he got back to Houston, he resigned. He said he could not fly any more after seeing the crash site in Mena.

Continental Crash at Stapleton Airport, Denver: On August 7, 1975, Continental Flight 426 was departing from Denver Stapleton

PEOPLE AND EVENTS

airport on Runway 9 to the east. I talked to the First Officer who was flying the aircraft. He told me the weather at the time of departure was VFR – okay. There had been some weather, but it had passed over the airport and was out to the west. After takeoff at about 160 knots, the airspeed dropped and the stick shaker activated. He pushed the throttles to the firewall. The aircraft continued to descend. When it became obvious the aircraft was going to impact the ground, he called for gear down. After impact, the gear collapsed as designed. The aircraft slid across an asphalt road and came to a stop in a gully.

The NTSB ruled the accident due to pilot error based on the crew lowering the landing gear. ALPA's Safety Committee investigated the crash. The Safety Committee located a truck driver whose 18-wheeler was blown off the same road that Flight 426 crossed just a few minutes before the crash occurred. Also a large billboard had been blown down about 100 yards from the crash site. After two years, the NTSB reversed its findings and re-classified the accident as caused by wind shear.

Texas International Crash at Stapleton Airport, Denver: On November 16, 1976, Texas International Flight No. 987, a McDonnell Douglas DC-9-14, crashed after rejecting a takeoff from Runway 8 right at Stapleton International Airport in Denver. A new Captain aborted his takeoff on Runway 8 because when he reached rotation speed, and started rotating up, the stall warning stick-shaker activated after the aircraft had rotated for takeoff. At that time the approach lights were not breakaway lights; they were made out of railroad track. The airplane ran off the runway, across drainage ditches and hit the approach lights. The crash sliced one of the wings in half and the airplane caught on fire. All the passengers and crew made a successful evacuation. The only available evacuation exit was through the tail cone. The flight attendant dropped the tail cone off and opened the door. One male passenger stepped on the flight attendant and got off ahead of others. Eighty-one passengers and five crewmembers evacuated the aircraft; 14 persons were injured. The aircraft was a total loss and that was the last aircraft lost at Texas International.

World War II Pilot, Bailey Gordon: I was fortunate to fly with several World War II pilots and many of their stories were interesting. Bailey Gordon went through cadet training in Victoria, Texas. He knew he couldn't navigate but the last thing they had to do before they got their wings and released from cadet training to start flying in the Army Air Corps, was to make a night cross-country trip, from Victoria to Corpus Christi to San Antonio and back to Victoria.

Four planes were making the flight. Bailey said, "I knew I was going to get lost if I got out there by myself."

Bailey climbed up over Victoria and circled. He stayed there, circling, and each time the other three airplanes reported in, Bailey reported in with them – when they were over Corpus Christi and San Antonio. When the other three airplanes returned to Victoria, Bailey came in and landed with them.

Bailey got his wings and later he was in North Africa, flying P-39 fighter planes. Bailey said the briefers would tell them where the German antiaircraft fire was located and how to get around it to shoot the German tanks. Bailey was so afraid of getting lost that he never took any evasive action. Bailey would take the heading he used to take him out there, shoot what was there, turn around, and fly back. After about six or eight weeks, Bailey knew he would get lost out there. The desert in North Africa all looked the same.

He went to his squadron commander and said, "Hey, I need to get on a B-17."

The B-17 has a navigator. After much persuasion, they released him and he got on a B-17 operation. On a B-17 flight over Czechoslovakia, the aircraft took a shell through the wing from antiaircraft fire. The plane caught fire and the Captain gave the signal for all to bail out. Bailey turned off all the switches and bailed out. There was no need to turn off the switches; the plane was going to crash. Due to his training, when you get out of the airplane, you turn off all the switches. When he got on the ground, the Germans were looking for him and a lady came out, got him, took him to her home, and hid him in the crawlway under her house. She contacted the underground, and they came for Bailey after about two weeks. Over the next 30 days the underground contacts walked Bailey back to Allied lines. In 1974, he went back to Czechoslovakia and met the lady who had hidden him in her home. He said it was an emotional meeting.

I remember flying a trip with Bailey Gordon. We were coming out of Mexico up to Houston. When we got close to Houston, Houston Ops called and said they wanted us to go to Dallas, not Houston.

Bailey said, "Okay."

I said, "Bailey, we need to take a look at our fuel situation here and I'll calculate the fuel, get the weather, and find out how we can clear customs in Dallas. I'm not sure it's an international airport."

I did all that and we landed in Dallas.

Bailey said, "Well, Jim, I think you were the Captain on this flight instead of me."

It was good to fly with Bailey.

World War II Pilot, Les Zollars: Les was laid back and had many good stories to tell. He was an easy guy to fly with – congenial and just a good guy.

Les Zollars was a big guy and he claimed he used to be roommates with Ernest Hemingway – I don't know if it was true. Les was a colorful character. In one of his first adventures, he was flying a P-38 over Louisiana at night. The plane caught fire; Les bailed out and landed in a swamp. He said he imagined that the swamp was full of alligators and snakes. It was night and he couldn't see in the dark, but he did see one little light in the distance. He was afraid to walk across the swamp to the light because a water moccasin or an alligator might get him. Les found a stump that he could perch on and stayed on that stump all night long. The next morning he walked out.

Les went to Europe where he flew P-61s that were big twin-engine airplanes with a lot of firepower. He said there were free-fire zones where you could fly in and shoot anything you wanted. Les found a canal where the Germans had put barges and he would go in and shoot it up. He was not only doing well but was also having a lot of fun because he could see the water splash up as he shot the barges. One day Les made the run, went again the next day, but on the third day the Germans were waiting for him with antiaircraft fire. He said they shot holes all through that airplane. When he got back to his base and landed, the hydraulics were gone.

World War II Pilot, Buddy Benedict: Buddy was really laid back. I made one trip with him to Denver. At the time, airways had VOR stations to fly over; the pilot must turn to a different airway from each VOR station crossed. The airplane had a mode on the autopilot that could be turned on so that it would follow the airway – the autopilot would be locked into the airway. Close to the VOR station, the needle became sensitive and started going left, then right. The airplane would start going left, then right. Most pilots would just turn off the navigation mode when they got close to a VOR station. After the airplane flew over the VOR station, the pilot turned the heading bug to go out the next airway. When the plane was past the VOR station, the pilot would flip the switch back on to navigation mode on autopilot.

Buddy was flying the airplane. One of the first things Buddy liked to do when the airplane leveled off was to smoke a cigarette and read the *Wall Street Journal*. On the heading to Denver we approached a VOR station. Buddy had the airplane's heading bug turned to go outbound from the VOR station. Then the airplane started drifting out to the right side of the airway that was to the east. I told Buddy he needed to change his heading.

Finally, ATC called and said, "Hey, Texas, you're about three miles east of the airway. Make a heading correction."

Buddy reached up and turned the heading bug. We intercepted the airway and start heading toward the other side.

ATC called and said, "Hey, Texas, you guys are now about three miles to the west of the airway. How about making a heading correction?"

Buddy said, "Hey, Jim, I've got it."

Buddy picked up the mike and said, "I'm doing the very best I can."

Buddy was 23 years old when he became aircraft commander on a B-17 and he was the oldest guy on the crew. Buddy had 240 hours total flying time. They were going to Europe to join the 8th Air Force. Fighter planes will not pursue if you stay in tight formation — start straggling off and they'd pick you off. After Buddy flew several missions, they had to change all four engines on his plane. After the engine changes, Buddy departed on a mission. As they were going in for the bomb run, Buddy had to keep adding power to keep up because the engines were so tight. After he pulled off the target, Buddy started getting low oil pressure lights. The plane started going down with the maximum power they could pull and it was still sinking about 300 to 400 feet a minute. The crew threw overboard everything that would weigh them down – machine guns, helmets, everything not tied down. The plane was still drifting down, drifting down, drifting down. When they reached 4,000 feet, after flying for some time, it sounded like they had run into a hailstorm. Buddy realized he had flown over the front lines in France and every German that had a pistol was shooting at them. Buddy told his crew that he would fly about another 10 minutes to the Allied side of the front lines and then all could bail out. He crossed the front line and flew 10 minutes and told the crew to bail out. But they all just stood there looking at him. Buddy turned the plane on autopilot, got out of his seat and opened the navigator's hatch. The air hit him when the navigator's hatch opened.

Buddy said, "God, I've talked to you many times, just let me live through this and I'll be in church every Sunday."

Buddy said he promised God everything he could think of before he bailed out. Then the rest of the guys bailed and everybody's chute opened. The plane went on a couple of miles, then two engines quit on the left side and the plane made a big circle.

Buddy thought "Oh my God, the plane's coming back and it's going to run over us!"

When Buddy got on the ground, a Frenchman came up and gave him a bottle of wine. Buddy sat there and drank the whole bottle before he moved.

The GI's got the crew back to their base. Buddy told the base commander what had happened.

The base commander asked Buddy, "Where's the Norton bombsite?"

The Norton bombsite was a high tech, top-secret bombsite that had to be recovered. The CO sent Buddy back to the crash site to get the Norton bombsite out of the airplane.

World War II Pilot, Eddie Andreas: Eddie Andreas flew 51 missions out of Africa in a B-24. He came out of World War II very nervous – he talked in a constant stream and was always moving, couldn't keep still. Once during negotiations when he was responsible for the retirement benefit portion of the contract, he had little to do so he went out to lunch. He came back and told us he found us a good place to eat that night – really good steaks. So we all went together for dinner in Eddie's new place, and placed our dinner orders. While waiting for our order, we began to notice that the place had only men in it and many were holding hands. Eddie had found a gay bar! We got our dinner, ate it really fast, and left.

I flew with Eddie Andreas quite a bit and Eddie was nervous in the cockpit. Anytime a switch was flipped, he had to look and see what happened. "Who did that?" "What did you do?" But he was a great guy, but nervous as a cat on a hot tin roof. It was fun to fly with him because he was a stickler for watching everything and making sure everything was done. If he heard a noise, he wanted to know who did it and why it was done.

Other Pilots: Most of the pilots were professional and beyond belief good stick and rudder guys. They were up and down all the time shooting approaches on the Gulf Coast that involved a lot of fog and weather. Only the jets had autopilots while the DC-3s and Convairs had to be flown by the pilots, most of whom were outstanding. A few are at the other end of the spectrum. J.V. Sclifo, the Chief Pilot, and I agreed that 95 percent of problems were caused by 5 percent of the same pilots. As union representative, it was my duty to represent all the pilots, even the 5 percent pilot population responsible for 95 percent of the problems.

Here is a glimpse of a few of those pilots who were out in left field.

Other Pilot, Ground Loop: A few of the Captains I flew with were really not the best pilots. The first was a Captain who was deathly afraid of a ground loop. A ground loop occurs when flying the DC-3. If you get a little wind or get crossways of the runway when landing, the DC-3 tail wants to swap ends with its nose. This Captain had a ground loop happen to him in a Lockheed Lodestar before going to work for TTA and left him deathly afraid of a ground loop happening upon landing. He made all the takeoffs and landings. The only thing he would allow his co-pilots to do was fly en route while the Captain made all the takeoffs and landings. One day he was landing in Louisiana. He came off the runway onto the taxiway at a pretty high speed and the airplane ground looped on him. Soon he was going across the ramp backwards. He got it stopped and unloaded the passengers, but it was comical to hear the ground agents talk about seeing the DC-3 coming across the ramp backwards.

Other Pilot, Stickler: Another Captain was a stickler. When you flew with him, he would take forever to taxi out to the runway. You would run the approved checklist only to learn Captain Stickler had another 15 to 20 personal items added to the checklist. After that, he would be ready to go. He would gouge the company whenever he could. He was always slow. He never would hustle. If he was behind schedule, he was just behind schedule, he would not try to make it up. In the nose wheel area, there is a light that can be turned on if you need to see if the nose gear is down and locked. If the nose gear doesn't come down, you look for line marks, and it's a "no go" item if the lights are not working. The guys on the ground in Houston said the Captain knew the light was burned out before he left for Mexico City. When he got to Mexico City, he wrote up the burned out light. As a result, the company had to arrange to replace the light and it took a six to seven hour delay in Mexico City to get the light bulb replaced. That repair would have taken about 30 minutes in Houston. After that the company called me in to talk about this Captain. They asked me to talk to the Captain and tell him they would pay his salary but they wanted him to stay home and not fly anymore. I went to the Captain's house and presented the company's proposal to him. He saw right through the proposal. He said if they kept him out long enough he would no longer be current to fly and would have to go through training again. Then the company would have a shot at washing him out. He was stubborn. When a strike came on and a buyout was offered, a pilot had to sign a waiver that he would not sue Continental if he took the buyout. The Captain's buyout was $160,000. He refused to sign the waiver and decided to fight the company in court. He lost his $160,000 buyout and never got any satisfaction out of Continental Airlines.

Other Pilot, No Go Joe: The next Captain was called No Go Joe. He had a reason for being afraid of thunderstorms. His brother was killed in the Navy flying through a thunderstorm. The saying about No Go Joe was that if he walked out on the ramp and saw a puddle of water, he wasn't going. One day he was sitting in Lake Charles and other flights were going in and out but No Go Joe sat there and refused to fly because of the weather. His nickname was well deserved.

Other Pilot, Captain Lizard: Another Captain who fit into this category was called The Lizard. The flight attendant, who made it her goal to sleep with all the pilots until she got religion, fell in love with the Lizard. He was flying a trip down to Mexico City and she went down on the flight to spend the night with Captain Lizard. This occurred after she converted to the "talking in tongues" religion. When the couple reached the airport the next morning to get on the return flight to Houston, they learned there were not enough seats on the flight for the flight attendant. She had a departure at noon in Houston so she had to be on the flight. Captain Lizard suggested that she go sit in the bathroom. That was fine until they cleared Customs in the United States and there were more passengers than there were seats available. Captain Lizard was turned in to the FAA. He went over to the FAA to respond, and was given a slight reprimand.

Captain Lizard's next incident involved a wingtip landing in McAllen. You really have to work to scrape a wingtip in a DC-9 during a landing situation. I called Captain Lizard and his co-pilot to explain how this happened. They delivered their story and it was obvious they had a cross wind and overcorrected. I told them we would have to meet with the FAA.

I told the Captain what I wanted him to say: "I thought it was a little rough but I thought it was within the parameters."

I told Captain Lizard and his co-pilot not to say anything more, but to let me do the talking.

When we sat down with the FAA, the examiner asked what happened and I explained it to him. The FAA examiner said that sounded reasonable. Then he asked the Captain what he thought. Captain Lizard started talking and talking and talking, while I was kicking him under the table. Finally, I said we needed to take a break.

I got Captain Lizard out in the hall and told him this thing could be settled if he would just keep his mouth shut. I told him, "The way you are talking you are about to lose your license!"

We went back to the meeting and finally got the matter resolved so that he did not lose his license. However, Captain Lizard was always in some kind of trouble.

* * *

Furlough: I flew for about seven months before the airline started having trouble and started cutting the schedule back. I was in Fort Polk one night and one of my classmates came out, banged on my plane, and said "We won't have to be flying this junk next week."

I said, "What do you mean?"

I thought maybe we were going to get checked out on the Convair or a jet.

He said, "No, we're going to be furloughed next week."

I went back to Houston, very downhearted. I called Dick Barker and told him it looked like I was going to be furloughed and he said to come on back to Pan American Sulphur and I'll get rid of this guy. I flew there for about nine months and then returned to Trans Texas. It was a good thing for me because I was making about $500 to $600 per month; I went back to flying the Gulfstream making $1,000 per month. That got my savings back up a little bit and helped a lot.

CHAPTER 16

Labor Relations and ALPA

Let me explain a little about the unions. There are good unions, bad unions and a lot in between. The Air Line Pilots Association ("ALPA") is a unique union: There is a national president, an airline pilot who is elected by the pilots of all the airlines represented by ALPA. Each airline's union is run by its own pilots. The first item in the ALPA Code of Ethics is:

An Air Line Pilot will keep uppermost in his mind that the safety, comfort, and well-being of the passengers who entrust their lives to him are his first and greatest responsibility. [See Appendix C: ALPA Code of Ethics].

National ALPA Governance: At TTA and TI, two representatives at each crew base – Houston and Dallas – were elected to run the TI union. With most national unions, such as the Teamsters or AFL-CIO, the union is represented by a person appointed by the national office and that person is not an employee of the company. At TTA and TI, each crew base had a captain's representative and a co-pilot's representative. This was the local executive council ("LEC"). Two LECs, when they met, became the Master Executive Council ("MEC"). The pilots on the MEC elect one in their group as the Master Executive Council Chairman ("MEC Chairman").

Local ALPA Governance: When I first started at TTA, the guys elected were the guys who bad-mouthed the company the loudest. That's the guy the pilots wanted to go tear up the company representatives so the pilots could make lots of money. That approach made everybody feel good but it didn't accomplish much.

In the beginning, I was on reserve most of the time, which meant I was at home and they would call me out when they needed a pilot because an airplane broke down, a pilot called in sick, or something of that nature. While at home, I read the contract agreement between TTA and ALPA from top to bottom. I knew that contract inside out. While sitting around the crew room, pilots would come in with contract issues and ask if I knew about a particular provision. I would tell them what the contract said and what it meant. I got the reputation of knowing the contract really well.

I was flying with Captain Ken Smith. Ken had been a contract negotiator and he asked if he nominated me as a first officer rep, would I take it, and I said, "Yeah, I'll take it." I was elected first officer's rep and the captain's rep was Captain Adams, who had been a B-36 instructor pilot. He was a good guy, calm and didn't yell about the company. Dallas also had a captain's rep and a first officer rep. We had the first MEC meeting with both councils. I noticed that the first officer from Dallas agreed with the Captain's rep from Dallas regardless of what he said. I would hold my hand up and say, "Hey, guys, I don't think that is quite fair or quite right." It was apparent right away that the first officer's rep from Dallas was afraid to talk in front of his captain's rep or say anything bad.

HIMS Program: When Stan Pointer was the MEC Chairman, several places in the industry were beginning to start a program of treatment for alcohol and drug abuse called Human Intervention Motivation Study (HIMS). Stan was successful in bringing the HIMS program onto the property. The problem at that time was that no one wanted to turn in a pilot because, generally, pilots turned in lost their license to fly and no longer had their livelihood. Alcohol and drug abuse, thus, was tolerated as much as possible until the problem was turned over to the Professional Standards Committee.

When the HIMS program came along, there was a way to deal with problems of alcoholism and drug abuse. There would be an intervention with the alcoholic pilot in which the pilot is told that that we were not doctors but that the pilot had shown signs that often indicate a problem with alcohol or drugs, such as no sick leave available, unable to get along with crew members, etc. The FAA requires that after rehab the pilot must be off line for two years, during which the pilot would be tested every month to confirm no alcohol or drug intake. The problem with this treatment is the pilot didn't have the means to support himself or his family for two years. As a result, there was reluctance for pilots to go into the program.

I looked at the rehabilitation issues and discussed them with Don Breeding, Vice President of Flight Operations. I told Don that we had to do something more in order to rehabilitate the pilots. By the time we reached these guys, they have used up their sick leave, depleted their savings, and the wife and the family are trying to protect the pilot and his job. We needed to tell these guys in our intervention that we realize he will be out of a job for two years because the FAA will not allow the pilot to fly for two years after the intervention. We needed to find the pilot a job within the company where he could work and earn enough to survive. I proposed that a pilot in rehab be permitted to use sick leave in advance. In other words the company would establish a bank of sick leave time. If a pilot did not call in sick for a month, four or five hours are added to his sick leave bank. Pilots with alcoholism or drug abuse problems would use up sick leave every month because they would be hung over and call in sick.

Don agreed to the plan and the program became successful on the property. Following is a report from the November 1977 issue of *The Straight Bull Sheet:*

HIMS REPORT
Rehabilitated Pilots Return to Flying

The Human Intervention and Motivation Study (HIMS) has successfully completed almost three years of program activities. During the first 30 months of operation, approximately

250 pilots have received advice and assistance for a variety of alcohol-related problems. Fourteen percent of the cases were self-referred, 72% were referred by ALPA personnel, 5% were referred by management or company medical departments, and 9% were referred by friends, family, FAA and others. Until that point, 73 pilots had been referred to in-patient treatment, while the others have been referred to out-patient counseling, AA, self-help programs, or sought treatment on their own. In some of these cases, we were advisory only; in others, the problem was not alcoholism. The Aeromedical Office presented 74 cases to the FAA for certification. Seventy-three were recertified. No pilot was denied on the basis of alcoholism alone. Denials are based upon poor prognosis, continued drinking, or the presence of other disqualifying illnesses. 89% of those who received our medical endorsement and were recertified maintained sobriety, while the 11% who returned to drinking are again off flight status and in some phase of further rehabilitation.

Professional Standards Committee: ALPA's Professional Standards Committee was put together to resolve problems that pilots were having. When a Captain and First Officer were in dispute or conflict, the Committee tried to take care of the problem before it became an issue with the company. When the company was handling an issue, an ALPA rep would go to the company and request that the company allow ALPA to attempt to resolve the issue first. There were people on the Committee from every seniority group so if a Senior Captain was having an issue, he or she could talk to a Senior Captain on the Committee; if the person was a medium seniority person, either Captain or First Officer, then they could find their counterpart on the Committee. Junior seniority levels also had a representative on the Committee. Once a pilot went to the Committee and asked for help, the one helping would write down all details of the problem and then go to the other party in the dispute or conflict and discuss it with him, talk again with the complaining pilot, then get both parties together to discuss the issue in an effort to resolve the dispute or conflict.

When I was MEC Chairman, I went to the company and asked them to tell us of any problems so we could intervene in an attempt to resolve problems before the company got involved. This included operational problems, or someone abusing the system or someone not conforming to standard procedures. The Professional Standards Committee did a lot of good for the airline and for the pilots by following standard procedures for dispute resolution.

Scheduling Committee: The Scheduling Committee would receive the trip pairings from the company and place them on the lines each month. Occasionally they had to deal with trip pairings that were not legal.

Grievance Committee: If a pilot had a grievance with the company, he would go to the Grievance Committee and, in turn, the Committee would file the grievance with the company. Next would be a grievance hearing. If the issue was not resolved at that step, it would go to what was called the System Board. This Board – comprised of two people from the company and two from ALPA – would attempt to work it out. If the System Board failed to resolve the conflict, then a "Neutral" would be called. A "Neutral" would be a professor or someone along that line. Some did this part-time and some full-time. The Neutral would sit on the System Board along with two pilots and two company personnel. If the company personnel voted one way and the two pilots voted another way, then the Neutral would come down with a decision.

Accommodations (Hotel) Committee: This committee would look at how far the hotel was from the airport and the accommodations for providing meals when there were late arrivals. Another issue that occurred with late arrivals in some hotels was the deployment of housekeeping service early in the morning and the hallway noise made by housekeeping. It was impossible for our crews to rest in such accommodations. We were successful in most hotels in getting rooms in a section of the hotel that had already been cleaned, were quiet, and housekeeping would not be on the floor until much later in the morning.

The people who served on these committees were pilots. They volunteered to serve on these committees on their days off. They were not paid for service but their service contributed to creating better working conditions for all flight crews. If a meeting was scheduled and the pilot could not get his flight changed to attend the meeting, the MEC budget would be used to buy the pilot's trip. Many dedicated people worked on the various committees.

CHAPTER 17

Based in Dallas

On February 18, 1973, when I returned from vacation, I called Crew Scheduling, and was told I had been transferred to Dallas. They told me I was scheduled on a flight out of Dallas the next morning. I drove to Dallas and checked into a hotel near Love Field for the trip the next day.

Flying out of Dallas was a unique experience because it was different from the crew base in Houston. Dallas flight crews were away from headquarters and the uniforms were not regulation. None of them wore hats, but all wore cowboy boots. Procedures were not followed as in Houston. It was just a different group – they all owned ranches. One Houston pilot was in Dallas and they asked him if he had a ranch and he said "yes." They asked how many head he had, and he said "18." They asked how many acres, and he said "half an acre" – and told them his "18 head" were kitty cats.

Ultimately, the Dallas crew base was closed because the company lost its feed-in to Eastern Airlines. The Dallas LEC insisted on a face-to-face meeting with Frank Lorenzo, President of Texas International, without the presence of any Houston ALPA representatives. They had their meeting with Frank. That didn't stop the company from closing the Dallas crew base.

I had memorable experiences with a particular Captain in Dallas. The company hired Jerry when he was 19 years old. His Daddy was a big wheel with the FAA and the company was trying to make some points, I guess. When Jerry was 23, he was checked out as Captain. I flew with Jerry on my first or second trip out of Dallas on the Convair 600 that used water methanol on takeoff to get extra power out of the engines. Use of water methanol was limited to two to three minutes on takeoff and then the throttles were pulled back and the water methanol disengaged.

Captain Jerry flew the first leg as we departed Dallas. After the first three minutes the water methanol was still running.

I said, "Jerry, we're still on the water methanol."

Jerry said, "Oh yeah, I always keep full power with the water on until we get leveled off."

I said, "Jerry, that's really not the procedure. We're going to burn these engines up. Then some pilot will get on this plane and have an engine failure."

He said, "No, I've been doing it ever since I've been flying the 600. It's no problem."

I said, "I'll tell you what, Jerry. You may have been doing it since you've been flying this plane, but I'm not going to fly this way. You either pull those throttles back or when we get to our destination, I'm going to get off, call the company and tell Crew Scheduling to replace me."

He said, "Okay, I'll do it."

Jerry pulled the power back and flew the rest of the trip following the standard procedure for pulling the power back after three minutes.

There were several other incidents with Jerry but I never thought much about it. Later on someone turned him in to the Chief Pilot, probably one of the other Houston co-pilots that had been bumped back up to Dallas. Jerry came to me and said, "You SOB, you turned me in!"

I said, "What are you talking about?"

Jerry said, "You turned me in for using water methanol all the time!"

I said, "No, Jerry, I didn't do that. I told you what I was going to do and that's what I did. And if I had a problem with you, then I would have gone to the Professional Standards Committee and talked to them. I would not have gone to the Chief Pilot."

I don't know if he ever believed it or not but that was part of my adventures in Dallas.

When I first moved to Dallas, I stayed in an apartment with one of the other pilots. Later I bought a house for my family in Carrollton and paid $57,000. The house we had in Houston, we built from scratch, really liked it a lot and paid $17,400. So it was quite an increase in cost. The kids did not like their school in Carrollton and I was not thrilled flying out of the Dallas base. We lived in Carrollton for about a year and I finally got a bid in Houston so we could move back.

CHAPTER 18

Enter Frank Lorenzo

Trans Texas Airlines ("TTA") started having problems. TTA was started by the McKaughan family. McKaughan, Sr. stepped down as President and he put his son in, McKaughan, Jr., who was a good friend of the Chief Pilot in Dallas. The company had jets on order – DC-9s. McKaughan, Jr. and the Chief Pilot cooked up a scheme where TTA would buy a jet Commander, an executive airplane, so that Trans Texas pilots could become familiar with flying jets. The only time I know it was flown was when the Dallas Chief Pilot and McKaughan, Jr. loaded it up with flight attendants and flew it to Acapulco on weekends. McKaughan, Jr.'s tenure as President didn't last long. When the jets were delivered to TTA, the company had been awarded the route from Houston to Dallas under the old CAB rules. That was a lucrative route dominated by Braniff for years. When they put the jets on that route, TTA's performance was poor. The company tried to determine how to increase the passenger loads on those flights. At a Board of Directors meeting McKaughan, Jr. said, "I know how we're going to fill these airplanes. We're going to put topless flight attendants on the Houston-Dallas route, and I know the flight attendants who are willing to do this." That was end of McKaughan, Jr.'s tenure as President of Trans Texas Airlines. As the jets came on line, the company didn't know how to put them in places where they would generate revenue.

TTA hired a consulting company – Lorenzo and Carney. They had been consulting for British West Indies Airline (BWI) and then for Mohawk Airlines. In the course of restructuring Mohawk, Lorenzo and Carney decided they would like to take over Mohawk, so they made an offer. However, Mohawk's Board agreed to accept a stock-only offer from Allegheny Airlines. Bob Peach had been the key person in building and running Mohawk for more than 27 years and could not bear to watch his airline disappear. He walked out of the boardroom before the Board took its final vote. Peach resigned one week later. Less than two weeks later on April 20, 1971, Peach, aged 51, was found dead from a self-inflicted gunshot wound at his home in Clinton, New York.

Lorenzo and Carney were hired by TTA to restructure the company and make it profitable. As they went through the company and straightened out the route system, they put the jets where they became profitable. Lorenzo and Carney made the same offer to TTA that they had made to Mohawk. Lorenzo and Carney had fees due of about $800,000 for their consulting work and they asked that the $800,000 in fees be paid in company stock. They borrowed more money and made an offer to buy TTA – I forget the actual purchase amount. TTA held a board meeting at the Bank of the Southwest in Houston to entertain the Lorenzo and Carney offer to purchase its stock. During this meeting, Hughes Air West, which was owned by Howard Hughes, sent an offer for TTA's stock which was about $20 more per share more than Lorenzo and Carney were going to pay – Hughes' offer was a cash offer, not just a payoff. It was rumored that there was a fist fight at the Board of Directors meeting over taking the Hughes Air West offer. At the end of the day, Lorenzo convinced the Board that since Hughes offer was sent by telegram, it was not a real offer.

As a result, Lorenzo and Carney took over Trans Texas. At that point, I called ALPA and asked them to do a background check on Lorenzo and Carney to see what the deal was and what kind of people they were. The report revealed that Carney and Lorenzo had gone to

Harvard together. Carney was well off – I think his family was involved with U.S. Steel. Lorenzo grew up poor in New York City and got a scholarship to Harvard to get his Master's Degree. After Lorenzo graduated from Harvard, he was employed in the accounting department of TWA Airline for two years and then moved to Eastern Airlines for another two years. After his stint of accounting at two airlines, Carney and Lorenzo each contributed money to form a company called Jet Capital. They planned to lease executive jet aircraft to oil companies. However, the oil boom was over and they didn't have any place to lease airplanes, but they had cash to start a business. They did not pursue the airplane leasing business but they got into the airline consulting business.

CHAPTER 19

Lorenzo Takes the Helm

In 1972, when Lorenzo came on board at TTA, the name was changed to Texas International Airlines ("TI"). Lorenzo was aggressive toward the labor unions. Lorenzo wanted to squeeze the labor contracts down to the minimum; he wanted the labor unions off the property.

ALEA Strike: Ground agents were represented by Air Line Employee Association (ALEA), the union that represented most of the ground personnel in the industry. The ALEA contract was up for negotiation. During the ALEA negotiations, the company continued to pressure for more concessions from labor. If an agreement was reached, Lorenzo would change the terms in such a way that ALEA could not agree. This went on for several months until finally ALEA went on strike. The airline pilots decided to honor the ALEA strike. The airline was shut down. At that time in the industry, when an airline shut down, there was a system whereby other airlines would overfly the striking routes and pay the striking airline the money for those flights. The ALEA strike continued for four months, which was the longest strike in the industry at that time. During those four months, Jet Capital or Texas International made a $16 million dollar profit, although TI never flew an airplane.

As the ALEA strike reached its endgame, the National Mediation Board said the matter needed to be settled. ALPA sent Jack Bavis, J.J. O'Donnell's assistant. The Mediation Board took the union representatives to Miami, put them into hotel rooms, and would not let anyone leave. It took two weeks before a settlement was made with all the unions. Floyd Carpenter was chairman of the pilot negotiating committee. ALEA was still talking, talking, talking... Floyd and Jack Bavis would go out and come back and we would ask where they had been.

And they said, "Oh, we were just seeing what was going on..."

We learned later that Carpenter and Bavis were negotiating to get the airline restarted, giving concessions out of the pilot's contract to help get the ALEA contract glued up. As a result of this negotiation, the only thing they were able to do was to get the salaries up on the DC-9 that matched the salaries at Delta. But that concession to the pilots didn't kick in until a year and a half after negotiations and the contract was extended by another two years. When we brought this back to the pilots, it was disturbing and the pilots were upset with the contract negotiations. I promised myself that it would never happen again when I was on the MEC negotiating committee – one man would never go over and negotiate all the contract provisions without the presence of the full committee.

After the ALEA negotiations, I became MEC Chairman and implemented a new policy. The ALEA negotiation illustrated the potential for another union on the property to jeopardize the pilots' ability to work. I set up a monthly meeting of representatives from each union on the property [Interunion Relationship meetings] to discuss and resolve problems before they became issues that affected our ability to work. I appointed Rick Hundley as Chairman of the Interunion Relationship group. Rick then reported the results of each monthly meeting for MEC review.

Jim McCartney, MEC Chairman at Texas International

Sometime later the ramp people represented by ALEA became unhappy with the ALEA leadership on the property. They voted in the Teamsters to handle their representation. From that time on, the ramp people were not represented at the monthly Interunion Relationship meetings. The Teamsters sent a young kid down to run the union for the ramp people. The ramp people presented him with their list of grievances. The Teamsters representative tore up the grievance list and told the ALEA members they didn't have any grievances.

Lorenzo Missed Connecting Flight: After the 1974 ALEA strike, Frank Lorenzo was the most hated guy at the airline for sure and probably was the most hated guy in the airline industry. Before the strike, if Lorenzo was on board, the Captain would let him ride in the cockpit. After the strike, none of the pilots would let Frank ride in the cockpit. I was flying a trip from Houston to New Orleans and saw Frank get on.

I said, "Frank, come on up and sit in the cockpit."

We took off and climbed through 10,000 feet where the sterile cockpit rules did not apply and started talking. "Sterile Cockpit" means no conversation about anything other than the flight at hand.

I told him, "Frank, take care of your people and they will take care of the dollars."

His reply was, "I can write the manual to make you guys do anything I want you to do. I don't have to coddle you guys."

The cockpit has a voice recorder that records the last 30 minutes of any conversation in the cockpit. Before Frank would speak, he would get out of the jump seat and put his hand over the mike pickup so he couldn't be recorded. When we landed in New Orleans, we were still talking and arguing. All the passengers got off and all the new passengers were loaded.

Finally, the ground agent came up and told Lorenzo, "If you don't get off, then this flight delay is going to be on you." Frank left.

I flew back to Houston and didn't think anything more about it. According to newspaper reports, on June 24, 1975, Eastern 66, was on its final approach into New York's John F. Kennedy International Airport at 4:05 pm EST, when the aircraft crashed into the approach lights short of Runway 22L. There were 124 persons on board the aircraft; the crash killed 113 people; nine passengers and two flight attendants survived, all with serious injuries. In Houston I learned the company had sent some people to Lorenzo's house to tell them Frank had been killed. Lucky Frank, he and I argued for so long on the ground in New Orleans that he missed Eastern 66 to New York. Back in Houston, I was afraid to tell anyone that I was responsible for Frank missing his flight because I knew I would get whupped up on. Neither Frank nor I ever spoke of this incident.

Bottom of Industry Pay Scale: Because TI pilots were at the bottom of the industry pay scale, many had a little business on the side to supplement their income. One of our pilots, Bill Moore, sold and installed water softener systems. J.V. Sclifo bought a water softener and Bill went out to install it for J.V. While he was working on the water softener system, Bill told J.V. that he dreamed that he had Lorenzo in a cage and he was poking him with a stick. Bill said it was the best dream he had ever had.

Strike Fallout: During the ALEA strike, ALPA told the pilots they could file for unemployment. The strike pay from ALPA was 3 months late. J.V. Sclifo, two other pilots and I drove to Conroe in J.V.'s Mercedes to file for unemployment compensation benefits.

Many pilots felt the financial hardship caused by the strike, some more than others. One pilot's wife was distraught about the strike. One afternoon while her husband walked the picket line, she went to the beauty shop and had her hair done. She went home and shot herself. When her husband got home, he opened the mailbox and found the check from ALPA for his 3 months of back strike pay. He went inside and found his wife's body.

After the company filed its first bankruptcy, it cancelled the health insurance for its employees. A week or so later, the pilots went on strike. One pilot's daughter needed open heart surgery. Because the company insurance was cancelled, the open heart surgery was cancelled. The pilot's daughter died.

CHAPTER 20

Operational Problems with Lorenzo

Cockpit Resource Management (CRM): Ken Smith was the Captain I flew with in the DC-3 that hit the goose on approach into Fort Polk. Ken was a check airman for the company and he would always brief me when we got into the airplane.

On our first flight together Captain Smith said, "Look, I'm the Captain but if you see anything that I'm doing wrong or anything that you don't understand, you stop me and ask about it and we'll discuss it."

I used the same tactic when I became Captain. I would always tell the First Officer the same thing Ken Smith had taught me years before. At the time there were three aircraft in the industry – not with our company – that hit the ground with the co-pilot knowing that something was not right but did not take any action to correct the situation and did not make his concerns known to the Captain in a forceful way. The co-pilot might mention a concern in a tone that did not require attention. When Ken became check airman, we started discussing the issue and we decided that we needed to see what was happening with our flight crews. So we set up a scenario in the simulator in which we would have a check airman Captain fly the left seat and call a First Officer on reserve and have him fly support for the Captain taking the check ride. The scenario was: when the Captain was flying and reached 200 feet on a landing approach, the Captain would have a passive heart attack, which meant that he simply stopped flying the airplane. We tested ten co-pilots, and seven out of ten took no evasive action, and let the simulator hit the runway in an uncontrolled condition. As a result of this test, we changed procedures to add calls by the non-flying pilot to the flying pilot so that at 1,000 feet on approach, the non-flying pilot would call, "1,000 feet" and the flying pilot must respond saying, "Roger." The call and response was repeated at 500 feet. At the decision point at 200 feet, the non-flying pilot would call out "Minimums." If the Captain were flying, his response would be "Landing" or "Go Around." If the co-pilot were flying, his response would be "Landing" or "No Contact." If the response was "No Contact," only the Captain can make the "Go Around" decision. This new procedure was reinforced at recurrent training for all pilots.

One of the things I noticed was that we had many pilots that were good stick and rudder guys but some didn't have management skills. Those pilots were usually the ones that came on board during a big hiring spree. They flew co-pilot for a short time, then were checked out as Captains. I talked to J.V. Sclifo, the Chief Pilot, about the need for leadership training to teach our Captains how to manage the airplane and the crew. We discussed the issue with Human Resources and a budget was approved to develop a training program. First, Human Resources hired a consulting firm to present a program. It was a psychology-driven program where we played card games and put together teams to play against each other. It was a "feel good" experience but not on target for what we wanted to accomplish. J.V. did some additional research and located Robert L. Helmreich, Ph.D. Helmreich was head of the Psychology Department at the University of Texas in Austin. He was also connected with NASA Ames Research Center. Dr. Helmreich became interested in our issues and agreed to help us. First Dr. Helmreich wanted to fly the line to observe interactions between the captain and the crew. We obtained permission from the FAA for Dr.

Helmreich to ride the jump seat in the cockpit. At that time, Cockpit Resource Management ("CRM") was in its infancy. I believe United was working on it a little bit and perhaps Pan Am. Where CRM was implemented, it proved to be an excellent program. What amazed me about CRM was tests in simulators proved that when looking at malfunctions and crashes, the best way to manage a situation was to turn over the flight duties to the co-pilot, while the captain managed the situation. This should not have surprised me because I knew that peripheral vision is narrowed by stress and cognitive ability is negatively impacted by stress.

There was a simulator test based on a Pan Am flight out of New York on a 747 going to Europe. Crews were put into a situation in which the 747 was loaded to the maximum, which meant the airplane could not come back without dumping fuel. The scenario was: as the airplane climbed out, it would lose a generator. It was not a big deal; it was a trip generator. The crew would go through the checklist on the generator loss. Later the airplane would lose an engine that would require the pilots to dump fuel and return to the airport. Fourteen crews were tested on this scenario. The results were that some captains would take control of the situation, fly the airplane and do everything required by the situation. Some did, but most didn't. In one scenario, the captain took off, the generator was lost, the engine was lost, and many tasks were dumped on the engineer. The flight engineer was instructed to: (1) run the engine out checklist, (2) check the fuel balance, (3) check the landing weight and (4) calculate how much fuel had to be dumped, which meant to calculate how many minutes you would hold the fuel dump chute open. The captain continued loading tasks on the flight engineer. As a result, the flight engineer calculated that fuel must be dumped for 12 minutes. After six minutes, the flight engineer said he had made a mistake and six minutes was enough. When the simulator landed at Kennedy, the airplane went off the end of the runway because it was overweight. This happened because the flight engineer was overloaded with tasks, rushed, and stressed to the point that he made mistakes.

The CRM program was implemented and was effective – one of the better things accomplished at TI.

Descent Procedure: Most DC-9 pilots knew how to get the airplane down in the most efficient manner possible from 35,000 feet.

The procedure that most pilots adopted was: start descent and drop 3,000 feet per minute, look at the miles, and calculate how many miles out you needed to start your descent. At 27,000 feet you could pull the power all the way back to idle and continue down to 10,000 feet at 320 knots; go 10 miles, and you would be slowed down to 250 knots – then you are in position to shoot the approach. It was an efficient operation. Speed below 10,000 feet is restricted to 250 knots. However, company engineers decided it would be more efficient to let down at 250 knots from 27,000 feet to 10,000 feet to save more fuel.

The engineers thought 250 was the maximum lift with the least drag; any time you increase lift you increase drag. There are three ways to increase lift: (1) increase speed, (2) increase angle of attack, or (3) extend flaps. However, when going into places like Los Angeles, Denver, or any high traffic areas at 250 knots, all other traffic is at 320 knots at 10,000 feet. Air Traffic Control will put the slower traffic behind the faster traffic.

I told the company, "We need to get this changed. I believe the company is losing money, if you calculate crew cost, delays and such."

The company argued about it for a while and I said, "Let's go to the simulator and do let downs from 35,000 feet to 10,000 feet at 250 knots to see which is the most efficient procedure to follow and how much money we can save."

The first problem we ran into was that no one had the same number for the operating cost of the airplane. Marketing had one figure, Maintenance had another figure, and Flight Operations had a third figure. It took the company six weeks to reach agreement on the cost to be used, which was $1,800 per hour. Today's costs are much higher. After 40 let downs from 35,000 feet to 10,000 feet in the simulator, we found the difference was $1.75 savings at 250 knots vs. the high speed let down. In one minute, each time an airplane was turned out of traffic, the company lost much more than it saved.

Drift Down Procedures: Another procedure implemented was necessary coming out of Denver. Drift down procedure is defined as the maximum power you can have on the good engine when you slow to 250 knots, then the aircraft drifts down to the altitude it will maintain. One route from Denver to Salt Lake City crossed the Rockies. If the weather was bad and maximum gross weight and anti-icing were required, the route was diverted up north where the mountains were lower and each ridgeline crossed had airports where the airplane could land. However, if you lost an engine going across the northern route with anti-icing in operation, the airplane could not maintain clearance altitude. The airplane would stop descending around 12,000 feet – below the mountains. According to the instructions, if an engine is lost in one area, the airplane must land at the specified airport in that area; if the airplane is a few more miles along the route, there is a different specified airport; another few miles, another airport is specified. In such an event, the pilot had to look in five different places in two different books to locate the alternate airport. I worked on the problem and altered the charts so there were arrows pointing to alternative airports for landing along the northern route. All you had to do was look at your Distance Measuring Equipment ("DME") to see the airplane's location and that eliminated the paperwork. The last time I was on a Continental airplane as a passenger, the drift-down procedure put together in 1970 was still being used.

Cost Containment on Fuel: At TI I developed a plan to save fuel and have the company reimburse the pilots half of the cost savings. I took the plan to Cathell and he took it to Jim Arpey. Arpey liked the fuel savings part of the plan but didn't like having to pay the pilots. Arpey implemented my fuel savings program, but instead of paying the pilots half of the savings, each month the Captain with the best fuel savings would receive a week's vacation as an award. As a result, one Captain tried really hard one month to get the vacation award. The Captain would taxi out on one engine; on final approach he would shut down one engine. Upon landing, the Captain would not use the thrust reversers because that would increase the fuel burn. The Captain would just ride the brakes until the airplane stopped.

Most jet aircraft have a tire pressure of 180 to 225 psi. On the DC-9 there is 200 psi. When the tire on a DC-9 blows out, it is like a stick of dynamite going off in the wheel well or on the landing gear strut. Engineers looked at the problem and decided they couldn't have the tires blowing out, if the brakes are too hot. The engineers put on a melt plug or fuse that would melt if the temperature got too high. The fuse plug would melt and let out the air pressure instead of blowing out the tire. The tires were flat, but no blow-out sound occurred.

On one trip, the Captain pulled into the gate, got off, and went on his way. The next crew came on and all the tires were flat because the incoming Captain had ridden the brakes so hard, the melting point was reached on the fuse plug and all four tires went flat. After that incident, the fuel savings program and the monthly vacation award ended. The program was scrapped until ALPA was off the property. Later the fuel-savings program I developed was once again implemented, but this time the pilots were paid part of the savings as an incentive.

CHAPTER 21

Weight and Balance Issues

Beginning of Weight and Balance Issues: In the beginning, management was not hard to deal with on the operational issues because there were not many operational problems. The airline didn't have a lot of revenue or a lot of passengers on its flights. There were DC-9 dash 10s with dash 7 power on them and DC-9 dash 30s with dash 15 power. For each engine, the bigger the number on the dash, the more power in the engine. When the "peanut fares" were implemented, the company got what it wanted: bigger passenger loads. However, with increased passenger loads, it became apparent in a lot of places that revenue did not increase, because of restrictions on the power available on the DC-9s. Weight and balance problems began to occur.

Allen Kelley, a good friend of mine, was well known as being the type pilot who always made sure that everything was done according to established procedure. Allen and I evaluated problems with the Weight Balance Form as we felt the issues were getting out of hand.

We analyzed the weight and balance issues to determine what could be done to alleviate the problems.

The Weight Balance Forms were normally destroyed after the completion of each flight. Allen requested all pilots to put their Forms in his box for a period of time. Allen took the Forms home and his wife, Sue, sorted the forms according to each issuing station. Next the forms as issued by each station were reviewed and the errors made by each station were noted. Some errors made by the ground stations were: (1) FAA regulations permit the airline to count each child on board as a half-weight. Sometimes there may be 16 half-weights on the form, yet when the flight attendant checked, there may be only four children on board; and (2) The temperature on the form was adjusted so it would appear that the aircraft could lift off with more revenue. The higher the temperature, the less dense the air, the less power is generated by the engines, and the wings are not as efficient in hot air. In cold air, wings are more efficient in obtaining lift and the engines can generate more power. For example, in Albuquerque the temperature on the Weight Balance Form may indicate a temperature 15 degrees cooler than it actually was on the runway.

As part of our study, we talked to the ground station agents in Lafayette because we had good rapport with them. They had been told by their management that they could overload any airplane up to 1,500 pounds, but if they had to go over 1,500 pounds, then they had to get an okay from the supervisor. Speed is based on weight and the balance must be such that if a two-engine airplane loses one of its engines after reaching the V-1 speed, the plane must still be able to fly with only one engine. Basically the company was willing to gamble that we would never lose an engine. This was confirmed by the information we received from the Lafayette agents that it was okay to overload by 1,500 pounds.

Weight determines the takeoff speed of the aircraft so the Weight Balance Form must be accurate. There are three stages in takeoff: **V-1** – the Captain can abort on the runway before reaching V-1 speed; **VR** – [VR speed is close to V-1] the pilot pulls the yoke back to rotate the nose up to fly; and **V2** – the safety climb speed. These three speeds are calculated on the total gross weight provided by the Weight Balance Form. There is a flip chart that contains the V-1, VR and V2 speeds for

WEIGHT AND BALANCE ISSUES

various weight ranges for all the various flaps and slats settings. FAA regulations state the aircraft must be loaded such that the aircraft could fly with engine failure at V-1.

As the problems grew, the breaking point came when Allen Kelley was flying a trip out of Houston to Austin. The Weight Balance Form had the elevator trim setting so that the aircraft, when rotated to nose up position, would climb and perform according to the manual. Kelley set the trim, flaps settings per the Weight Balance Form, and took off. When Kelley rotated, he really had to pull on the yoke to get the aircraft air borne. When Kelley leveled off, the trim was really off as to what it should have been. Kelley called ahead to the Austin ground crew and told them to take all the cargo out of the bins and not take anything inside until he checked the contents of all cargo bins. Allen had a reputation for always making sure that everything was right.

At that time, Bob Lemon had been hired by Breeding in the Flight Department and Bob was as aggressive toward the pilots as he had been toward management when he was the MEC Chairman. The ground agents called Bob Lemon and told him the flight was going to take a delay because the Captain wanted to pull off all the bags and check them. Lemon told the ground agents to have the Captain call him when he was on the ground. When Allen got on the ground, the ground agents told him to call Lemon, and Allen said that's fine but you go ahead and start taking the bags off. With the bags removed, Allen found a 6,000 pound drill bit in the baggage bin. It had been there for four days because it had not been unloaded at its destination. After the drill bit was not unloaded, it faded from the paperwork. The airplane had been flying four days with an extra 6,000 pounds and had been flying out of hot airports – Albuquerque, Denver and Mexico City. Those 6,000 pounds of undeclared weight were critical to the operation of the aircraft.

As a result of Allen's incident and other factors we uncovered, Allen and I went to Breeding and told him he must fix the weight and balance errors. The first fix was to put computers in every station. This brought some improvement, but there were still problems getting enough lift in the high hots with the engines we had. The company bought new airplanes with bigger engines and put more powerful engines on the existing aircraft. It helped but we still had problems in Denver, Albuquerque and Mexico City when the temperature rose. Douglas came out with a way to increase lift at the high hot airports with an optimum over speed takeoff. The optimum over speed takeoff required that you take off with the slats only. Normally on takeoff, it was slats and flaps 15 or slats and flaps 5. The optimum over speed procedure required rotation speed (for nose up) of 170 to 177 knots, which is quite fast. The Weight Balance Form would show whether the pilot was limited by the second segment climb, tire speed, or runway length. Frequently it would be tire speed. The tires were rated for 225 knots and if you went above that speed there was a good chance you would throw the treads off the tires.

The company did not have ground school on optimum over speed takeoff. However, the company distributed to all pilots a 15-page memo of instructions with respect to optimum over speed. For example, the instruction sheet stated you must check the tire pressure and each tire must be at least 200 psi [psi means pounds per square inch] and all tires should be at a psi within 20 pounds of each other. The memo was distributed to the pilots the night before the new policy was implemented. So if you had an early flight to a high hot airport such as Mexico City, Albuquerque or Denver, you would have to read and understand the memo en route. If you had any question, you couldn't ask the memo.

Allen and I continued to work on the weight and balance problems. We worked with the company's Weight Balance Form that was prepared by the ground agents. The ground agents had the sheet the way they wanted it, but the pilots had to look all over the sheet, maybe in five or six different places, to obtain the required data. Breeding was finally convinced that the pilots were the end users of the Weight Balance Form. The pilots wanted a summary line for the data required for takeoff: flaps, slat settings, temperature, trim settings, runway and aircraft total weight. It was my practice to calculate the total weight in my head – take the Operating Empty Weight (OEW), amount of fuel on board, the number of passengers multiplied by 200, and that would always be close to the gross weight of the airplane.

Once as I taxied out for takeoff in Mexico City, I read the summary line and it was way off from my calculation. I told the co-pilot to turn around and go back to the gate. I called Operations and told them we couldn't take off because we were overweight.

I was told, "No, sir, that can't be."

So I told him to have the station manager come out and meet me. The station manager and I looked at the paper and figured out how they managed to get their numbers. We had a full load of passengers and 160 bags. The ground agents changed the OEW (operating empty weight) of the aircraft to accommodate the revenue and cargo.

The station manager said, "Oh, Captain, that's the new OEW of the aircraft."

I said, "Here's the book with the weight of the aircraft and that's what we're going by."

He said, "Yeah, I guess you're right, I just wrote the number down wrong."

I said, "What are we going to do about it?"

And he said, "Well, we're going to take all the bags off."

I said, "Now this is an international flight. We have 115 passengers going to Houston on an international flight and you're going to send them up there with no bags? They're going to kill us. You need to get on the PA, if that's what you're going to do, and tell them exactly what's happening, that you are going to ship the bags on the next flight."

The station manager got on the PA and made the announcement in Spanish. The baggage bin doors came open and closed and they brought us another Weight Balance Form that had the correct OEW with maximum weight to the pound. We took off to Houston. As we crossed the Gulf of Mexico, I started thinking about it and I called J.V. Sclifo, the Chief Pilot.

I said, "J.V., I want you to meet me at Customs and let's do a baggage count."

We were supposed to have zero bags and they took off 160 bags. As a result of this incident, the station manager in Mexico City was fired.

Romance in the Cockpit: We had an incident in Baton Rouge that really shouldn't have happened. We had a Captain who made some gross errors and was unprofessional. The Captain was married and he was flying with one of our first female First Officers. She was married. They had a little romance going and were flying together every time they could bid trips together. As they approached Baton Rouge, the weather was really bad, it was raining heavily and ceiling was down to about four or five hundred feet.

The aircraft was cleared for an ILS (Instrument Landing System) approach. The Captain was flying and, at the outer marker, about five miles from the end of the runway, he was trying to tune his Automatic Direction Finder (ADF). The ADF could be tuned to receive commercial radio stations. While flying the approach into Baton Rouge, the Captain was tuning the ADF because he was losing his country music station. When the aircraft crossed the outer marker the pilot put the gear down and he was supposed to arm the auto spoilers. It was a requirement of the airline that the spoilers be armed for every landing. Any exception was at the Captain's option: if landing on a dry runway with 6,000 feet of runway available, after touchdown the pilot must manually deploy the spoilers. Some Captains like to do this because when the spoilers come up on touchdown, it causes the airplane to squat down, and it is not a smooth landing. The company went along with this notion of not arming the auto spoilers if you have 6,000 feet of dry runway. That was not the case on this flight. The Captain was at the outer marker. The First Officer did the checklist and called for the auto spoilers.

The Captain said, "Nah, we don't need them."

The approach continued and the tower continued to advise that it was raining extremely hard. Upon touchdown, water was on the runway and the brakes did not respond. Even after not arming the spoilers for auto deployment, the spoilers were not extended manually when the aircraft touched down. The airplane ran off the end of the runway and the gears could be heard breaking off on the CVR. The airplane went through some gullies and stopped. The passengers were safely evacuated; and there were no fatalities. However, one of the passengers had a heart attack in the terminal and died.

The company was concerned about the aircraft being overloaded. The first thing the company did was remove all the bags from the airplane, which is against National Transportation and Safety Board ("NTSB") rules. The airplane was totaled. The company bought the airplane from the insurance carrier and brought it back to Houston. The fuselage of that airplane now sits in the Continental simulator building at Houston Intercontinental Airport. The fuselage is used to train flight attendants in emergency evacuation procedures, and can be tilted 70% on its side and filled with smoke.

The company made a $1.6 million dollar profit for that quarter, a direct result of the insurance payout on the crash of the airplane.

The crash of that airplane and the concern about getting the bags off lit the fire enough that the company decided to get with ALPA and resolve the weight and balance issues. The weight and balance problems were magically resolved.

Allen Kelley was well known throughout the company for making sure that everything was done according to established procedure. Kelley had been a thorn in the side of the company over the recurring weight and balance issues. But Kelley had made his point effectively enough that when this accident occurred, Don Breeding, the Vice President of Flight Operations, said, "If Allen Kelley had been on this flight, the crash would not have happened."

CHAPTER 22

Two-Man Crew Issue

The two-man crew issue came up in our integration negotiations with Continental pilots. Continental had a lot of flight engineers. The TI pilots told the Continental pilots that we did not want the pilots to be integrated with the flight engineers because those jobs would go away. The Continental pilots were adamant that the flight engineer positions would not go away. That argument was null and void after the seniority list was put together. This issue came to a point where it had the potential to split up ALPA.

History of Crew Reductions: We put together a history of crew reductions from the time the flying boats started out. When the flying boats were flown by Pan Am across the Pacific, they had a pilot, co-pilot, flight engineer, radio operator and navigator – five crew members. As time passed, the navigator and radio operator positions were eliminated. That left the pilot, co-pilot and flight engineer in the cockpit.

One needs to understand the politics of ALPA to understand why the two-man crew was such a big issue for pilots and almost split ALPA.

United Airlines had almost 6,000 pilots at the time the two-man crew became a major issue. The President of ALPA was elected by each pilot group. Each pilot group had a vote and their vote was directly related to how many pilots were in each pilot group. United was the largest carrier at the time so United could almost dictate who would be the President of ALPA if they talked to one of the other major airlines such as Northwest or Continental. The President of ALPA had to be sure that the United pilots were happy with him.

Flight Engineer on Deck: The FAA required a flight engineer on aircraft that had a maximum gross weight of 88,000 pounds and above on takeoff. That was fine as long as you were flying DC-6s, DC-7s and Constellations. When the twin-engine jet came along the FAA and Air Transport Association ("ATA") got together and decided that the twin engine jet would have only two pilots on board although the weight exceeded 88,000 pounds. Then the 737 came down the pike, and the DC-9s, which were two-man operations – a pilot and co-pilot. There was no station on board for a flight engineer in the newer airplanes.

In the new aircraft, the function of the flight engineer was automated so a flight engineer was no longer needed. Back in the piston days, the flight engineer was critical because the job was to monitor all the systems and advise the pilot when a problem occurred. There was an engine analyzer so the flight engineer could see what a spark plug was doing so that if a plug fouled out, the flight engineer could tell maintenance what cylinder and which plug was involved. When the twin-engine jets came out, the flight engineer was replaced by a system with Master Warning and Master Caution lights.

If you look in a cockpit, above the instrument panel there is an 18-inch glare shield. This eliminated the glare that made it impossible to read the instruments. There were some emergency lights in case the lights went out on the instrument panel – flip the switch to turn on the lights on the instrument panel. There are two buttons in front of each pilot – Master Warning that was Red and Master Caution that was Yellow. When these lights come on, the pilot looks at the overhead panel. The annunciator panel is the first item. All the systems of the airplane are represented on the overhead annunciator panel. When the yellow Master Caution light goes on, the overhead panel might say, "Cabin Pressure Approaching 10,000 feet." Every system had a light and a message. The Red Master Warning lights are for emergencies like "pressurization failed and cabin above 10,000 feet." The pilot must push the master light out and look at the overhead panel to see the problem. Then the pilot refers to the QRH – Quick Reference Handbook. If it is the generator, the pilot turns to the generator section, and the instruction may be to take the switch, put it to "reset," then see if it is on. If not, then it is turned off for the crosstie. If the crosstie does not work, the pilot starts the Auxiliary Power Unit and puts the generator on that system. These tasks were previously performed by the flight engineer. The engineer would say, "Captain, the generator is tripped. What do you want me to do?" and the Captain would reply, "Reset the generator." That was the circumstance that involved the FAA in eliminating the rule that all aircraft 88,000 pounds and above had to have a flight engineer. After that, it was based on the workload in the cockpit.

There was only a place for the pilot and co-pilot in the DC-9 and 737 aircraft. The Master Caution panel and a Master Warning panel were developed to announce problems on the overhead panel so the pilots could see and handle the problems instead of having a flight engineer behind the pilots looking at gauges.

The United pilots – in what I characterized as a feather-bedding operation or "make work" operation – forced into their contract that all 737s must have a three-man crew. United pilots took the issue to an ALPA Board of Directors meeting. United, with one or two other carriers, got a resolution passed that any new airplane coming along must have a three-man crew. That became ALPA's policy because of United's vote. The policy didn't bother us at TI because the company did not have any aircraft on order that exceeded the DC-9. Then Douglas came out with the MD-80 and that aircraft became a source of friction between all the other operators of DC-9s. ALPA's policy was in place as Texas International was looking at purchasing the MD-80s. Southern and some of the other carriers operating with the DC-9s started putting in orders for the MD-80. ALPA wanted to force Douglas to build the aircraft to accommodate a three-man crew.

Dennis Higgins and I were on the two-man crew committee at Texas International and United sent down someone to talk to us about the advantages of having a three-man crew.

Southern pilots were invited to Douglas to look at the MD-80s. Dennis and I were invited to Douglas the week after the Southern pilots visited the Douglas plant. We went to Los Angeles, toured the plant, and looked at the airplane. The President of Douglas gave us a talk. Dennis and I looked at the MD-80 and we thought our pilots would fly the airplane. It is laid out much better than the DC-9 and it flies just like the DC-9 except it has a better autopilot, better flight director, and better systems.

As mentioned earlier, the two-man crew issue came up in our negotiations with Continental pilots. I called the MEC Chairman at Hughes Air West. Hughes Air West had just completed their seniority list integration following a merger. I asked if I could come out for a couple of days and ride in their 727 aircraft to observe and film the duties performed by their flight engineer with my video camera. The Hughes MEC Chairman granted permission for me to do this. When I returned to Houston, I turned over the footage I had taken over a period of two to three days to a professional film company to produce a film about the two-man crew issue with someone doing the voice over commentary. The completed film explained the progression in aviation from the flying boats to modern jet aircraft, and how the number of people in the cockpit crew had decreased over the years. The film then looked at the flight engineer's job in the 727 and in the DC-9 to see how the flight engineer's job would be eliminated. I lost my copy of the tape but it was presented at one of the meetings on the integration negotiation of the seniority lists between TI and Continental pilots.

Dennis and I called J.J. O'Donnell, President of ALPA at the time, and flew to Washington DC to meet with him. We told O'Donnell, "Look, ALPA can pass any kind of resolution saying it would only support a three-man crew, but our pilots are going to fly a two-man crew. We can't stop it and ALPA can't stop it." Dennis and I suggested to O'Donnell that we needed to get a fix for this.

Pete Conrad, a former astronaut working for Douglas Aircraft, came down and met with Cathell, Vice President of Human Resources, to discuss the two-man crew issue. Cathell called me to meet them for lunch to discuss the issue. Conrad was a really nice guy but his experience was with the military. Douglas wanted to keep the two-man crew status in its aircraft.

ALPA Approves Two-Man Crew: Eventually, J.J. saw it was a political issue and he would have to bite the bullet on it. ALPA put together a solution that we would abide by a committee of experts who would settle the issue. The expert committee came back with the finding that a two-man crew would be a safe operation. Today, the 747, 777, 767, 757 and all the European airbus aircraft are operated with a two-man crew. But it was hard for people at the time to see into the future.

CHAPTER 23

Flight Operations at TI

Purchase of TWA Airplanes: The company bought five TWA DC-9s that we were going to paint in our colors and put on the line. When they brought them in, ALPA representatives went out, looked at the planes, and noticed that the overhead switches were backwards from what they were in our Douglas airplanes. TWA had more Boeing airplanes, so the TWA Chief Pilot had the switching changed in their DC-9s to be the same as TWA's Boeing airplanes. To the TI pilots that meant the switches in the TWA DC-9s were 180 degrees from how the switches were configured in TI's existing DC-9s. ALPA went to engineering and asked them to flip the switches to be consistent with the switches in TI's DC-9s. Engineering said it couldn't be done. We had a meeting with Lorenzo and told him about the switching problem. We told Lorenzo we thought it might cause an accident.

Lorenzo said, "That's why I have insurance."

The TI pilots passed a resolution saying we would not fly the DC-9s purchased from TWA until the switches were made standard to the existing DC-9 configuration at TI. The switches were changed.

Bear on Board: One incident that happened on a flight was comical but sad. Allen Kelley was flying a trip out of Dallas to Waco. In the Convair, the galley was at the rear of the airplane. The baggage bin was aft of the galley. There was a plexi-glass window so if you had a fire in the baggage area, you could go back to the galley, turn on a light in the baggage area and see what was going on back there. The bathroom adjoined the galley and if you opened the bathroom door, there was a kick out panel that you could kick out to gain entry to the baggage compartment to fight a fire or whatever you needed to do.

After takeoff when the plane leveled off, the flight attendant came up and said, "There's something bad going on in the baggage bin."

Allen said, "What do you mean something bad?"

She said, "I don't know, but there's something bad going on back there and I'm not going back there to fix coffee or anything until you come back and take a look."

Allen went back to the galley, put his nose on the plexi-glass window and turned the light on. And WHAM! A bear paw hit the plexi-glass!

Allen said, "Oh, my God!"

A bear broke out of its cage and was loose in the baggage bin. Allen's first concern was that the bear would come through the kick out panel into the cabin. He locked the bathroom door and told the passengers that the restroom was out of service. Allen called ATC and told them he was returning to Dallas. The passengers got off the plane in Dallas and Allen saw the ramp people going toward the baggage area with a rope.

Allen told them, "You don't want to try to catch that bear with a rope."

A couple of hours later, animal control arrived. They opened the baggage bin and shot the bear with a tranquilizer gun and that put the bear to sleep. The bear was the mascot for Baylor University in Waco. There was also a cocker spaniel in the baggage bin in a kennel. The cocker spaniel's barking annoyed the bear. The bear broke out of his cage, tore open the cocker spaniel's kennel and ate the cocker spaniel.

While the bear was being subdued, newspaper people were in the airplane taking pictures of the bear through the plexi-glass. There were so many people in the tail end of the airplane that Allen thought it was going to drop on its tail. This incident made *Paul Harvey News* the next morning and gave Allen and Texas International about 15 seconds of fame.

J.V.'s Comical Mouse Story: There were those comical moments that had nothing to do with flying: When he was Chief Pilot, J.V. Sclifo was sitting in his office which was partitioned off from a larger area that served as a waiting room for pilots waiting to see J.V. On one occasion, J.V. was on the telephone with the Airport Manager in Beaumont regarding a runway problem. While on the phone, J.V. noticed a mouse running across the floor. J.V. continued his telephone conversation until he realized the mouse was running up his leg inside his pants. J.V. dropped the phone, jumped up, yelled and grabbed his crotch. He felt three of what should have been only two. He started to squeeze the third "ball" – thankful that he grabbed the right one. His secretary ran into his office as J.V. was jumping around, yelling, squeezing his crotch, then he kicked his leg and out flew the dead mouse! That gave all the waiting pilots a big laugh and became an oft-repeated story throughout the airline.

Simulator Check Ride Incident: Captains are required to take a check ride every six months; First Officers are required to take a check ride once a year. At first TI did not have any simulators and all check rides were in the airplanes – without passengers. Later, TI leased simulator time from Eastern's facility in Miami. The cost was $700 per hour, which was much cheaper than using the airplanes. The first simulators did not have visuals. The simulator windshield just had opaque glass. As the technology progressed, visuals were added that made simulator training more realistic – so realistic that one of TI's pilots had a humiliating experience on his check ride. In the simulator, the plane took off with engine failure scheduled before he reached V-2, and he lost control of the airplane. The aircraft started to roll and was falling toward the hangar. The pilot peed his pants.

Captain Goes Round the Bend: One TI captain went off the deep end. The captain started out saying he was still active in the CIA. He must have believed that, but I don't think it was true. The Captain hired a private detective. He would buy the detective a ticket to wherever the Captain would spend the night. The detective would sit outside the Captain's hotel room door on his overnights. This went on for several months.

On his last flight, the Captain was flying back from Los Angeles to Dallas. The Captain disconnected the autopilot and started hand-flying the aircraft. Next the Captain started mumbling. The First Officer was experienced and he heard the Captain say:

"Now, baby, I'm going to roll you over and we're going to go kiss the ground."

The Captain started to roll the airplane. The First Officer grabbed the controls and told the Captain to turn loose of the controls and push his seat all the way to the back, which he did. There was a pilot in the jump seat and the First Officer told him to pull out the fire axe, and if the Captain touched any of the controls, the pilot was to hit the Captain with the fire axe. The First Officer did not want the Captain to touch anything.

When the flight reached Dallas, the Captain was taken off the flight and that was the end of his flying career.

First Meeting with J.V. Sclifo: When I first met J.V., he had just been elected as the Captain's representative for ALPA. We were meeting at J.V.'s home regarding labor issues. I was accompanied by the secretary-treasurer of the Local Executive Council ("LEC"). The LEC were representatives for a single crew base. The MEC were the representatives for all crew bases. The secretary-treasurer didn't have much flying time and was one of the first to cross the picket line. J.V. didn't exhibit much interest about the issues but did say he believed in doing the right thing regardless of what was written in the contract. The secretary-treasurer resisted, but I said I would go along with J.V.

From then on J.V and I became really close friends. When J.V. retired, I spoke at his retirement dinner and recalled that he was one who always did the right thing.

J.V.'s family came from a small area in Italy that is known for the longevity of its residents. During World War II, J.V.'s father and his brother emigrated from Italy. J.V.'s father went to the United States and settled in Shreveport, Louisiana. His brother, J.V.'s uncle, went to Argentina. Sometime in the 1970s, J.V. contacted some of his family members in Argentina and flew to Argentina to meet the part of his family that he had never seen. The Argentina branch of the family told J.V. they would meet him at the airport. When J.V. got off the plane, he was met by 200 family members living in Argentina. He was overwhelmed to see so many relatives in one place. He expected perhaps 10 to 15.

J.V. retired early from the airline because of medical reasons. A garbage truck hit the rear end of J.V.'s Mercedes. J.V.'s back was injured and he could no longer pass the medical to fly. J.V. is 84, still plays golf as much as he can, and has called me frequently during my illness.

Guest Passengers: Crew scheduling was a recurring issue. The crew schedulers and management had no idea about the fatigue level on the trips we were flying. I frequently invited people in management to come out and fly with me on the jump seat. Ed Cathell, the Vice President of Human Resources, volunteered to go.

I said, "Ed, I don't want you to just go out and ride one leg with me. I want you to ride the whole sequence because we have a three-day trip here."

We started out late in the evening and flew to Dallas. As we put the gear down coming in to Dallas, we got a red light on the nose wheel light, it didn't turn green, so we recycled the gear, finally got a green light and landed. We wrote it up in the logbook so Maintenance would take care of it and see if we needed to change airplanes. Maintenance looked at it, signed it off, and said it was okay for further flight. We took off from Dallas heading to Amarillo. As we neared Amarillo, a weather front was coming through. It was snowing and blowing. We started the approach, put the gear down, and got the red light again. We had to recycle the gear until we finally got a green light, the same as we had in Dallas. It had not been fixed.

After we landed, we boarded the van and went to the hotel. Ed said he would buy dinner for the crew. So we all went to the restaurant and ate dinner. When we got to our rooms, the weather was still bad. In the middle of the night, the power went off and the room became icy cold because there was no heat. I put the covers from both beds over me but I was still freezing. The next morning when I got up, the water in the commode was frozen. We couldn't shave or anything, so we went to breakfast. We discussed the bad weather. At the airport Ed said, "I'm not going any further." He got off at Dallas and went back to Houston. Our point was made.

One other time I had an opportunity to get someone to ride in my jump seat. I was at a meeting in Washington, D.C. with a group of pilots discussing crew fatigue and scheduling. Langhorne Bond, the FAA head at that time, was in our meeting. Flight Time and Duty Time were on the Agenda. I said I would like for Langhorne Bond to come and ride on my jump seat for a three-day trip. He never showed up. Many trips were tiring. Management, supported by the FAA, would not look at circadian rhythms or any other pertinent data. They were just getting the flying done.

FedEx Fatigue Study: The FedEx guys, who fly all night, were really fighting the fatigue problem. They got NASA to come in and take a look at the issue. Some of the pilots wore rectal probes for a year or so. NASA was looking at the core temperature of the body. On a four-day trip, the core temperature kept dropping. That indicated that the fatigue level of the pilot was going higher and higher. As a result of the study, the FedEx pilots did get some relief. But airline pilots did not get any benefit from the FedEx study.

Red Headed Kid: An incident in Lafayette, Louisiana amused me. We were sitting in the cockpit as the passengers were loading for the next leg of our flight. A little boy came through – he was probably 5 or 6 years old, red headed and freckle faced. I asked him to come up to the cockpit and look around, which I always do for children on board if time permits. We let him look around at the instrument panel, get into one of the seats, and turn the wheel.

I was talking to him and said, "Well, I guess they call you Red."

He said, "Yeah, they call me Red."

Later in the conversation, I said, "Well, Red, are you married?"

He said, "What the hell's the matter with you, man? Are you crazy?"

QC Airplane Cargo Door: Throughout the industry, the Air Force paid the airlines to have what were called QC – Quick Change – airplanes in the fleet. The Air Force subsidized the airline so much a month to fly them. On a QC airplane, next to the regular passenger entrance door is a second door that is 14 feet wide and about 8 or 9 feet tall. It opens from the bottom and the door is raised to the top of the fuselage. That way you could remove all passenger seats and load cargo onto the airplane. There were two reasons the Air Force wanted these airplanes: (1) they wanted to be able to get to these planes in case of a national emergency; and (2) they would use airline pilots to crew the planes. TI had six of these airplanes. The cargo door was heavier and the floor had to be reinforced to hold cargo. These airplanes weighed about 6,000 pounds more than our regular airplanes, and there was an increase in operating costs.

On a TI flight, the airplane departed Houston to Mexico City, to McAllen, and back to Houston. Captain T.K. Lee took off and the crew got a warning light on the cargo door. Captain Lee picked up the mike, called Houston Maintenance, and told them the light was on.

Maintenance said, "Yeah, that's a microswitch and the light has been coming on and off. We've capped all the hydraulic lines to that door and there is no way it can come open because there is no hydraulic pressure to it."

The flight continued to Mexico City and back to McAllen, both legs uneventful. Out of McAllen, the co-pilot was flying and they climbed up to 10,000 feet. Below 10,000 feet, there is a 250 knot speed restriction. At 10,000 feet, the nose is lowered a little bit and speed is accelerated to 320 knots to climb. As the nose was lowered, the aircraft started picking up speed and the cargo door popped open. About a third of the fuselage was open. When rapid decompression occurs like that, everything not tied down goes out the open door. The overhead bins (then) did not have doors. All the papers in the cockpit flew out. First, the power was pulled back, then the pilot tried to make a left turn, but the aircraft would not turn left. Because the large cargo door was open, it was like having a rudder right up front.

Captain Lee said, "I've got it." He tried turning around to the right. He looked toward the back and he could see people had been cut up by the stuff flying around the back and people were bleeding. Captain Lee called the company and said he needed all emergency equipment out because he had an emergency and was coming back in to McAllen. The airplane started coming around and he kept the speed up considerably higher, and made the approach and landing. As he was coming down for landing, the door began coming down. One passenger next to that door was being held in by his seat belt; his legs were flapping outside the fuselage. As that door started coming down, Captain Lee was concerned about the door's coming down and cutting the passenger in half. As it happened, the door was warped enough that it did not close, and the passenger was only slightly injured – his legs were banged up. They landed and got everyone off. The irony of the incident was the passenger hanging outside the aircraft refused medical treatment. The crew insisted he be checked to be sure he was okay since they felt he would be filing a lawsuit. But the passenger said all he wanted was to get on the next flight to Houston. He was down in the Valley with his girlfriend and he was afraid his wife would find out where he had been. He never sued the airline.

Captain Lee and his First Officer received awards from the FAA and ALPA for saving the aircraft. That was a good outcome for that incident.

Rules for the Ordinary Pilot: A Captain was flying into Lafayette. It was raining, wind was blowing, and they had to shoot an ILS approach. The tower advised the Captain that he had a tail wind of 12 knots gusting to 15 knots. He continued on, touched down, and hydroplaned off the end of the runway into the mud. He called Lafayette Operations and told them to bring a truck and some rope to pull the airplane back on the runway. That didn't happen, but they got everyone off.

When they went to the FAA hearing on the incident, the FAA examiner asked the Captain, "Do you realize the limitation for a tail wind on this airplane is 10 knots? You were told twice that the tail wind exceeded that. Why did you continue?"

The Captain replied, "Well, that's for the ordinary pilot."

Harlingen Incident No. 1: A crew flying into Harlingen had been cleared for an ILS approach to the Harlingen Airport. The Harlingen Airport did not have a tower. The co-pilot was flying. They broke out of the clouds at 1,100 feet. The co-pilot saw something out of the eyebrow window and felt a little tug on the airplane but couldn't figure out what it was. The flight landed, taxied into the gate, and put the stairs down. One of the ground crew ran up into the cockpit and told the crew, "Something big fell off your airplane when you landed." The crew walked around the airplane and everything appeared to be intact. He insisted that something had fallen off the airplane when it landed. They got into a truck and drove to the touchdown area on the runway. They saw a man walking along the runway. He was soaked with gasoline and seemed disoriented, and said, "Where am I? What happened?"

They got him into the truck, drove a little farther down the runway, and found a crashed Piper Cherokee – a little single engine airplane. As the TI flight broke out of the clouds on its approach to the runway, the Piper Cherokee had been scud-running under the clouds. The DC-9 was on the ILS glide slope and flew under the Piper Cherokee. That was what the co-pilot saw out of the eyebrow window. The TI DC-9 hit the Piper Cherokee. The only damage to the DC-9 was a black streak all the way down the top of the fuselage of the DC-9 left by the tire of the Piper Cherokee. The Piper Cherokee lodged on the T-tail of the DC-9. When the DC-9 touched down and the thrust reverses engaged, it dislodged the Piper Cherokee, which fell off to the side of the runway. The lucky Piper Cherokee pilot survived the incident.

Harlingen Incident No. 2: The TI crew spent the night in McAllen, and it was about a five-minute flight from McAllen to Harlingen. The crew took off and shot their approach into Harlingen. They went over the top of a house, hit a tree in the front yard, went through a power line, pulled up and missed the approach. They realized the airplane wasn't pressurized so they flew at 10,000 feet to Houston and landed. The Captain wrote up the incident in the logbook as a bird strike.

The mechanic said to the Captain, "Bird strike, my ass! There is a power line hanging out of your left wing."

Upon investigation, it was learned that the crew had been drinking across the border until about 2 in the morning. The flight crew didn't check the weather or anything. Just got into the airplane and took off. Visibility in Harlingen was zero/zero. The Captain was terminated.

CHAPTER 24

In-Flight Emergencies

Pilots are always concerned about safety because they are the first one at the scene of a crash. While doctors bury their mistakes, pilots die with theirs.

One thing that helped the accident rate go down was installation of the flight cockpit voice recorder ("CVR") and the flight data recorder ("FDR"). Both are stored in the tail of the aircraft. These so-called "black boxes" (even though they are actually neon orange) are stored in the tail because the tail usually survives a crash. The CVR records cockpit conversations on a 30-minute loop of tape. If the airplane crashes, the last 30 minutes of cockpit conversation is preserved. The flight data recorder records the flight data from the beginning to the end of each flight and must be operational for every flight.

The CVR holds the potential for a lot of abuse. ALPA got an agreement with the FAA that the cockpit voice and flight data recorders would be read out only in the event of an accident. That was the Golden Rule and I don't know of any that were read out except one. Captain

Bob Lemon decided that one Captain had been dragging his feet or not following proper procedure – I'm not sure what initiated his action. Nevertheless, Lemon decided to pull the voice recorder out. As soon as he took it to the radio shop to get the technician to read it out, the technician called ALPA and told us that he was reading out the voice recorder. The ALPA MEC members went in and confronted Lemon. The technicians prevented Lemon from telling any stories about what was on the voice recorder because they had been right there listening and he had to admit that he had read out the voice recorder. As a result of that, ALPA revoked Bob Lemon's ALPA membership. That didn't really hurt him, but perhaps made him feel bad for a minute or two.

Engine Failure Procedure: If you lose an engine, the procedure is: (1) IDENTIFY the engine that failed (when you lose an engine, the plane wants to turn toward the dead engine; plane veers to the right if the right engine has failed. In that case, the pilot pushes the rudder of the good engine to maintain runway heading – dead foot, dead engine.); (2) VERIFY with other pilot. Pull throttle back on the failed engine, if nothing happens that is verification that it is the failed engine; and (3) SHUT DOWN the engine and announce "Shutting down No. 2 engine."

Engine failure requires that the flying pilot follow procedure for the established sequence of actions described above. In a propeller-driven aircraft, the procedure includes "feather" of the failed engine. To feather an engine, engine oil is pumped into the prop dome and that turns the blades of the propeller so that they are perpendicular to the airstream. That decreases the drag on the aircraft as it continues to fly with the remaining engine. The steps in the process for all aircraft are (1) Identify, (2) Verify and (3) Shut Down. Jets do not require "feather" since there are no propellers. Engine shut down for all aircraft require that in sequence you must (1) retard the throttle to idle, (2) pull fuel mixture control back to shut off fuel flow to the engine which shuts down the engine, and (3) feather the engine on propeller driven aircraft.

August 15, 1967, Engine Failure: The first engine failure that I had while flying at TI occurred on a DC-3 with Captain Harry Hales on a charter from Houston to Amarillo. We were cruising along near College Station, when the right engine swallowed a valve. The engine shot a smoke ring in front of the cockpit. The airplane was vibrating so hard that it was difficult to reach the feathering button overhead. But we got it feathered, went back in, and got another plane. We proceeded to Amarillo and finished our trip without further incident.

July 20, 1969, Engine Failure: The next engine loss was in a Convair 600 with Captain Washburn. One of the check airmen told me that the only thing faster than the speed of light was to watch a pilot when he loses an engine reach over and shut it down. His hands move so quickly you can't see them.

Captain Washburn reached over but got the wrong lever and shut down the good engine. The bad engine was still running. I tried to get the condition lever back up to keep it from feathering, but it went all the way in. So we had to do a restart that takes two or three minutes. We got it restarted and back on line.

Then Washburn said, "We better feather the other engine."

I said, "Look, we've already feathered this one. If we feather that one, we will really have scared the passengers to death and they'll think they're going to die! Just pull it back to idle so it is not over-temping and we can go in to land." That was what we did.

Washburn was a pretty good Captain. He got into racing airplanes. He went to Reno in 1975 to race in the T-6 category. He bought an airplane and spent a lot of money getting the engine souped up. He took his girlfriend, mother and father to the race and they were in the stands. As he was coming around one of the pylons, he clipped the pylon with one of his wings; it took the wing off, and he crashed upside down. He was killed instantly.

November 2, 1969, Engine Failure: Lynn Lowe and I were departing Lake Charles in a Convair 600. Just as we broke ground, the No. 2 engine started over temping. Quicker than a flash of light, Lowe had that thing feathered. We went around, came in, and landed.

I said, "Lynn, you're supposed to verify those engines, don't just reach up there and shut it off. Let me know you're going to shut it off. You scared me to death."

This incident was typical of the engines over temping.

February 22, 1970, Engine Failure: The next engine failure was in a Convair 600 with Captain Jerry Riddle, who was reluctant to make decisions in the cockpit. This guy bad-mouthed the company all the time. Any time he had a chance to gouge the company, he would do it. We had him in the Professional Standards Committee several times and he had been bumped back to co-pilot for a year because of some of his shenanigans. Jerry and I were going to New Orleans and the right engine was over temping.

I said, "Jerry, we need to shut it down."

Jerry said, "No, no, we can't shut it down. Dispatch will be all over me. Call dispatch and tell them what it is."

I said, "Jerry, the engine is going to melt out there and I'm going to shut it down."

I feathered the engine. Then I said to Jerry, "You know, you're the Captain on this thing and you ought to act like a Captain."

December 15, 1970, Engine Failure: I was the Captain on the next engine failure. We were flying out of Dallas in a Beechcraft 99, a small 19-passenger airplane. We were in heavy rain and the fire warning came on. I shut the engine down and fired both fire bottles. The fire warning remained on. We turned around and landed back in Dallas.

Five Engines Feathered in Three Days: Rick Hundley and I flew a three-day trip when we were flying DC-3s. The company had 25 DC-3s but only three in operation. The company was not maintaining these aircraft. If one broke down, they would just go over to the bone pile, get another one, and put it in service. On that trip, we feathered five engines in three days. I think that was a record – at least it was for me.

Backward Overhead Switches: As mentioned earlier, TI purchased some TWA airplanes with the backward overhead switches. Maintenance changed all the switches but the two essential radio bus switches. They were still backward. I was on a flight that took off out of Houston Intercontinental. The procedure was that you get clearance to 5,000 feet then you are turned over to Departure Control who can clear you up to 15,000 feet.

When I reached 5,000 feet, Departure Control said, "Climb and maintain ..."

We lost communication with Departure Control. We continued to maintain the 5,000-feet-runway heading. I started looking around and figured out that both radios were dead. I looked up and there were those two switches. The other pilot looked up and saw that they were backward. He flipped them but didn't tell me. I flipped them back and restored our communication. We continued our trip with no further incidents.

Baltimore Trip Fuel Over Burn: One of the more dramatic trips I had was a flight from Houston to Baltimore. This was just prior to the first march in Washington, DC commemorating gay pride. We left Houston with a full load because of our cheap fares going to Baltimore – a good jumping off point to Washington, DC. All the passengers were gay except for one guy. The flight attendants kept coming up to the cockpit to tell us what was going on – they were holding hands, kissing, etc. It didn't bother me. But the one straight man on board stood in the galley for the whole trip.

This particular airplane, Tail No. 3505, had burned about 10 percent over the fuel burn. The company had gone to the FAA and got our reserve fuel load cut down from 6,000 pounds to 4,500 pounds. They also got what was called No Alternate Required ("NAR"). Normally we have enough fuel on board to go to our destination and then on to an alternate destination if required and still have 45 minutes of fuel. We were still having the weight problems discussed earlier. The company requested the FAA and obtained consent so that if the weather forecast is 6,000 feet with 10 miles visibility, the flight can be dispatched with No Alternate Required ("NAR"). The Baltimore flight was dispatched with an NAR dispatch release. The fuel burn was over projection at every checkpoint.

When we were within 150 miles of Baltimore, the weather information broadcast in Baltimore reported it was ceiling zero/visibility zero. It had been forecast to be 6,000 feet or better. I called Richmond, Virginia. They were down. I called Washington National. They had 300-feet-ceiling overcast and ¾ mile visibility. I told them I needed to head into Washington National, shoot the approach, and land. ATC said our flight would be number 19. I said we could not accept that position and I declared minimum fuel. ATC put us in the number 3 slot. We landed and had 1,100 pounds of fuel left when we arrived at the gate. That was eleven minutes of flying. That was a close one.

There was television coverage to meet our passengers that had been diverted to Washington National from Baltimore. When the passengers deplaned, the one straight passenger asked if he could get off the plane with the flight crew. We said, "Sure."

Problem Not in the Books: There are routine things that we do in the simulator – almost any problem you can think of can be duplicated for simulator training. I had one incident coming out of Denver that wasn't in the books. We were going to Houston. You could pretty much fly straight to Dallas and then start your arrival route into Houston that requires a right turn into the Houston arrival route. I reached up to turn the autopilot heading bug and the aircraft did not respond. It just kept heading straight. I disconnected the autopilot and got my hands on the yoke. But I couldn't move the yoke. So I called Air Traffic Control ("ATC") and told them that I was going to hold my heading because I had a problem. I called Houston Maintenance and told them what had happened. They told us to do everything that we had already done.

I said, "We need to talk to somebody at Douglas. Get a Douglas engineer on the phone and patch us through."

So we got the telephone patch in and the engineer said, "Where did you guys take off?"

I said, "Denver."

He said, "What was the weather like?"

I said, "It was clear."

He said, "What was the runway like?"

I said, "It had a little slush on it."

He said, "Well, I know what your problem is. Just go on down until you get to where the temperature is above freezing and it will go away."

The Douglas engineer was right and the problem was resolved. As the gear was raised upon takeoff, the slush the tires had gathered from the runway was thrown into the wheel well. When we reached higher altitudes, the temperature was 40 degrees below zero and the slush had frozen inside the wheel well. The wheel well contained flight control cables and that is why the yoke would not move. That was an unusual event. I was glad that I had that experience because I knew how to handle the situation when it happened to me two more times while I was flying for Evergreen.

March 12, 1971 Both DC Generators: The next failure was on March 12, 1971. I had been bumped back to co-pilot because the number of daily flights had been reduced. I was flying co-pilot for Ken Smith and we lost both DC generators. The engine failures discussed above were situations we had practiced in the airplanes. When we got the jets we practiced these situations in the simulator. Because of that training, they were routine situations. However, when you start losing electricity, it is a little more concerning. We shut down all nonessential electrical and returned to the departure airport. When we were close, we turned on one radio to make our landing.

Anti-Skid Brake Failures: All modern aircraft now have anti-skid braking systems. When the wheels lock up, it releases that wheel so the tire doesn't tear off the rim. I had two incidents with failure of the anti-skid braking system. The first one was in Austin. The first flight of the morning we had to do what is called an "AC/DC cross tie lock out check," a procedure to confirm that if a generator goes out on one side or the other that the remaining generator would pick up the load for the failed generator. We performed the procedure and the test failed. That meant one of the relays was stuck. The procedure is performed with both engines running, both generators on line, and external power disconnected. We announced to the passengers that we were shutting down the electricity and both engines to resolve a little problem and it should take just a few minutes. We shut everything off and the airplane was dark. We started the engines, and got everything on line. Again, we performed the AC/DC crosstie lock out check and it worked. We taxied out for departure and started to take off. Just before we reached V-1 the master caution light came on and we started to abort. I saw the anti-skid light blink once. We taxied in to have maintenance take a look at the problem.

Maintenance came to the cockpit and said, "I don't know what your other problem is but your No. 4 tire is gone."

The anti-skid had failed. As a result of the various delays and problems, we departed Austin with no passengers. If I had been a passenger on that flight, I would also have gotten off!

The next anti-skid failure I had was upon landing in Merida, Mexico. It was right after a thundershower and puddles were all over the runway. As we came in for landing and gently put the brakes on, we scuffed off a tire because the anti-skid system failed. We taxied in and it took a two-hour delay while we negotiated with Mexicana to rent a wheel from them so we could fly back to Houston and ship the rented wheel back to them.

Bomb on Board: Back in the 70s when Cubans (and others) wanted to go to Havana, there were charts in our airplanes with rings around

Havana in 100-mile increments so we would know the distance from our location to Havana. There was an event in the Middle East where they blew up three airplanes. We were constantly concerned about having a bomb on the airplane. I was flying one day and received a message from dispatch that we had a Code 67. What's a Code 67? We got the book out and it said "Bomb on board."

We called dispatch and asked, "What's the confidence level?"

Dispatch said, "It's high."

That means that whoever called it in knew the flight number and also may have known the tail number of the aircraft. As a result we immediately asked dispatch, "What should we do?"

Dispatch asked, "What's the nearest place you can land?"

"Texarkana," I replied.

Dispatch said, "Go in to Texarkana and we will have the FBI come out."

We landed in Texarkana. Any time you have a bomb on board, they don't want you around the terminal or other aircraft so we taxied out to a closed runway and shut it down there. They sent a bus out and we unloaded the passengers and put them on the bus to the terminal where we waited for the FBI. The FBI showed up about two hours later.

The FBI agent said, "Well, Captain, why don't you go out and inspect your aircraft?"

I said, "I thought that was your job."

The FBI agent said, "No, we are just here to advise you."

We opened the baggage bins and looked everything over in there. While we were flying, we informed the flight attendants and asked them to discreetly take a look through the cabin without alarming the passengers, but we searched again. Everything was clear, no bomb was found. After a three- or four-hour delay, we continued our trip.

Near Mid-Air Collision: I was flying from New Orleans, cruising along at altitude. At that time the aircraft only had a transponder. There was no altitude reporting. Air Traffic Control ("ATC") always relied upon the pilot to report their altitude. When controllers made a mistake, they would call out "Lost radar contact," which meant the controller didn't know where everything was on the radar screen.

As we were cruising along, we received a "Lost radar contact" call and I told the other pilot, "Let's start looking. There's somebody close."

IN-FLIGHT EMERGENCIES

About the same time, a twin Beech executive aircraft with about 10 to 12 seats in it, appeared in our windshield. It was so big and close that all I could see were the engines in the windshield. We pushed the nose over and I turned off the transponder. ATC called about three times.

I said, "Let's not answer it right away."

The voice from ATC reached a higher pitch with each call.

After a few minutes, I called and said, "Well, we missed it."

Clear Air Turbulence: Ken Smith and I were flying to New Orleans and we were coming up on a line of weather. We called the flight attendant and told her to make sure all passengers are buckled in and that she must get buckled into a seat and stay until we release the seat belt sign. We told her we were going to have some weather, we didn't know how bad, but it looks like it is going to be pretty rough. As we got closer to the weather line, we were on top and saw a "saddleback," which is a hole in the weather. We turned and continued through the saddleback where we could pass through the line of weather in the clear. About halfway through the saddleback, we hit turbulence that was extremely strong. I saw my Coke come across the windshield – just the fluid and ice floating across the cockpit. Then we hit the bottom of the turbulence and BAM! I couldn't get any communications with ATC but I discovered that the turbulence had G forces enough that our headsets came unplugged on both sides. We couldn't communicate with ATC because our headsets were unplugged. We remedied that, called New Orleans, and landed.

After landing, the flight attendant would go down the stairs and thank the passengers for riding with us as they deplaned.

That time, as we sat there, Ken looked out the window and said, "Oh my God! She just fainted."

A ramp agent caught her before she hit the ground. We got out of the airplane to send her to the emergency room, and she told us what had happened. When she went back to the cabin, one of the passengers with a small child said the child needed to go to the bathroom. So the flight attendant took the child back to the bathroom. The flight attendant was with the child in the bathroom when the turbulence hit. It threw the flight attendant and the child out of the bathroom. As both were in midair, the flight attendant caught the child and her back slammed against a seat back while she was holding the child who was not hurt.

The flight attendant's back was injured, but she did not call and tell us what had happened. I went back and looked inside the cabin. The commode contents had come out into the cabin and it was a mess back there. It took several hours to get it all cleaned up.

J.V.'s *God Is My Co-Pilot* **Flight**: On his first trip as a Captain, J.V. Sclifo had a trip from El Paso, to College Station, to Houston. His co-pilot was Bob Rosenfeld. They spent the night in El Paso and headed to College Station the next evening. From College Station they flew to Houston. There was no radar on board. They were flying at 3,000 feet and encountered rain and hail. The hail was so hard that the co-pilot's windshield broke. Visibility in College Station was zero. They were unable to maintain altitude. Harry Williams was in the jump seat. J.V. called San Antonio Center and told them he was in bad weather and holding an easterly heading to Houston to escape the weather and that they would go direct to Houston when they broke out of the weather. J.V. said his heart was jumping out of his chest. The leading edges on the wings were flat from the hail damage and that destroys lift. J.V. was concerned about landing with the flat leading edges. He sent someone back to check on the passengers and they were all asleep. J.V. called the company and told them he had severe damage and needed assistance. T.K. Lee, the Chief Pilot, met them as they landed. J.V. said his legs were shaking. The plane was so badly damaged they had to remove the wings. There were six holes in the fabric and three or four window panes in the cabin were cracked. J.V. went home and went to bed. Then he heard a thunderstorm. He thought the thunderstorm had followed him home.

Lightning Strikes: During my career I was struck by lightning two times. The first time I was downwind in a 757 in Phoenix. Normally before a lightning strike, you start getting St. Elmo's fire build up. St. Elmo's fire looks like little lightning going across the windshield. We had a lot of that and on radar, it looked like there was a unicorn spike coming out of the St. Elmo's fire, then all of a sudden, WHAM! In the cockpit the CRTs (TV screens for our instruments) lost all the color and started fading. The screens stayed gray for several seconds and I thought we were going to lose all the data. The color came back on, we returned to the airport, and landed the airplane. Normally, when you have a lightning strike, you get two holes in the aircraft, one where the lightning enters and one where the lightning departs.

The second lightning strike was in the MU-2 that I flew for Joe Taylor in Newport. I was flying in the clouds and there was a lot of electrical activity. We had St. Elmo's fire and BAM! The lightning hit! We returned and landed in Newport to check the airplane. They only found one hole on the left side wing tip. It was the portion that doesn't carry any fuel, it is just aluminum.

Safe Transportation: While knowing the type of things that can occur may be disconcerting, remember that none of the incidents cited here resulted in a crash. A scheduled air carrier is still the safest form of transportation – safer than driving a car and safer than walking down the sidewalk.

CHAPTER 25

Labor Relations at TTA, TI and Continental

My years at Trans Texas, Texas International ("TI") and Continental were educational because I learned about negotiating, unions – things that I never thought I would have to deal with. I was just happy flying airplanes. However, during those TI years, I served as the co-pilot representative for two terms, MEC Chairman for two terms, Chairman of the Negotiating Committee and, after the 1975 Contract, I served on each Negotiating Committee until the Continental strike. I was Chairman of the Negotiating Committee for the Integration of Pilots' Seniority Lists of Continental Air Lines and Texas International. The next order of business was to combine the two pilot contracts and I was on that committee as well.

During my time with TI, I served on committees for the negotiation of the following contracts:

February 1, 1970 to February 1, 1972
June 1, 1975 to October 1, 1977
1977 to 1980 [do not have copy of this contract]
July 7, 1981 to February 1, 1983
1981 to July 7, 1981, TI and Continental contract integration

The Federal Aviation Administration ("FAA") dictates the management structure of an airline. It requires that there be a Vice President of Flight. At the time that I came on board, the Vice President of Flight had to be a pilot who had an ATR rating and he also had to be rated in the type of aircraft that the airline operated. The airline also had to have a Chief Pilot. When I was hired at Trans Texas, the Vice President of Flight was A.J. High and the Chief Pilot was Bill Moody. The rumor was that Moody was somehow related to A.J. High. I don't know whether it was true.

As time passed, Don Breeding became the Vice President of Flight and he hired my good friend, J.V. Sclifo as the Chief Pilot. Breeding did not have the qualifications required by the FAA. However, before Breeding became Vice President of Flight, the companies in the industry approached the FAA to change the rules so they could hire a Vice President of Flight who was not a pilot but had airline management experience. That was a cost saving to the airline so they wouldn't have to pay the Vice President of Flight the salary of a senior Captain at the airline. I first met Breeding in the third contract negotiation. He was sitting in the corner doing calculations on the cost of each item as it came across the table. He had survived Lorenzo and always did a pretty good dance between Lorenzo and the pilots.

Prior to becoming the MEC Chairman, I noticed that the pilots were not very well informed. Union meetings were held once a month or once every six weeks or so. Only the non-flying pilots attended the union meetings. After attending a union meeting, one could sit in the crew room and hear four or five different versions of what was said at the meeting. When I became MEC Chairman, I decided to establish a program to keep all pilots informed not only about what was going on at the union meetings, but also what was going on operationally within the company. That is the reason I started *The Straight Bull* sheet. The

Straight Bull newsletter was issued monthly to keep the pilots in the loop about everything that came within the purview of the MEC. [See Appendix D: *The Straight Bull* newsletter]

After training, pilots receive information about the operation of the company through a mailbox before and after flights and through the "grapevine." Pilots are largely unseen and very isolated in the cockpit, except when someone from management rides in the cockpit jump seat. Pilots have little or no interface with management. A pilot can go for months without seeing anyone from management. *The Straight Bull* was an effort to bridge that communication gap between management and its pilots.

CHAPTER 26

Contract Negotiations

MEC Chairman Lemon: Bob Lemon was elected as the MEC Chairman, and Bob had a temper. It was beyond belief. He would get mad at the company. He went to crew scheduling over an issue and they had the door closed. He kicked the door in, went in there, and cussed them all out. He had a low boiling point and was a holy terror.

When contract negotiations came up, they would normally elect a captain and first officer from each base to become the negotiating committee and the MEC Chairman would be an unofficial member of the negotiating committee. I was elected to be a contract negotiator for the first time. ALPA National sent a professional negotiator from Washington, DC whenever we had a negotiation. Most of the time, this person was also an attorney. This time we had a guy that Bob Lemon really liked and his name was Gorgos. The reason Lemon liked him so much was because he jabbed the company all the time at the negotiating table, called them liars and stuff like that. It was not productive but it made Lemon feel good. As we continued through this negotiation,

J.J. O'Donnell, President of ALPA National, uncovered some problems with Gorgos. I don't know whether it was on his expense account or what, but ALPA fired him. It made Lemon so mad that he took the whole MEC to Washington, DC to force J.J. O'Donnell to reinstate the guy. J.J. O'Donnell listened to what Lemon had to say.

O'Donnell said, "Well, Captain Lemon, that's fine, but that's my decision and I'll give you another negotiator."

In my first contract negotiation I observed more than I provided any input because co-pilots were not supposed to say anything, just sit and look.

The next contract negotiation came about without any trouble. We sat down with the company and I had a little bit more to say in that one. It was over pretty rapidly because there were not many issues. We were low man on the totem pole for pay scale in the industry. We looked at what other contracts had in them and we thought that was where we would wind up. The company knew that; we knew that. The negotiations were smooth and uncomplicated.

After my second contract negotiation, I had the opportunity to attend Negotiator Training at MIT in Boston. Later I went to similar training at the AFL-CIO's George Meany Building in Washington, DC The training was extremely valuable. In each of these sessions, they split us into two teams – one representing the company and one representing the pilots. There was an observer who sat through all negotiation sessions. When the negotiation was complete, the observer would critique our performance.

Wage Increase Limit: The next contract negotiations in 1972 were conducted when Jimmy Carter was President. We were under a 1.6 percent wage increase limit mandated by federal law. That contract negotiation was short because everybody knew that 1.6 percent was what we were going to get. With the 1.6 percent wage increase, we made sure it was a short contract period so we could get back in and negotiate a wage that was closer to industry standard.

Best Contract Gains: The negotiation I conducted with Ed Cathell in 1977 was the best contract gains and the company received the best productivity. It was because we were able to deal fairly across the table. Cathell would hold up for the company side and he made sure that the company did what they said they would do. It was a good negotiation.

Kansas City Contract Negotiation: In our next to last contract negotiation at TI, we had been in Kansas City negotiating for months with a national mediator. We reached tentative agreement in Kansas City and went back to Houston to write the language. In Houston, the process dragged on and on. Finally, we went through a 26-hour session and reached an agreement. We had been up all night and all the language for the open items was put together. When we finished, I told Cathell, VP of Human Resources, to talk to Lorenzo. Each time we negotiated a contract and signed off, Lorenzo reneged on part of it. I told Cathell I wanted him to talk to Frank, get him on the phone, and make sure everything is okay. The company group left and were gone for about four hours. Cathell returned and said they had everything squared away and Frank agreed to every item. I went home, put out a tape to the pilots that we had an agreement and more information would follow. I had been up about 30 hours. I told my wife not to wake me up unless the house was on fire. I went to bed about eight in the morning. At ten she woke me up and said I had to get up and talk to Ed Cathell. I got on the phone and asked what in the world was wrong.

Ed said, "Frank called this morning and said he could not go along with three or four items in the contract."

I said, "You guys talked to Frank last night and he signed off on this in front of the mediator, and we're not going to back off on this. You've got the problem – not us. You have agreed to this."

The next morning, Sunday, Ed Cathell and Don Burr, President of TI at that time, Don Breeding and several others went over to Frank's house and told him if he did not stand behind his word that they would all resign.

Frank said, "Well, I'm getting screwed. But I will go along with it since you guys feel this strong about it, but I am really getting screwed."

Difficult 1980 Negotiation: John Adams was there for the 1980 contract negotiation. I watched him during the negotiation and Adams was having a difficult time conforming to what Lorenzo was telling him to do. One day as I watched Adams, he made the decision to go with Lorenzo. Adams became a stone wall. He would not budge one inch on anything. He would sit there like a rock. If asked a question, John would look at the wall and not say a word.

One could wave a hand in front of his eyes and say, "John, are you in there?"

He wouldn't talk. Maybe ten minutes later, he would say something. It was a difficult negotiation. We finally got through the negotiation but it was a really tough operation. We got down to national mediation. The National Mediation Board (Board) was there for about a year with us to see if we could resolve the issues. The Board said they would give us a cooling off period of 30 days, then the pilots would be able to go on strike or the company could go into lockout.

I called Jack Bavis in Washington and said "If we go on strike, what happens to our scope clause?"

The scope clause in the TI contract stated that all flying by TI or its affiliates will be done by TI pilots. ALPA National said the scope clause would go away if we entered mediation.

I said, "Can you stop the release for self-help?"

Jack Bavis stopped the release for self-help by the Board; the cooling off period didn't occur. We continued to negotiate and finally reached an agreement.

Slowdown: During the 1980 negotiation, the pilots pulled a slowdown. What some of the pilots were doing was bad like putting the flaps down 20 miles out trying to burn fuel, being late – really beyond what they should have been doing. What we asked for was a "by the book" operation. Some of the guys went way out into left field. The company sued ALPA for having a work stoppage or work slowdown. During contract negotiations, we put out a tape every night to tell the pilots what was happening. We would add a nonsensical comment at the end of each tape. For example, "The clouds are in the west;" "Off, open and split" (the shutdown checklist for the DC-3); or "Keep the blue side up," (which had no meaning). None of the comments had any real meaning. They were added to make the company wonder. We were never sure it was effective until we reached the trial in federal court. The company called in a group of pilots to testify.

The pilots were asked under oath, "What does it mean? Keep the blue side up?"

The pilots didn't have a clue what they were talking about. It was comical to learn when we put "Off, open and split," (the DC-3 shut down check list), that the company thought it meant we were going to shut down the airline. The day after that comment was on the tape the company had all the check airmen and management pilots in the crew room ready to fly in case the pilots didn't show up.

We didn't understand what was going on when the company came to us and wanted us to fly the Dash-10 airplanes at a cut rate. If we did that, the company would expand our flying time. Floyd Carpenter was still chairman of the negotiating committee and didn't want to talk to them.

I said, "Floyd, not talking to them is not a good policy. We ought to listen to them."

He said, "No, I don't want to talk about it."

During his tenure with TI, Floyd Carpenter had been Captain's representative, Vice President of Flight, Chairman of the Negotiating Committee and MEC Chairman.

New York Air: We had some MD-80s that were supposed to come to Texas International. When we didn't have any negotiations over this, Lorenzo got really upset. John Adams was head of Human Resources at this time, and we were at loggerheads with Lorenzo and his operation. We learned that Lorenzo was going to take the Dash-80s to New York and call it New York Air, which was being bought and paid for with TI money. We had a pretty strong scope clause – one of the strongest in the industry – that said that any flying by TI and its affiliates or any company that took over Texas International would be done by TI pilots. This issue came to a head. While we were in negotiations, ALPA hired Mike Mann, with Corporate Campaign, to help us out. Mike Mann was a pivotal character in the movie *Norma Rae*. Mann was effective in what he did for us. We started buying shares of stock and attending stockholders meetings. We were generally questioning what was going on with the company. This put a lot of pressure on Lorenzo but it didn't make him change direction. New York Air started up and left ALPA pilots holding the bag.

When Frank Lorenzo started New York Air, the first operation was started out of LaGuardia. We obtained permission to set up a picket line and many TI pilots and pilots from other airlines walked the picket line around the LaGuardia terminal building for the first flight. Lorenzo invited the Mayor of New York City and other public officials for the inaugural flight of New York Air. The first airplane ran off the taxiway and didn't take off.

That evening I went to a cocktail party given by ALPA. Former astronaut Frank Borman, President of Eastern, looked me up and introduced himself.

I replied, "I'm Jim McCartney, MEC Chairman at Texas International."

Frank Borman said, "Well, Jim, if there's anything we can do here at Eastern to help you get rid of that scab operation, we sure would be interested to help you with anything you need."

The first morning we walked the picket line with our signs, TV cameras were out there as people started coming in. Lorenzo came in a big limo. Gloria Steinem came up and one of the flight attendants picketing with us went over to her and told her:

"Gloria, you represent women. Our flight attendants are only making half of what other flight attendants make. Are you going to fly?"

Steinem just blew off our picketing flight attendant and went straight through the picket line to get on her flight.

Dennis Higgins and I were walking the picket line when a limo pulled up. The door opened and a black lady got out with the shortest mini skirt I had ever seen. Then a black gentleman got out, walked up to us, and said:

"What's going on?"

We told him we were picketing New York Air because it's a runaway shop. ["Runaway shop" is a union term for work that is given to a new work force instead of the existing work force. The TI pilot contract had a scope clause that stated that all flying by TI or its affiliates will be done by TI pilots.]

He said, "Well, I don't cross picket lines."

He gave us his business card and he was a councilman for the City of New York. He said, "If you guys come down to my office in the morning, I'll see what I can do to help you out."

Dennis and I put the card away. We got up the next morning, put our suits on, and caught a cab. The councilman had asked us to be there at 8 a.m. and, being pilots, we were early. We gave the address to the cab driver, and he said:

"You guys don't want to go down there. That's down in Harlem."

I said, "Yes, we do."

CONTRACT NEGOTIATIONS

He said, "I'll take you down there but no cab's going to come down there and pick you up."

I said, "Well, we'll deal with that later."

The cab driver took us to Harlem and it was really a rough place. We found the Councilman's office but there were bars across the door with a chain and lock. The cab driver offered to wait until the Councilman showed up. We saw a grocery store across the street, told the cab driver we would go across the street, get a cup of coffee, and wait until the Councilman got to his office. We crossed the street to the grocery store. Dennis got a cup of coffee and I got a coke. Finally, we noticed the chain was off and the door was open. We walked back across the street and went up the stairs to the Councilman's office. We told him what was going on and the Councilman told us what he could do.

We heard the door rattle and he said, "Hold it, guys."

The Councilman pulled out his desk drawer and took out a pistol. I thought, oh my God.

Then we heard him say, "Mary Lou, you know to tell me before you start up those stairs."

It was his secretary. After we finished talking, seeing what he could do, which was little, we said we needed to go back and asked if he could get us a cab. He said cabs don't come down here, but I'll send you back in my car. That was my venture into Harlem.

Protracted Negotiation Resolved: In 1980, when we were negotiating our contract, we had been in negotiations for two years. Suddenly, the company was more than willing to settle the contract and we didn't have any idea why. Jim Arpey, Vice President of Operations, called me one morning and asked me to meet him for breakfast at his country club. He asked me to meet him alone. I called J.V. Sclifo and told him that Arpey wanted me to come alone and I didn't know what to do. J.V. said to go ahead and find out what they want. Arpey asked me, "Jim, what's it going to take to settle the contract?" We went over the issues and almost magically, we reached agreement on the contract terms we were requesting. At the time, I didn't understand the company's motivation to settle the contract issues. Later the company announced it was deeply involved in the takeover of Continental Airlines.

During the contract negotiation before the company announced it was buying Continental, I was living in Kingwood. All the utilities were underground and we had a two story house with two telephone lines, one downstairs and one upstairs for the kids. One day it had been raining hard and when the telephone rang, it rang on both lines, upstairs and downstairs. After the water receded, we still had the telephone problem, so I called AT&T to resolve the problem. AT&T came out, looked, and told me I needed to go out and look at the problem. They found a transmitter that tracked all the telephone calls to and from my house. AT&T told me all calls were transmitted to some other location within a five-mile radius from my house. My home telephones were bugged. AT&T removed the transmitter. I called ALPA and told them about it and they said there was nothing I could do about it. I don't know how long the tap had been there, but it was during the contract negotiations for sure.

* * *

Good People in Management: We were fortunate to have some good people. Ed Cathell was head of Human Resources and he hired John Adams as his assistant. Don Burr had become President of the airline and he hired a guy named Bob Galloway as Vice President of Operations. Galloway was the only guy I could deal with who would be straightforward and not evasive.

Galloway said, "Jim, I'm not going to lie to you, but I'm not going to tell you." Anything he told me was as good as gold.

Burr was more of a people person with everyone in the company and tried to make peace with the unions. Burr came up with the "peanut fares" concept. The DC-9 dash 10 originally came out of Douglas with 65 seats with a first class section and the Dash-30s with 90 seats and a first class section. Burr put the peanut fares into effect and stripped out the first-class sections. The planes with 65 seats now had 90 seats, and 25 seats were added to the Dash-30s. The program was successful. The airline was making money.

The rumor was that Burr was fired but the public statement was that he resigned to "pursue other interests."

Lorenzo got crossways with Bob Galloway and let him go. Galloway ran the BART System in San Francisco, California, for about three years. Frank got into trouble again, and Bob Galloway was lured back. When Bob arrived in Houston, he called me from his hotel.

Galloway said, "Hey, Jim. Come on over and let's talk."

We sat down and I told him I was glad to see him back, but I asked, "Why in the hell did you come back to Frank's operation?"

Bob said, "Well, Jim, here's the deal. If he fires me this time, my severance package is such that I'll never have to work again."

CHAPTER 27

Purchase of Continental

A few weeks after we signed the 1980 contract, Texas International announced they were making a takeover bid for Continental Airlines. As the purchase negotiations progressed, the President at Continental, Bob Six, hired Al Feldman from Frontier Airlines. Feldman had a good reputation for being able to deal with the unions and run a good airline. The Continental pilots urged management to start an Employee Stock Ownership Plan ("ESOP"), so they could buy Continental stock at a discount and make an alternate offer to buy the airline. Continental management complied with the request. The pilots used their pension plan funds to buy stock and gave Continental an increase in productivity. Instead of the whole group taking a hit, Continental decided to furlough just the bottom 425 pilots. It was a decision that would later come back and haunt the Continental pilots. The furlough took place and the bidding war began, back and forth.

Eventually it was getting close to the endgame and it looked like Texas International would take over Continental Airlines. Feldman, sitting in his office in the Los Angeles hangar, shot himself. There was speculation whether Feldman used the same gun Peach used to shoot himself. There were questions from the mechanics working at the hangar in Los Angeles about events that occurred on the evening Feldman shot himself.

Negotiating the Seniority List: On October 31, 1982, Continental Airlines merged with Texas International, and retained the Continental name for the merged entity. After Lorenzo won and started to integrate Continental with TI, the two seniority lists had to be combined. Both TI and Continental pilots belonged to ALPA. I was elected chairman of the TI Negotiating Committee to integrate the seniority list. I picked a Captain's rep, J.V. Sclifo, who had been Chief Pilot. J.V. was a good friend, honest and upright, who would look the situation over and try to be fair. We had a First Officer rep that was in the middle of the seniority pack of first officers so that we would have senior people represented by J.V. and junior people represented by the First Officer in the middle of the pack. The negotiations went on for several months and the Continental pilots really wanted to put the TI pilots on the bottom of the list. They came up with proposals; we came up with proposals. No agreement was reached.

Jim McCartney with evidence collected to merge pilot seniority lists

We followed the ALPA policy for merging seniority lists. Ultimately, if you could not agree, the matter went to arbitration. We entered arbitration. Marcia L. Greenbaum, from MIT, was the arbitrator. I thought she did a good job of putting our list together and it didn't hurt anyone's career.

During the negotiations, the Continental pilots clearly did not think the TI pilots were good pilots or good people. We didn't know how little they thought of us until the end of the arbitration of the seniority list. When it was over, the lawyer for the Continental pilots said he would like to meet with the TI pilots the next morning after the Continental representatives left town. The next morning the lawyer said he was embarrassed to do this, but that the Continental pilots insisted that he deliver this message to us so we would know how they felt. The lawyer told us that the Continental pilots thought we were unprofessional, didn't know how to be a big airline, and that the TI pilots were "functional illiterates." You can imagine how well that went over with the TI pilots.

Integrating the Two Airlines: After integration of the seniority list, the next step was to consolidate the two contracts. As this was going on, the two airlines were being integrated operationally and it was becoming a total disaster in the way it was managed. I flew several trips into Denver and was left waiting for a gate, sometimes for two hours, because the planning was not right. They would park us out away from a gate and bring a bus out to haul the passengers into the terminal. Conditions kept deteriorating and it was obvious there were serious operational problems. The cash flow was really bad. Both Continental and TI MECs met in Washington to discuss what could be done to save the airline. The company approached ALPA to request a substantial pay cut.

Lorenzo made an offer to the TI and Continental pilots before the strike. He talked to the Continental MEC Chairman and told him he wanted to cut their pay. I believe he wanted to cut the pay to Captains to $3,260 per month. That number may not be exact. If they took the pay cut he would put $200 million dollars that Texas Air had into the operation of the newly merged company. The Continental MEC did not respond to Lorenzo's offer. The Continental pilots didn't want to talk to Lorenzo at all because they thought they had the power.

The Continental pilots said, "We can take Lorenzo and put him to his knees. We'll just go on strike."

I told them in front of the lawyers and everyone, "Continental is going to declare bankruptcy."

They said, "Oh, you're just a spy for the company." I still had pretty good relationships with the company people. I said I knew it for a fact.

They said, "No, they will never let it go bankrupt."

I said, "I'll tell you what I know. I know the secretary of the President of Texas International is typing up the papers to present to the court for bankruptcy."

They just laughed.

I told our MEC about the speech the Continental pilots' lawyer made about the seniority negotiations in which they called us "functional illiterates." I also told them that Frank was going to cut through these guys like a hot knife through butter.

Bankruptcy Filed: On September 23, 1983, Continental filed for bankruptcy protection in the federal bankruptcy court in Houston. Because I had been one of the pilots involved in a lot of management decisions, the company called me and asked me if I would fly a trip down to Mexico City. The company had to continue to fly its international routes during the bankruptcy or lose them. On the way back from Mexico City, I heard that ALPA had gone on strike. I said I would not cross the picket line.

My co-pilot said, "Well, I am, and I'm going to take your job." That was the last trip I flew for Continental.

When I got back to Houston, I went to see Breeding, Vice President of Flight Operations, and told him I would not cross the picket lines.

"Jim, you understand that the management pilots like yourself will not take a pay cut, you will stay at your old salary. But all the rest of the pilots will take a pay cut."

I was making $7,305 per month and the rest of the pilots would be cut to $3,200 per month. The company wanted to keep a corps of check airmen on board getting their pre-strike pay and it would be a tremendous sacrifice if they gave up their job as check airman. The company wanted to use the check airmen to bust the pilots that they did not want on the property.

When the strike came down, they critically needed flight engineers – hard to come by because the required time in heavy aircraft for the flight engineers rating was difficult to get in the civilian world without airline experience. The 425 pilots furloughed by Continental crossed the picket line in droves and that allowed Continental to start up the operation and successfully end the strike.

Bomb Plot: During the strike, Captain Charley Hall and another pilot concocted a plot to plant a bomb. None of the members of ALPA's MEC Committee knew about their plan. Fortunately, the company got wind of the plan and foiled it before anyone was hurt. Hall and the other pilot put together some type of bomb device and were on their way to place the bomb. I think the company knew where they were headed because they had wiretaps on many of the pilots, including me. The company told the police about the plan. The police set up a roadblock and several people from the company were there to identify the two. They spotted the roadblock, turned around and headed in the opposite direction. They tossed the bomb out of the car but it did not detonate. They were just trying to get rid of it. The police recovered the bomb. Hall and the other pilot were indicted, convicted and each spent two years in the Federal pen.

Charley Hall's wife divorced him while he was in the pen. Charley had been adopted and his father was President of Eastern Air Lines, but Charley flew for TI/Continental. After Hall got out of the pen, his father died and Charley inherited several million dollars. His wife returned and proposed they get back together. Charley declined.

Post-Strike Incidents: After I refused to cross the picket line and left Continental, Frank Lorenzo called me to meet him for lunch at The Houstonian to discuss some issues. Instead, Frank just wanted to convince me to cross the picket line and return to work. Frank said the company was going to do great things. I declined his offer because I still could not cross the picket line.

After the strike started, I left my flight kit (with my initials on it) in the pilot crew room. My flight kit had my logbook inside. There was a part-time employee of the company that pilots hired for $20 per month to update their instrument approach plate books. He called me and told me that my flight kit was no longer in the pilot crew room. I believe it was stolen by one of the scabs that took the many empty places left by the striking pilots. I started a new logbook, but I regret the loss of my record of 2,000 to 3,000 hours of flight time.

On June 30, 1986, Continental emerged from Chapter 11 bankruptcy protection.

Strike Settlement: Two years after the strike started, ALPA negotiated a settlement. In the settlement, ALPA would not be on the property, but all the pilots had an option: come back to work and be placed on the seniority at the same place they would have been prior to the strike, or take a buyout.

Many pilots went back; many pilots took the buyout. I decided I had known so much about the operation that I could not bring myself to go back to Continental Airlines, so I took the buyout. The buyout I received was $60,000 or $80,000 – I don't remember the exact amount.

My personal feeling with respect to pilots on strike was that it is never in your best interest to go on strike. As long you have the throttle of the airplane in your hands, you are in control of your position. Nothing much can be accomplished if you are walking a picket line.

* * *

My good friend, Gary Portzline, was a unique guy. He was a good Captain at TI for a long time and we had walked the picket line together for two years. He decided he would go back and fly for Continental. He flew DC-9s for TI previously and when he went back they put him on a 727 so that meant he had to go through simulator training in the 727 and get a type rating in the 727. When he went to the simulator to take the type rating, of course, the FAA was there to make sure everything was right. They were the ones to say up or down whether you get the type rating or not. Well, the check ride went fine and the FAA guy said "fine job" and the company check airman, as I predicted when they kept their high salaries, said, "Well, you didn't pass the check ride and didn't meet our standards." They refused to let Gary back online. Gary went to ALPA and told them his problem. It took ALPA a year to get the issue resolved and get Portzline back into the cockpit. He got a year's back pay when it was resolved. While he was out, they had a base bid and the company bid Portzline for Guam. Portzline flew out of Guam for quite some time.

I remember one thing about Gary when we were walking the picket line and telling war stories. When he graduated from high school, Gary weighed only 116 pounds and he joined the Army. He was trained as a paratrooper. On the first parachute jump, everybody bailed out. Gary said all the other guys passed him with their parachutes opened, but he was so light that it took him forever to get on the ground. Everyone else was on the ground with chutes packed and put away before Gary touched down.

CHAPTER 28

Lorenzo Makes a Run for Eastern

When Frank Lorenzo was taking over Eastern Airlines, there were many problems caused by changes made by Texas Air. The news team, McNeil-Lehrer, called to do a background interview with me and J.V. Sclifo, who was Chief Pilot at the same time I was MEC Chairman.

The people who came to interview us asked questions and we answered them on camera. When the piece was aired on television, Robin McNeil or Jim Lehrer asked the questions and it looked as though we were in the studio answering the questions. We described the problems we were having with the weight and balance issues and that it was a problem that the company knew about. I gave them copies of memos that I had written to Lorenzo telling him about the overloaded airplanes. J.V. did the same thing when he was interviewed.

When I watched the McNeil-Lehrer interview on television, they had Lorenzo on the program and he said, "Well, I never heard anything about overweight airplanes or airplanes not being within weight and balance limits." McNeil-Lehrer had copies of the memos that J.V. and

I gave them, but did not use them to challenge Lorenzo's denial of knowledge about the issue.

After that, I swore never to give another interview. I had confidence in McNeil Lehrer from watching them previously. I was disappointed that McNeil-Lehrer did not use the documentation we provided to the show's producers to challenge Lorenzo.

CHAPTER 29

Trans Star f/k/a Muse Air

I had been thinking about what I would do if I didn't go back to flying. I talked to my friend, Bill Baker. We had been racing motorcycles together for many years and been on all kinds of adventures together. I asked him if he would be interested in setting up a maintenance shop specializing in brakes and front ends. We were going to copy the business plan after Brake-O. We started Brake Test, got it up and running, and I worked there for about two years managing the place.

But I was antsy and wanted to get back in the air. My friend, Allen Kelley, who did the Weight and Balance analysis and also did Safety work at TI, had been flying for an operation called Muse Air which changed its name to Trans Star.

Allen said, "Jim, why don't you come on over here?"

I said, "Well, I think I might."

I called John Hodge, the Vice President of Flight, whom I had known from TI. After John retired, I helped him get a job in the Chief Pilot's office as an assistant or go-between for some of the pilots. I called John and told him I needed a job and he said he would put me in the next class. So I started at Trans Star. It was an operation based in Houston that ran the old National Airlines routes over to Florida, Miami and Tampa. Sometimes it would stop in New Orleans, then back to Houston and then to many airports on the West Coast. That was its primary route structure. They were flying DC-9s Dash 30s, DC-9s Dash 50s and DC-9s Dash 80s.

I flew at Trans Star from December 17, 1986, until October 1, 1987, when the company went into bankruptcy.

CHAPTER 30

Evergreen Airlines

After Trans Star ceased operations, I called a friend of mine at Midway Airlines in Chicago. We had worked together at Texas International and when he left there, I had written him a letter required from a union representative saying he was a fair and impartial guy so he could become an arbitrator, or neutral, for grievance hearings. I told him I was out of a job and wondered about getting a job with Midway. He said he would get me right into a class and to come on up and take the physical. I called my friend, Allen Kelley, and asked him to go with me to Midway. Allen said he didn't want to go over there because they give a pretty strict physical and his blood pressure is always questionable when he goes in for a flight physical. Allen suggested we go to Evergreen Airlines. I said I didn't know anything about Evergreen. Allen said it was a freighter operation and there were several guys up there from TI and Continental flying 747s, DC-8s and DC-9s. We called Evergreen and they said to come on up.

We talked to the Chief Pilot of the DC-9 operation, and he said he thought he could hire us as Captains but asked us to go over and take a simulator ride in Portland, Oregon. We were at the Evergreen headquarters in McMinnville, Oregon. They gave us a van and we drove to Portland for the simulator ride. The instruments were not installed in a basic T pattern. [See Appendix E: T-Pattern Instrument Panel]. It was an old T-33 simulator that was a piece of junk. The flight director didn't work — that is the instrument that tells you if you are left or right or up and down for an ILS approach. The guy said if you look up at the top you can see if you are left or right and if you look at the bottom you can see if you are up or down. When you put the gear and flaps down on the simulator, you had to go to 100 percent power or it would just quit flying. It was in a terrible state of maintenance, or the lack thereof. I flew it first and Allen flew it. I told Allen I didn't do well and he said he didn't, either. It was so difficult to fly IFR because it was so different from anything I had ever flown.

Allen Kelley and Jim McCartney at Evergreen Airlines

We went back to McMinnville and the guy in charge of the simulator had already called and told the Chief Pilot that we couldn't fly instruments. We were discouraged. The Chief Pilot drove us in the van to drop us off in Portland so we could go home. As we were driving along and talking with him, we told him one of our flight attendants used to fly as flight attendant for Elvis Presley out of Memphis on a Convair jet. He said, "Oh, I used to fly co-pilot on that plane." He asked who she was and we told him her name. He said he knew her.

By the time we got to Portland, the Chief Pilot said, "Okay, you guys, I'm going to hire you. That simulator must be a piece of junk for you guys to have trouble with it."

I said, "I think you are wasting money to send anyone over there to see if they can fly instruments in that simulator. That thing is so out of tolerances."

He hired us and we started work at Evergreen on November 10, 1987. Evergreen hired us as Captains. This was my first interface with the military as a pilot. I had been in the military as crew chief on a B-47 but I really didn't know anything about military flight operations. Allen and I were both based out of Wright Patterson AFB.

Evergreen had log air operations for hauling freight to air force bases from the parts depot at Wright Patterson AFB in Ohio. There were also parts depots at Kelly AFB in San Antonio, Hill AFB in Salt Lake City, and in Tulsa and California. Our flights out of Wright Patterson AFB were up to Pease AFB, which is a little north of Boston, to Loring AFB in Bangor, Maine, then to Griffiss AFB in New York, just off Lake Ontario near Syracuse. Then we returned to Wright Patterson AFB.

At night, the airplane would be used for mail. Evergreen had a contract for delivery of the mail at that time. The mail was sorted in Terre Haute, Indiana. The route was to fly from Wright Patterson AFB to O'Hare Airport in Chicago, pick up the mail, and take it to Terre Haute for sorting. We would wait four hours in the middle of the night while the mail was sorted. When the mail was loaded we returned to Wright Patterson AFB to be there first thing the next morning to start the log air operation. At Evergreen, we worked a week on and a week off.

My first trip out of Wright Patterson AFB, I didn't know anything about base operations. I just knew we went to base ops to get our paperwork. I filed a flight plan up to Pease AFB and told the Tech Sergeant that I needed the weather for Pease AFB and alternates.

He said, "Well, I'll read it to you."

I said, "No, just give me the piece of paper." At that time it came off the teletype.

He said, "No, you're not authorized."

I said, "What do you mean, I'm not authorized?"

He said, "You're not authorized to read the weather."

So we had it around and around. The tech sergeant read me the weather for Pease AFB and for Loring AFB in Maine. Next, I asked him to read me the weather for the alternates. He asked what alternates I wanted. I named three. He said he could only give me one. I said I wanted all three. We had another big argument until finally I got the weather the way I wanted it.

Then he said, "You have to file a flight plan."

I said, "I already did."

He said, "No, you can't file a flight plan. The civilians over here have to file your flight plan."

So I went over and cancelled my flight plan. They gave me a form, I filled it out, and the civilians filed my flight plan.

It was amazing to learn how the military operates. My first impression was that I didn't know how we ever won a war. It was interesting flying, because each AFB had different rules and the controllers were not always standard. For example, each air force base had different definitions as to what constitutes hot cargo – stuff that might explode. At some air force bases, shotgun shells were hot cargo. In other places, rockets were not hot cargo. If hot cargo was aboard you must taxi to a remote area. In the event of an explosion, there would be no damage to airport facilities or other aircraft. Usually when we arrived at Pease AFB, we would go to base operations, get the weather and pick up a box lunch for $1.75. It was a good lunch, had half a chicken in it, more than enough to eat. At Pease AFB, they had C-5s and F-111s, a swing-wing airplane.

When we got up to Loring AFB, it was a Strategic Air Command (SAC) base with B-52s. Loring was different. The plane was refueled while cargo was unloaded from the aircraft. At Pease AFB, the airplane was shut down, the electrical power turned off, and ground wires connected. No one could be around the airplane except the fueling crew. When fueling was complete and the crew returned, we had to touch the ground wire before they would allow us to get on the airplane.

At Loring AFB, all operations could be going on at the same time – fueling, unloading, and loading cargo.

Next stop was Griffiss Air Force Base in New York where they had fighter jets. I think they had F-15s when they were new. We dropped our cargo and returned to Wright Patterson AFB.

One week we flew cargo; the next week we flew the mail. The mail was tricky. If an airplane had a mechanical, operations would have to re-route flights. Instead of going back to Wright Patterson AFB, it would be necessary to go to Cincinnati and drop off the mail, then back to Wright Patterson.

On one trip into Pease AFB, it was pretty windy. We landed and taxied to the hot cargo area. We went to base ops, got the weather and our box lunch, and got on the bus to go back out to the airplane. In came an F-111 and it ran off the runway and one of the swingwings folded up. The airplane caught fire and the grass caught on fire. We had a three-hour delay until they got the fire out so we could continue our trip.

One time when we landed at Griffiss AFB, it was snowing hard. When we were ready to de-ice for departure, we couldn't get it de-iced enough from one truck. We went out to the edge of the runway, and they brought out two trucks to de-ice the airplane, and we took off immediately.

When Allen and I were flying out of Wright Patterson AFB, the air force base was really nice to us. We would go to the Bachelor Officer's Quarters (BOQ), they would let us stay in wonderful rooms, and the cost was just $5 or $7 per night. Evergreen had one aggressive co-pilot who spoiled this great accommodation. He came in one night and the BOQ did not have rooms available; they were occupied by officers. The co-pilot raised hell with the OD (officer on duty). As a result all Evergreen pilots were kicked out of the BOQ. We had to go to Fairborn, Ohio, to find a hotel. Allen and I found a hotel and were sitting there one night. Allen looked at me and said, "Jim, we've hit the bottom of the barrel. It can't get any worse than this." It was a terrible hotel. We all resented the co-pilot for getting us kicked out of the BOQ. Allen often referred to Fairborn as Stillborn.

When Allen and I started our training, we had a check airman who was a stickler for maneuvering speeds. We had flip charts listing what the speed should be when flaps were at 15, flaps 5, flaps retracted, slats only, and clean maneuvering speed. After determining the weight of the aircraft, the crew would refer to the speed charts, and then flip to the appropriate aircraft weight and configuration to determine the maneuvering speed. The check airman we had – Captain Jerry McCall – wanted the precise, exact maneuvering speed. He was really over the limit on his tolerances.

After we had been there for two months, Allen and I became check airmen. That was a good experience. I did a lot of work on simulators at TI on projects like let downs, optimum over speed takeoffs, training first officers to speak up when they had a question or concern, and first officer performance when the Captain was incapacitated. Evergreen rented simulators in Tampa. Sometimes we used U.S. Air simulators and various other locations all over the country. One thing I liked was, when we picked up a student, we would take him from Day 1 right out of the classroom and have the student until we released him to fly. We got to know the students, their abilities and weaknesses. We got to work with the new pilots until we were ready to sign them off to fly the line. These guys were usually sharp. They had been flying commuters, doing a lot of hand flying, so they could fly the airplane pretty well.

We commuted to work on the jump seat. We would go out to Evergreen, get on the jump seat, and go to work. When Allen and I became check airmen, Evergreen would buy our ticket on the airline to fly from our homes in Houston to Wright Patterson AFB. Most of the time rather than waste the money, Allen and I would ride the jump seat on Evergreen whenever there was a flight in Houston. None of the guys wanted to see Captain McCall get on the airplane because he would always give them a check ride.

If there were two people standing by to get on the jump seat, Captain McCall would say, "Well, I'm a check airman so I have to go before you because I have to give these guys a line check."

They didn't necessarily need one, but this was just a way he could get the jump seat ahead of anyone else. Jerry was really into the numbers and not thinking beyond what was in the book.

Crash at Evergreen: Captain Jerry McCall's co-pilot was going to go to work for United. On his last day at Evergreen, Jerry and his co-pilot were departing Carswell AFB. The freighters had a door that opened up one-third of the fuselage. When the cargo door was closed, it was the Captain's responsibility to be sure the cargo door was secure. It was night; it was dark. Jerry sent his co-pilot out to make sure the cargo door was secure. It appeared the door was closed. Right after takeoff, the cargo door popped open. Normally, the No. 1 radio was used. It was the top antenna so you could talk to the tower and ground control. The antenna on the bottom was used for radio No. 2. Once you were air borne, No. 2 radio was used for communication and No. 1 radio was put on the company standby frequency. As they were coming downwind, the cargo door broke the top antenna off and they couldn't talk to the tower. Jerry was so busy he didn't think about switching to the No. 2 radio that used the antenna on the bottom. I am not even sure he was aware of that. Downwind as Jerry was slowing to maneuvering speed, the aircraft stalled prior to reaching maneuvering speed, rolled upside down, went straight in and killed Jerry and his co-pilot.

Depressurized Cabin: The DC-9s, as I mentioned earlier, had a tail cone that would drop off for emergency evacuation. Prior to the tail cone, there was a hatch back there for emergency evacuation. The older DC-9s had a plug hatch that you take out – like an over window hatch – for emergency evacuation. When removed, one can crawl out or step over it. The crew walked around the airplane to check it out and everything seemed okay. They took off and the airplane was not pressurized. The Captain said, "Oh, I remember, that pressurization plug was not in." He told the co-pilot to keep climbing the airplane and he would go back and put the plug back in. He had to climb over the freight that was stacked to the ceiling. He took an oxygen bottle with him and he climbed over the freight to get to the back of the airplane to put the plug back in. The co-pilot continued to climb, leveled off but the Captain did not return. The co-pilot yelled at the Captain then rocked the wings back and forth in an attempt to get the Captain to respond.

The co-pilot finally declared an emergency and landed at Amarillo. They checked and found the Captain – dead. The Sheriff in Amarillo wanted to lock up the co-pilot for murder, thinking that he had done something to the Captain. The investigation revealed that the Captain had recently been scuba diving in the Caribbean. When the Captain was in the fuselage, he got the bends and died.

Delta Force: In Terre Haute where the mail was sorted, the military paid for an airplane to be crewed, fueled and ready to go for flight 24 hours a day for the Delta Force. We had a 727 that was sitting there, full of fuel, with 60 seats and the rest empty so the Delta Force could put all their gear with them in the cabin. Evergreen had authorization to fly anywhere in the world. If the Delta Force went anywhere, it would look like a civilian flight. I had a friend who was assigned to this operation, and he actually flew a couple of flights with the Delta Force on board.

Landing at White Sands: One time at Holloman AFB in White Sands, New Mexico, we landed and got to the freight ramp. A three-star general came into the cockpit and said, "Captain, how did you get in?" I thought, God, what did I do? I said I just shot the approach. He said, "Well, you're the first airplane we've been able to get in here in three days." That somewhat surprised me. Later I learned that a lot of the military aircraft, like the B-1 bomber, had neither anti-icing nor de-icing capability. One of the bases in our route, Malmstrom AFB in Great Falls, Montana, had B-1s stationed there. Once when going in there, we were told to over fly due to an accident. The next day when we went in there, we found that a B-1 had crashed about 100 yards south of the runway. The Air Force people told us it was due to air frame icing.

Approach into Minot ND: The weather was really bad as we approached Minot AFB. We worked hard and got in there, about 100 foot overcast and that was our minimums with ILS (Instrument Landing System) and GCA (Ground Control Approach). We got in with the wind blowing; I think the wind chill factor was 50 degrees below zero.

We taxied up and the unloading crew came up and said, "My God, why did you come in here? You're the only plane that has been in here in several days. We don't like to work in these conditions."

I said, "Well, I thought that's why log air operations were here, so we could get the supplies you guys needed."

They were upset that we had come in and they had to unload the airplane and load it back up.

Training First Officer: I was training a First Officer. He had been a flight engineer on a DC-8. There was some sort of union activity and they were going to make pilots out of the flight engineers so the flight engineers would not start their own union. Carlos was a really nice guy who looked to be about 18 or 19. When I started talking to him I found out he was 42 years old. Carlos said the human body is designed to live to 160 years and he said he intended to make it. He wouldn't drink cold water and took cod liver oil every morning. I thought he would do great in the airplane except he was not used to flying at all. Carlos had received a multi-engine rating about seven or eight years ago and had not flown since then. I cut him a lot of slack but after several hours training, he still could not plan his descent. He was not consistent in his landing approach – sometimes he would be at 10,000 feet and 30 miles from the airport or he would be at 3,000 feet 30 miles from the airport. He struggled with it. On the first landing I had with him, Carlos touched down, pulled the throttles all the way back; then he reached forward for another set of throttles to lift up and pull back to put the thrust reverses behind the engines. As the power is pulled, thrust reverses and slows the aircraft. It was a good thing we were on a SAC base and the runway was 10,000 feet.

I said, "Okay, Carlos, put it in reverse, put it in reverse!"

Carlos said, "They're broken, they won't come."

I said, "Let me have it." I put them in reverse.

I guess he was not used to doing it. I went through two weeks with him and wouldn't recommend turning him loose on the line. Allen Kelley rode with him and he wouldn't turn him loose, either. I don't know if he ever got signed off to fly the line or not. He was a nice guy, but should stay as a flight engineer; he was not a pilot.

Initial Operating Experience: Evergreen Management had promised one of their dispatchers that at some time they would make him a pilot, because he had flown in the Navy. After three years as a dispatcher, it was time for the dispatcher to move up to a pilot position. He was assigned to me after completion of his simulator training. We departed from Wright Patterson and I told him he could fly the first leg. He took off and everything seemed fine.

As we leveled off at our cruising altitude, he said, "I should be Captain on this airplane. I've got 1,600 hours, I'm nuclear qualified, and I should be the Captain."

I said, "Well, I can promise you we are not going to drop any nuclear bombs today."

As we approached Pease AFB, the weather had deteriorated, down to about 300 to 400 feet overcast with about two miles visibility. Air Traffic Control cleared us for ILS/GPS approach.

The co-pilot said, "I'll use the GPS approach. I've done it many, many times."

I said, "Well, let's tune the ILS up, too, just in case we lose the GPS."

Initially, he had problems getting the airplane configured for the landing. I told him he was high on the glide slope, and to increase the rate of descent. He worked on it but did not reach the glide slope. I finally told him I had to take the airplane. I put the airplane on the ILS glide slope and made the landing.

I thought it was amusing that he thought being "nuclear qualified" made him Captain material right off the bat. He was one of the more memorable guys I had on an Initial Operating Experience flight.

Loss of Mail Contract: Evergreen lost the mail contract that was a big portion of the DC-9 operation. It appeared we would have to check out on a different airplane or just not have a job. Or we would have to bump someone out of his seat. I was tired of freighting for the military and the hassles with the military.

CHAPTER 31

America West Airlines

When Evergreen lost the mail contract, Allen and I decided since we had some buddies (some Continental and TI guys) at America West Airlines, to see if we could find a job there. We were hired. We were in Houston and had a class date. J.V. Sclifo was in Phoenix as a SIM instructor for America West and he had an apartment. We told J.V. we had a class and he said to come on out and share his apartment. We split the costs because none of us would be there all the time. We looked forward to that and took off for Phoenix.

I bought a used car, a Chevrolet Impala, to drive to Phoenix. We got into the dessert and had a flat on the left rear tire. It was baking hot; the back seat and trunk were full of clothes. We had to unload the trunk to get the spare tire out. As I started changing the tire, flies came out looking for the moisture on our bodies. Allen was fanning as hard as he could to keep the flies off us while I was changing the tire. After the tire was changed, we went on down the road, stopped and bought a new tire.

While we were getting the new tire put on the car, there was a big sign that said, "No person beyond this point unless you are a mechanic!" I told the mechanic that I wanted the tire balanced within a quarter of an ounce. He told me, "Our balance machine will not do it within a quarter of an ounce." I said, "Oh, yes. I'm an engineer and I designed that machine. I'll show you how to do it."

He let me come back into the shop with him and I showed him how to manipulate the switch so that he could balance the tire down to a quarter of an ounce within balance. He was very happy to have learned that technique and I was very happy to have it done. But I was a bit sorry that I had to fib so I could go into the shop to show him how it was done. We got our tire balanced and away we went!

We arrived in Phoenix, drove to J.V.'s apartment and he welcomed us. We really felt good and had a good camaraderie there with J.V. On Sunday, we settled in and rested.

Allen Kelley and Jim McCartney, first day at America West Airlines

On Monday morning we put on our suits and ties and went to the classroom. The first thing on the agenda was a talk by Ed Beauvais, CEO and founder of America West, and Mike Conway, who had been with America West from the start. America West required that each employee purchase stock in America West. I bought about $3,000 worth of stock and paid for it up front. Allen took his stock on a payout with deductions from his paycheck. We lost this money when America West filed for bankruptcy protection.

Ground School and the Captain Did Me In: We were going through ground school with some guys who were upgrading to Captain and we were training as First Officers. One of the guys was pretty sharp in the ground school. Unfortunately, after ground school, I got paired up with him. He had been a Navy pilot. When we got in the simulator, it became obvious to me that he couldn't fly the 757. He had been flying the 737 and was pretty good with the flight management system that I struggled with. They had a training course and ground school on the flight management system but it was based on a little P.C. computer that didn't have anything in the world that looked like what was in the airplane. It did not function at all like it functioned in the airplane. I did not put a lot of effort in it because I thought I would get the training on the airplane. When we were in the airplane, the Captain was having all kinds of problems. As long as he was on autopilot, he was okay. If the autopilot came off, then it was "Look out, here we come!"

I took my check ride and passed. The Captain took his check ride. I had been an instructor and check airman for quite some time and knew he wasn't ready. The check airman said, "Yeah, he would have no problem." When he got in the simulator, it was terrible. Every time the autopilot was cut off, he would be in trouble. The check airman from the FAA wanted him to hand fly the approach. One time he was shooting an approach into Los Angeles on the simulator and he missed the visual descent point. The point at which you are supposed to start down is when you can see the runway. He started down early and landed on the runway with one main gear on the runway and the other in the grass. When the check ride was over, the check airman and the FAA check airman left immediately. We were still in the simulator shutting it down.

The Captain said, "Well, it was a little rough, but I think I got past the check ride." I said, "You're going to be lucky if they don't take your license away from you."

He failed. Not only did he fail, but I failed because of his performance. We went back to the simulator and I passed my check ride. The Captain stayed there for a while until he finally got his type rating.

Down the road about the time of the 1991 bankruptcy filing of America West, the Captain left America West and started flying for an Asian airline. The Captain landed a 767 so hard that the fuselage broke in half just aft of the wings. That incident probably ended his career. I lost track of him after that.

We got out of ground school and on the line. We had nice long legs flying Phoenix to New York, New York to Phoenix, and it was a great airplane.

First Officer Tambra McCartney: On November 5, 1990, my daughter, Tambra, was hired by America West. I had flown with her only one time before she came to work at America West. Just before she got her private pilot's license, I went out with her and right away I saw that she was going be a strong Captain. As we were flying along, I reached up to tune the radios for the next station. She said, "Don't touch those radios! I'm flying this airplane!" On May 2, 1991, Tambra and I flew together for the first time at America West. She flew as co-pilot on that trip. I know we were the first Father and Daughter in the cockpit at America West, but I think we may have been the first Father and Daughter team to fly in the cockpit in the industry. There have been a lot of Father and Son teams, and Father and Daughter, with Daughter flying as a flight attendant.

It was a real thrill to fly together – and great fun for both of us – the several times when Tambra and I flew together. We were competitive and always had a challenge as to which one of us could make the best landing, accurately guess the length of our flight, etc. On one flight out of California, I predicted the length of our flight to be 59 minutes and 52 seconds. The airplane captured the exact length of the flight from takeoff to touch down. When we landed, the length of the flight was exactly 59 minutes and 52 seconds! That really impressed Tammy – and me, too.

Besides being a great experience, our flight was written up in the company newspaper and also in the *Arizona Republic* in Phoenix. Tambra flew at America West until the bankruptcy was filed. She was furloughed from October 1992 until June 1994. During that time she flew for Piedmont Airlines. She was recalled in June 1994 and is still there. She is now Captain on the A-320 airbus. America West bought US Airways and the company is now known as US Airways.

Union Activity: When I arrived at America West, pilots were trying to get ALPA on the property. There had already been one vote for the union and it had failed. Later, they tried to get an independent union on the property. Eventually there was another vote and we got ALPA on the property. Captain Mike Martin, who spearheaded the effort to get the union on the property, was a great pilot and the MEC Chairman. He was pretty much bullet proof if they went after him because he was a check airman on the 757. Most of the 757 guys were pro-union. When the vote came down and ALPA was certified as the representative of the pilots at America West, I called Mike and told him he would have to negotiate a contract; that I had done several contract negotiations, probably six or seven labor agreements; and I would be glad to serve on the negotiating committee. He said that would be fine, and I became Chairman of the Negotiating Committee. Mike generously gave me his full support during the contract negotiations.

First order of business was to get a negotiating team together. I had read a paper written by one of the pilots on the financial situation at America West. I thought it was a good paper and suggested we look at him as a negotiator. He became one of the negotiators. Unfortunately, when we went to ALPA headquarters in Washington, D.C., I was talking to some of my friends up there and told them I really had a lot of confidence in this guy because of the financial report he had written on America West.

One of guys said, "He didn't write it, I wrote it. He just put his name on it."

That gave me some pause. We had a Captain appointed who had been at Continental Airlines. A First Officer on the committee gave us four on the Negotiating Committee. Next, Bill McCoy was appointed to the committee. McCoy was an expert on the computer and had really good knowledge of the company and scheduling procedures. That was our negotiating team.

The first objective was to get out a questionnaire to all the pilots and see what they thought were the priorities that needed to be negotiated in this contract. We went to Washington for about a week to prepare the pilot survey. The Continental pilot was strong in his opinions; wanted everything exactly his way; was rigid and difficult; and was confrontational on many of the issues. Finally, we reached agreement on the survey and everyone signed off on it.

When we got back to Phoenix a few weeks later, I found a note in my box that said the Continental Captain on the Negotiating Committee was a convicted felon. I didn't know anything about this so I took it to the MEC and told them to handle the matter because I did not want to know about, or be involved in, whatever this Captain's past record may have been. The MEC decided that with a felony conviction for tax fraud on his record, the Continental Captain could not be a credible negotiator on the Negotiating Committee. The Continental Captain was removed from the Negotiating Committee, and that left four of us. When Washington came down they said only three could be authorized to negotiate the contract. The junior First Officer on the Committee was disappointed. The MEC said they would take it as their part of the budget so he could stay on the Negotiating Committee. He would not have a vote but could express his opinion.

When we got the survey back, we had our priorities as to what the pilots wanted. The main thing was money, but it was stressful. The pilots wanted to know what the priorities were. I told them we would relate that information after the contract. We did not want to jeopardize our negotiations with the company by informing of our priorities in advance.

Wien Air Lines, based in Alaska, had ALPA pilots originally. The ALPA pilots at Wien took the position in negotiations that they would have a three-man crew in the cockpit just like United did. They even went on strike over the issue. Wien started hiring replacement pilots and they flew at Wien until the two-man crew issue was resolved. When that happened, ALPA pilots were back on the property. When the ALPA pilots returned to work, the strike breakers lost their jobs. At that time America West was starting up its 737 operations and hired several of the Wien strike-breakers. The Alaska strike-breakers were now senior Captains at America West. They had it set up so they would get credit for 100 plus hours per month and fly only 40 to 50. Their paychecks were $140,000 per year. That made it possible for management to brag that they paid their pilots $140,000 per year – though that was applicable to only a few pilots. The rest of the Captains were making $60,000 or $65,000 per year, and First Officers were making around $30,000 per year. The Alaska strike-breakers were anti-union and did not want the union on the property.

The Negotiating Committee started work and America West hired a professional negotiator out of Washington, DC – Jerry Glass. Jerry had negotiated a lot of contracts with ALPA for some of the smaller airlines and he came down for a meeting with the Negotiating Committee. I told Jerry that the first thing we wanted to do was to get some agreements up front before we started negotiating so this would not be a confrontational negotiation. I wanted to establish rules up front. He said, "That's good, let's talk about it." I said first we want to follow the ALPA contract sections – they are all laid out and we can go through it just as it is. Jerry said that's fine. Next, I wanted to eliminate dueling tapes at night where the company is saying one thing and we are saying another. I suggested that ALPA prepare a tape and submit it to Jerry. If Jerry found anything objectionable in it, then we would take it out or work it out. Jerry agreed.

I made another agreement with Jerry Glass prior to the start of negotiations. Many pilots felt that the airline had two sets of books – one for union negotiations and one for stockholders. I told Jerry I wanted the books opened up for us. Jerry said he thought he could arrange that and he did. We had investment bankers from New York go through the books to confirm the financial status of America West. I wanted this for the edification of our committee, and so our pilots could be confident that we were negotiating with a company that was really in bankruptcy. America West had been operating in bankruptcy since filing for bankruptcy protection on June 28, 1991.

One factor in the America West bankruptcy filing was the fact that America West bought two 747s to run a new route from Phoenix to Hawaii to Nagoya, Japan. The purchase of these aircraft occurred in the same time frame as the Gulf War, also known as Desert Storm, which lasted from August 2, 1990, to February 28, 1991. During that time people were afraid to fly, so many of the flights to Japan flew with only twelve passengers. Yet it was hard for management to shut down this route.

Contract Negotiations: We started negotiations in May 1994. The meetings were difficult at the start because management changed at America West. Beauvais and Conway, who had been with America West from the beginning, were no longer in charge. Before we started negotiations, Conway had not been relieved. Conway was deadheading on one of my flights and came up to the cockpit and said he understood I would be Chairman of the Negotiating Committee. I said yes, that's what I've been elected to do. He said he hoped we could get this put together, and he was going to work as hard as he could to get a good agreement for both the pilots and the company. A few days later, he was terminated.

Franke came in as the new CEO and he hired a law firm out of California that had a reputation as a union-busting firm. They sent a lawyer in with Jerry Glass and a couple of company people. The lawyer objected to everything we tried to get across the table. It didn't matter if it was a no-cost item. I finally got Jerry off to the side and told him we can't make any progress, yet the company wants an agreement, we want an agreement, and the company wants to get out of bankruptcy. Jerry said, "Just let me work on this. It may take a few weeks but I will get rid of this guy." Eventually he did get rid of the lawyer and negotiations started progressing.

On our side of the table, I was fortunate in that I called ALPA and asked the name of the best lawyer we could get to negotiate with us on the committee. They gave me Richard Domholt out of Seattle. Also, I wanted a specialist to look at the whole thing to see if we could put it together. ALPA sent Bob Christy, who had been an Eastern Captain and was then on the staff at ALPA National. When Frank Lorenzo put Eastern into bankruptcy and shut down the airline, Christy went to work for ALPA National. He was a most amazing guy – he could beat the computers. He had a Master's Degree in statistics. When the company came in with a proposal that required financial analysis, Christy would be within one or two percent right off the bat before the numbers could be run through the computers. Domholt and Christy helped structure an agreement that was probably the best agreement in the industry for our size airline at that point in time.

Long Term Disability: One thing we got in the America West contract was a long-term disability benefit. If you have any type of heart condition, you are grounded; you could be grounded because of any other disability produced by illness or injury. We proposed that the company purchase an insurance policy that would provide a pilot grounded for medical reasons with two-thirds of his pay from the beginning of his long-term disability until such time the pilot reaches normal social security retirement. Alternatively, the company could provide employment to offset the insurance payout, but the pilot could not be forced to move to Phoenix to accept such employment. I was proud that we got that in because it was such a good benefit for pilots.

Stabilized Paycheck: I wanted a stabilized paycheck in the contract. We had pilots flying 20 to 40 hours per months and getting paid $140,000 per year as described above. There was a second group of pilots we called "life style pilots," who flew only 20 to 40 hours per month and were paid for that amount of flight time – that's all the time they wanted to fly because any more would interfere with their life style. That meant the company paid insurance and other benefits for part-time pilots. So we proposed a "cap and bank system" based on a 28-day month. Pilots would be required to fly 16 days in a 28-day period and would be off 12 days in the same 28-day period. If you flew a 28-day period and got only 77 hours, the company would pay you the "cap" for 85 hours of flight. That meant you had a negative balance of 8 hours in your "bank." If you flew 88 hours the next month, again, you would be paid the "cap" of 85 hours and 3 hours would go into your "bank" and reduce your negative balance to 5 hours. If you flew 90 hours for a 28-day period, you were paid the "cap" of 85 hours and 5 hours credit would go into your "bank." The 85 hours "cap" worked out to be 5 hours and 15 minutes of flight time per duty. This also guaranteed the company that it would get 85 hours of pilot utilization out of each pilot over a period of time saving the company money. To stabilize the number of pilots on the property, we gave them two to three months per year in which they could fly three additional hours above the 85 hour cap if certain conditions were met. The provision also included a trip guarantee. If a three-day trip was cancelled for any reason, then the company paid the pilot for the hours not flown and the pilot was on standby during that time. If the pilot was called out on standby, then the hours flown offset the hours not flown. If the pilot flew more hours than the cancelled hours, then the pilot was paid for the extra hours.

A pilot's pay is based on flying. Per FAA regulations, pilots can fly only 1,000 per year, which works out to about 85 hours per month. Pilots are paid only when the aircraft moves; the pilot's pay starts when the engines start and stops when the engines stop. A pilot may fly a trip that keeps him away from home for 14 or 15 hours, yet may be paid only for six hours because he/she may be sitting in a crew room waiting for the next trip. The airline likes to mention that pilots fly only about 85 hours per month, but they leave out that it may take 180 to 240 hours per month away from home to get 85 hours of flying time per month.

The cost of the plan to the company proved to be minor. We got the 5 hour and 15 minute per day schedule. If a pilot went to work one day and flew only 4 hours, he/she still got credit for 5 hours and 15 minutes. In the old days, a pilot could go out one day and fly only one hour. In the DC-3 days, the FAA required one 24-hour break every seven days. Often, a pilot would fly all over the country and the 7th day off may be in El Paso. The pilot may fly another six-day cycle and not be home for two weeks. That is why "duty rigs" came about. The 5 hour and 15 minute "duty rig" would keep pilots from flying every day for only two hours per day. This contract also included a provision that if a pilot called in sick on a holiday, he must provide a note from his doctor. Some pilots bid lines that had a trip on Thanksgiving, Christmas, or New Years, then call in sick so a reserve pilot would have to fly his trip.

Cockpit of Boeing 757 at America West Airlines

The company flew three airplanes: the Boeing 737 (737), the Airbus 320 (A-320) and the Boeing 757 (757). If a Captain wanted to move up to a larger aircraft for a salary increase, that caused six training events to occur. This contract made the salary on each type of aircraft the same. There was no need to move to a different aircraft for an increase in salary. This was another area in which the company received the benefit of substantial savings under the terms of this contract.

The training events that – prior to the contract – were required in training a 757 Captain, (1) the company would bring up a Captain from the Airbus, and train him/her to fly the 757, leaving a vacant seat in the A-320. (2) A 737 Captain must be trained to be an A-320 Captain. (3) A 757 First Officer must be trained as Captain on the 737. (4) An A-320 First Officer must be trained as 757 First Officer. (5) A 737 First Officer must be trained as First Officer on the A-320. (6) A new hire must train as First Officer on the 737. It was an expensive undertaking. just to put a 757 Captain in place. I don't know the cost of each training event, but several years ago, the cost of training an Airbus Captain was $70,000. It was fair to use $70,000 as the training cost, realizing it would be more on the 757, less on the 737. Assuming $35,000 for training each First Officer, the total cost for training three First Officers would be $105,000. Assuming $70,000 for training each Captain, the total for training three Captains would be $210,000. The total for all six training events would be $315,000, to get one Captain on the 757. Making the salary the same on the three types of aircraft resulted in substantial savings to the company in training costs alone.

I believe the sale of Boeing aircraft was hurt when Airbus came out with the A320. A pilot trained on the A-320 is equipped to fly any Airbus. It is all "fly by wire" and everything can be made the same in each aircraft from the giant four-engine Airbus, all the way down to the A-320. The training cost obviously is much less if the entire fleet is made up of Airbus aircraft versus a fleet of Boeing aircraft, because each Boeing airplane has a different type rating. One reason why Southwest Airlines is a unique and profitable airline it has only one piece of equipment – the 737 – so its training costs are considerably less than the rest of the industry.

The cost of the contract to America West was $500 million for a term of five years. This cost was offset by the increase in productivity built into the terms of the contract. The cost to America West proved to be negligible – the per seat mile cost to the airline increased by $.002, less than a penny per seat.

Some pilots do not understand that the financial status of the airline has an impact on their paychecks. When I presented the terms of the contract to the pilots at America West, I said we had negotiated the contract without significantly increasing the seat per mile cost. One pilot got up and stated we should have negotiated more money and raised the seat per mile cost. Another pilot said he could not vote for the contract because of the provision that said any vacation time had to start on a Wednesday. This is an example of how some pilots are completely disconnected from the financial status of the airline. America West was in bankruptcy while this contract was being negotiated.

Captains averaged an increase of $40,000 per year and First Officers averaged an increase of $30,000 per year. Prior to this contract, Captains were making an average salary of $60,000 per year and First Officers were making an average salary of $30,000 per year. The contract provided salary increases for the pilots over a five-year period. Following are the average salaries for captains and first officers in May 1995 and April 2000 during the term of the contract:

	May 1995	Apr 2000
	First Year	Last Year
15 year Captain	$120,876	$137,086
10 year Captain	$114,787	$130,191
5 year First Officer	$ 70,444	$ 79,892
3 year First Officer	$ 58,225	$ 66,068

The salaries show this was a good contract for both the pilots and the airline. The contract negotiated in 1995 continued until the year 2000. When the year 2000 arrived, ALPA entered into negotiations that lasted for four years until a new contract was signed. America West was in bankruptcy while this contract was being negotiated. The purchase of U.S. Airways validated that the 1995 contract was good for both parties.

Two groups of pilots were not happy with the contract: the Alaska strike-breaker pilots who were paid $140,000 per year for flying 20 to 40 hours per month; and the "life style" pilots that flew 20 to 40 hours per month and didn't want to fly any more hours.

When I was getting close to the mandatory Age 60 retirement, the Manager and Instructor for the A-320 Simulator asked me if I would be interested in becoming a SIM (Simulator) instructor when I retired. I said yes. Those two groups of pilots, who were not happy with the contract, went to the SIM Manager and told him they would not take a check ride with me if I were a SIM instructor. My offer was withdrawn. The two groups got even with me.

Under Federal Air Regulation (FAR) Part 121, Captains require a physical every six months; after age 40 Captains must have an EKG every six months, and the results go directly to the FAA in Oklahoma City. First Officers had to have a physical once a year. Every six months, Captains had to go in for a check ride; every year First Officers had to go in for one. This put a lot of tension on pilots, with the possibility of failing a physical or failing a check ride. There was a lot of pressure any time a pilot went for a check ride. Many pilots would get nervous before the check ride, but most became used to it eventually and just settled into the routine of the recurring check rides. Pressure to perform really wasn't new. Pilots are scrutinized in everything they do. With the cockpit voice recorder, when we make a mistake or crash, everyone can see what happened, which is good for safety issues.

Continental Pilot Asks "Functional Illiterate" for Information: DeWayne Barton was a Continental pilot who went to Alaska Airlines. He was part of the group that called us TI pilots "functional illiterates." After the contract negotiations at America West were completed, Barton called me to find out how we did it. I was tempted to tell him that this functional illiterate couldn't possibly tell him how it was done. I suppressed the urge and told him what I could.

Virginia Flying: When Virginia and I first got married, she was a reluctant flyer. She had to wear pressure bands around her wrist to suppress nausea. It was really an ordeal. As time passed, she would fly with me during the summer when she was away from her job as school counselor. She would fly to Phoenix and go on trips with me. Once we spent the night in Ontario. The next morning we went to the airport and my flight was full. It looked like I would have to leave her in Canada, which put a strain on both of us because we weren't sure about clearing customs. The Flight Attendants said they would put Virginia on one of their jump seats, so she came with us. But I did have to leave her in one place in the states. She got bumped off because she was flying "non-rev," (free). I told her where I would be that evening. When I got there, she had already arrived. She figured out how to work the system and flew "non-rev" to my destination. I was proud of her ingenuity and glad to see her.

Once I took her to Searcy, Arkansas, rented a little Cessna 150, and we flew around a while. Several months later, my cousin, Dub Hall, who had been a flight engineer for years and lived in Phoenix, died. His wife, Bonnie, called and asked if I would bring his ashes back to Arkansas, take them up in an airplane, and drop them over the old McCartney farm place. Virginia and I rented another airplane in Searcy. We found the location of the McCartney farm and Virginia reached out the side window of the airplane and dumped the ashes into the slip stream. We returned to Searcy and paid for the airplane rental. As we were leaving, the ramp agent ran in and asked, "Man, what's all that gray stuff on the side of the airplane?" I never told him what it really was, but parts of Dub's ashes were washed off the Cessna 150 on the ramp at the airport in Searcy, Arkansas!

Rat on a Plane: Once a flight attendant spotted a rat on a 757. America West, which utilized its aircraft 12 hours daily, grounded the plane and called Terminex to exterminate the rat. Three days later the rat was once again spotted on the plane. Another attempt to exterminate the rat on the plane failed. Enough with Terminex. Two pilots took the plane up to 30,000 feet, put on oxygen masks and depressurized the cabin. That killed the rat. It was an expensive extermination but the alternative might have been more expensive: a passenger spotting the rat in-flight, screaming on board, guaranteed a public relations nightmare!

Bus Accident: We arrived in Flagstaff one night before our flight was to leave early the next morning. Our aircraft was supposed to come in around midnight. We woke to find everything snowed in. We got to the airport, but the airplane had not made it in the night before. We were sitting in Operations with all the passengers uncertain as they about what was going to happen. Finally, about 10 a.m. the company decided to bus everyone to Phoenix. All got on a Greyhound bus, the co-pilot, flight attendants and I in the back of the bus, and I was dozing. I heard yelling, "GD, god damn, god damn." We had come off the hills down into the valley into a nightmare scene: a creek down there had radiated fog all over the road and the highway was full of cars piled up. To avoid plowing into the cars ahead, the bus driver swerved off the Interstate and we were barreling through pine trees until the driver finally got the bus stopped. It was a miracle that we didn't hit any trees. We sat there about four hours before they got another bus to the scene. We still weren't rescued. The incline was too steep for anyone to walk up. They had to throw ropes down to pull us up, one by one. Finally, we got everything squared away and on the new bus. Company agents came down with the bus from Flagstaff, so I told one agent, "Now, look, when you get back to Flagstaff, call Phoenix and have someone meet this bus so they can accommodate these people." It didn't happen. When we got to Phoenix, no one was there to meet us. The bus driver just opened the door and dumped everyone out. I told the passengers to wait there. I went inside and got an agent to come out and accommodate the passengers, who – no fault of anybody involved in the flying – must have considered that whole experience their "flight" from hell.

Age 60 Rule: The mandatory Age 60 retirement rule was first raised in an American Airlines contract negotiation. C.R. Smith, President of American from 1934 to 1968 (except for time out during World War II), was trying to get rid of pilots by age 60 so American would not have to pay so much in retirement benefits. He couldn't get it done, but one of his buddies, former Army Air Corps Lt. Gen. Elwood "Pete" Quesada, was named the first administrator of the newly created FAA by his former military commander, President Dwight D. Eisenhower. Under Quesada, the FAA issued a mandate that all pilots had to retire at age 60. The Age 60 Rule, in Air Carrier Part 121, stayed in place until just recently when it was extended to Age 65. I served on a National ALPA Committee to see how many pilots actually reached age 60. The Committee found that only 40 percent of pilots reached age 60. Pilots usually died earlier from heart attacks or were grounded by heart conditions such as murmurs, arrhythmias, etc. – or by getting killed or hurt by their "toys," such as motorcycles, boats, airplanes, etc.

Pilot and His Airline: Any pilot is married to his airline. It is as much in the pilot's best interest for the airline to make money as it is in the best interest of the company and its stockholders. At 40 or 50, a pilot can't quit and go fly co-pilot for some other airline, so he's probably in the only place he will be during his flying career. Probably, but that didn't work out for me. Three airlines I worked for went bankrupt, I got tired of the military, and I retired from America West under the Age 60 Rule.

Final Flight: On my last flight before retirement, I took my wife, Virginia, and my daughter, Tambra. When we landed at Phoenix on the last leg of the last flight of my airline career, a fire truck met our flight and sprayed water over the aircraft as we entered the gate area. Then there was a little party for me. Without my knowledge or consent, the flight attendant had a copy of a poem I wrote to commemorate my retirement. She told us in the cockpit to stay off the PA for a few minutes. She read the poem I wrote and announced my retirement to the passengers on the flight.

Continental had a different program: on your last flight, you got to pick your crew. The company called ATC and got permission to get the 250-knot speed restriction lifted for that flight and got priority handling for the trip. One thing on their last flight that was really nice: the retiring pilot got to do a high speed flyby down the runway; across the end of the runway at 350 knots about 20 feet off the ground! Passengers were thrilled and everyone at the airport got to watch. I'm sorry I had to miss that, but it's about the only thing I missed about Continental.

My Retirement Poem: Retirement was the last thing I wanted. I still wanted to fly. To express how much I would miss flying, I wrote this poem in 1997:

Last Fling With My Beautiful Thing

Let me tell you about this mistress of mine
She is better than fine wine

She demands my best
I have passed all her tests

When I have trouble dealing with my life
She is always there ... more forgiving than any wife

I have followed her everywhere
She must know how much I care

I just couldn't let her escape me
Even when I long to be free

Together we have traveled the world without a care
Oh, what fun we had getting there

We have known the best
Now we are here at America West

I must make her jet engines whine
We must arrive on time

Now we are at the gate
And we are not late

I have enjoyed your every flight
Even those late at night

How can the Government be so cruel
To make this arbitrary age 60 rule

Unless the Government rescinds
This is the end

How quickly 35 years go by
Only she knows how much I love to fly

Please excuse this tear in my eye
It's so hard to say good-bye.

CHAPTER 32

The Captain Speaks

Negative on the Expletive: One incident occurred while in line for takeoff at Dallas Love Field when Braniff's home base was at Love Field. Wind was blowing strong and we were down to one runway. About 14 or 15 airplanes were in line to take off on the one runway. Then out came a Braniff airplane down the taxiway.

The Tower called and said: "Braniff, you go in front of the rest."

Someone in one of the planes keyed his mike and said, "That's bullshit!"

The Tower: "Who said that?"

Every airplane in line reported to the Tower:

"Continental 22, Negative on the bullshit."

"Eastern 16, Negative on the bullshit."

All the way down the line.

I'm sure the Tower operator never again asked, "Who said that?" Or, bucked the line for one favored plane.

Memorable Sites: All airlines want to make sure their flight deck crews make in-flight announcements over the PA system. It's a good public relations tool. However, many pilots have announcement talent; some don't, and should stay off the PA. One Braniff captain realized that and would never make an announcement. Management finally told him that if he didn't make an in-flight announcement on his next flight, he would be terminated. On his next trip out of Dallas to Seattle, he didn't make just one announcement, he made several. He pointed out every air carrier crash site from Denver to Seattle. He directed passengers to look at a certain site on the ground, told them that on [date] an [airplane type] crashed, then related all the details of each crash. Management called him back in and rescinded their order.

Proud of the Co-Pilot: At America West, Captain Tony Anger was especially talented on the PA; he kept the passengers informed and made them laugh. Truth was not a requirement. My daughter, Tambra Swan, was co-pilot for Captain Anger on a Dash 8 flight at America West.

Captain Anger announced over the PA, "We are so proud to have Tambra Swan as First Officer on this flight. Tambra was in the first Gulf War and was responsible for shooting down four enemy planes." [Pause] "Oh, not enemy planes? Well, we are very proud of her anyway!"

As the passengers departed the airplane when they reached their destination, one kindly little lady stopped to thank Tambra, and Tambra replied, "No, thank you for flying with us." The lady again thanked Tambra with tears in her eyes for her service in the Gulf War. Tambra realized the lady believed the story about Tambra's service in the Gulf War!

Proud of Flight Attendant: On another flight, Tambra became an unwitting co-star of Captain Anger's PA announcement. Captain Anger announced, "We are so proud to have John as one of our flight attendants today. John and his wife, Helga, are expecting their 8th child."

Again, as passengers departed the airplane when they reached their destination, Tambra was telling the passengers thanks for flying America West. Shortly, it became clear that Flight Attendant John got his revenge on the cockpit crew of two. John, who is openly gay, told the passengers that his wife, Helga, was the co-pilot. Helga/Tambra received congratulations from several passengers on her expected 8th child.

I trained Tony Anger as a Captain when I was a check airman at America West. Tony is an excellent pilot. I learned later that he is also an accomplished artist. Tony draws cartoons for the America West Airline newspaper.

Proud of Flight Attendant's Musicality: On a trip for Henson Airlines, First Officer Tambra Swan told the passengers, "We are so fortunate today to have Mary Ann as our flight attendant. She has been a songwriter for many years and has just recorded her first song, 'I'd Step On A Nail For Your Love Tonight.'" Tambra added that the song was doing well on the charts. As she served drinks to the passengers, they asked Mary Ann the name of her song. She tried to remember what Tambra said over the PA, and told them, "For Your Love, I'd Step On A Nail." Shortly after finishing her service to the passengers, she went to the cockpit to tell Tambra that she'd be getting even with her. They are still good friends.

View of Grand Canyon: Another pilot, flying over the Grand Canyon, decided to pull a joke on the passengers.

The pilot announced to the passengers, "We have a beautiful view of the Grand Canyon on the right hand side of the plane. And all those passengers on the left hand side of the aircraft will not be able to see it. I'm sure the people on the right hand side wouldn't mind if you step over and take a look out the windows on the right hand side of the aircraft."

The pilot looked through the peephole in the cockpit door and when passengers moved to the right side of the aircraft, he rolled the airplane to the right side and announced, "Oops! Not all at once! Not all at once!"

The Non Verbal Captain: A few months after the Lockheed L188 was placed into service, they began to break up in flight. One New York-based Eastern captain went into the chief pilot's office and told him he wanted off the L188. The chief pilot told him he had not completed his 12-month training commitment and he would not release him.

The Captain said, "You don't understand, I'm afraid to fly this aircraft. I will go back and fly the DC-6 or the L1049."

On his next flight (of course, on an L188) from New York to Miami, when they leveled off at cruising altitude, the Captain advised his First Officer he was going to the restroom. The Captain got out of his seat, opened a duffel bag, took out a parachute and put it on. Then he walked to the rear of the aircraft where the restrooms were located. The sight terrified some of the passengers. When they landed in Miami, several called to complain about Eastern issuing parachutes to the pilots and not the passengers. The Captain got a month's suspension without pay, but he did not have to fly the L188 anymore.

Part Five
Retirement Years

CHAPTER 33

Flight Instructor; Buying & Selling Airplanes

By the time I approached my mandatory Age 60 retirement, I had married Virginia Balch Landrum, my childhood sweetheart. It had been many years since I had seen Virginia. I left Arkansas in 1954. I saw her again when she visited my sister in Houston in 1958. Virginia and I were both married to other people. I sought her out in 1995 when I was twice divorced. For the first time we were both single. At my sister's urging, I called Virginia and told her I would be visiting Billy Tate and would like to drop by and take her to dinner. The spark was still there. It was a whirlwind long distance courtship that ended with our marriage on February 1, 1996, almost two years before my retirement on October 31, 1997.

Virginia had a house in Newport, Arkansas, and I was flying out of Phoenix. She was still working as Counselor in the elementary school in Newport, Arkansas. I sold my home in the Phoenix area and moved to Newport when we married. I was commuting from Arkansas back to Phoenix to fly my trips. I would drive to Little Rock to catch a flight to Phoenix. I tried to bid trips that I could fly out in the evening on the days I went to Phoenix and return in time to catch my return flight to Little Rock. I could tell as I neared age 60 that I would need to own an airplane of my own when I reached age 60. I'd have to have an airplane to fly. I had always had an airplane or access to an airplane. I bought a Cessna 152. Every couple of weeks, Virginia and I would fly down to my Mother's house in Buffalo, Texas, to mow the grass at her house, on an 84-acre farm with about four acres of yard around the house.

There was no flight instructor at the Newport Airport. The airport people said I should start teaching around there. Eventually I decided that might be a good idea, giving me more opportunities to fly. I started flight lessons, and I was pretty busy. Next I started teaching instruments. I obtained Certified Flight Instructor (CFI) and Certified Flight Instructor-Instruments (CFI-I) ratings, started instrument and primary flight instruction at the Newport Airport. It kept me occupied and in the cockpit.

While flight instructing, I had several outstanding students. Dr. Istvan Molnar had a good feel for the airplane. Most doctors I trained knew the theory behind flight and they really had that down. But when a doctor gets into an airplane, it is difficult for many to put that theory into actual practice. Dr. Molnar had a fine touch for the airplane – he was a natural. He got his pilot's license without any problem at all. Dr. Molnar visited me in Bloomington during my illness. Dr. Molnar does thyroid cancer research and now lives in New Jersey.

Another outstanding student was Mike McDermott. Mike owns a small business involved in agricultural irrigation. Mike is active in his church and travels throughout the world as a part of the volunteer staff of an overseas television ministry. Through this work he met a lady who owns a major sports team; she sometimes provides transportation for Mike on her King Air Super B 200 or her Hawker 750. But Mike is humble, down-to-earth, kind, and a thoroughly good person – also, one of the most fun guys you will meet. On top of all that, he makes the best barbequed ribs I have ever tasted. He has sent ribs to us in Bloomington via Federal Express. Mike visited me in Bloomington during my illness. He has his own airplane and I taught him how to fly. He is also a natural pilot. I had several good students – talented people.

I had another student that I simply could not train – a Presbyterian minister. He was a great guy but he was afraid of the airplane. He wouldn't tell me that and I would say, "Come on, let's fly." He just couldn't get the hang of it. He wanted to quit. I told him, "Let's go up at night." We flew under the full moon and it was so beautiful. He said he really enjoyed it but when we landed, he said he didn't want to fly any more. He just couldn't put it together. He was a nice guy but did not have the inclination for flying.

I called Bill Baker, my partner in Brake Test, and said, "I think we could make a little money buying and selling airplanes."

Bill said, "Well, let's explore that."

I talked to the mechanic at the airport and told him we were thinking about buying, reconditioning, painting and selling airplanes and asked if he would be interested in working with us for a share of the profit. Bill Baker and I would front the money for the purchase of the airplane and parts, and when we sold the airplane, we would split the profit. He was interested. The first airplane I bought was a Cessna 172. We painted it, fixed it up and I sold it to one of my students, Dr. Molnar. It was a nice airplane.

The next airplane we bought was a Beech Musketeer out in Prescott, Arizona. I went to Prescott, looked at it, felt it was a good airplane with a really good price on it, but it didn't have any radios. I thought we could paint it, put some radios in it, and sell it for a good profit. After inspecting the airplane, I planned to leave early the next morning to fly it back to Arkansas.

The guy I bought the airplane from said since there was no radio, he would let me use his GPS and handheld radio and I could ship it back to him via FedEx. I took off early the next morning. I had to de-ice the airplane before I could take off. I planned to stop in Truth or Consequences, New Mexico and refuel there. Then I would make one more stop in Arkansas. I took off.

With the handheld radio, I could only communicate when I was within 25 miles of an airport. As I was flying along I started picking up some clouds and I was getting pretty good overcast underneath. Finally I saw a place where I might get down into Truth or Consequences. I started down, looking at the terrain, and I had an altitude I was going to. If I didn't break out of the clouds by then, I would climb back out.

I started picking up ice. When I reached my altitude, it was still a solid deck so I started climbing out of the ice. The antenna was howling because of the ice accumulation. I got up into the clear, the ice dissipated, and I continued and decided to go on to Amarillo.

When I got close to Amarillo, Airport information reported 200 overcast and two to three miles visibility. I called and told them I needed surveillance approach, which is what they use to take a plane in on radar. They could line your plane up with the runway and every mile they would tell what the plane's altitude should be. The ceiling had come up and I broke out about 600 feet or so. I landed, refueled and the tower wanted me to call them. I called and they said they didn't think there would be an incident out of this, but asked for my phone number at home so they could call me if something came up.

I flew on and it started to get dark. I decided to stop at Fort Smith, Arkansas to get fuel and check the weather in Newport. I stopped at Fort Smith, called and got the weather in Newport and it was fine. I flew on to Newport without further incident.

We fixed the airplane up and Bill Baker came up to look at it. He really liked it, so he took it down to Houston to use to get his private license. Eventually we sold the airplane. I enjoyed that airplane; it was nice, kind of slow, but fun to fly.

Next we bought a Cessna 340, a twin-engine airplane that had been modified. It had a pressurized cabin so you could fly at 25,000 feet. We put it through our maintenance shop and got it fixed up as we wanted it. Bill called and suggested we go elk hunting. He got some of his buddies in Houston to go with us. I went to Houston in the 340, picked them up, and we flew to Colorado to go elk hunting. Unfortunately, the only elk we saw was walking around in a pasture on our return trip to the airport.

Another trip we took in the 340 was to Gainesville, Florida. Connie and Chuck lived in Gainesville, Florida when Claire, their first child was born. They had two cats and Claire was allergic to the cats. So they asked us to come down, visit and find a home for the cats in Arkansas. We flew to Gainesville and spent a couple of days visiting. We enjoyed seeing the little one and had a good time. We took the cats back with us in kennels and put them in the back of the 340 with the luggage. We covered the cats in the kennels with a blanket. We took off and

FLIGHT INSTRUCTOR; BUYING & SELLING AIRPLANES

started climbing out. As we started climbing, the cats started squawling! You could hear them above the engine noise – WAH! AWAH! WAH! AWAH! WAH! AWAH! WAH! AWAH! They kept it up all the way from Gainesville to Arkansas. It was a relief to get on the ground and get those cats out of the airplane.

Eventually we sold that airplane and it went to Canada. That was the end of our buying and selling airplanes. There was not enough profit in that venture to keep on doing it, but it was fun while it lasted!

CHAPTER 34

Aviation Program at Arkansas State College, Newport, Arkansas

By this time I was on the board of the Newport Airport Commission. There was a community college next to the airport, and I was trying to get an aviation program started there. I talked to the head of the school several times and he was agreeable, and said he was "really going to look into it." A year later he was still "really going to look into it." I contacted Kaneaster Hodges, a lawyer in Newport and ex U.S. Senator from Arkansas. His brother, Morrison, a heart surgeon, had been a classmate of mine when I went to high school in Newport.

I told Kaneaster of my frustration but still wanted to get an aviation program started at the college, as an opportunity to provide an exciting career path for kids in Newport and the surrounding farming area.

Kaneaster said, "Well, I guess we will just have to force it down their throats."

Kaneaster, well-connected with Wal-Mart, got some money funded for the school's aviation program. We bought a Cessna 172, fixed it up, and looked for someone to administer the program. We found Dr. John Kerr at a nearby community college. Dr. Kerr had his PhD and about 4,000 hours flying time. He said he would be glad to come over and run the program for us, so we hired him.

After the first semester (there were about 16 in the first class), all the students should have soloed and been well on their way to getting their private pilot's license. But that was not the case. The students were lagging behind in completing the schedule. We put together an Advisory Board to monitor and support the aviation program, and did a lot of other things to support the program. We went to Mississippi to look at their program. We got State funds to help out at the airport for the aviation program. We received a grant from the State to purchase a flight simulator, that was up and running. After the first semester, none of the students had flown nearly as much as they were supposed to have. We called Dr. Kerr in and asked him why. Dr. Kerr said, "Well, they just won't go out there and fly." We said, "You're supposed to be the guy leading this group and getting them out there to fly."

He was lackadaisical about it. The Advisory Board said we had to do something about this. Dr. Kerr was fired. The Advisory Board asked if I would take the program. I said I didn't want to go back and do this kind of everyday stuff. I said I would do it for one semester for free. The college said they would have to pay me – I don't remember how much but it was a small amount – and I took over the aviation program for one semester. We had the instrument portion of the program in place for the second year of the program. If a student completed the two-year program, he could come out with a private pilot license, an instrument rating, and 165 hours of flight time – almost enough for a commercial pilot's license.

During our investigation into Dr. Kerr's activities, we learned that he would fly the plane to Batesville and leave it there all day for an oil change or other maintenance work, so much of the time the plane was not available for use in the program. When I took over the program, I arranged for the mechanic to come to Newport and perform any maintenance work at night so the airplane was always available for the students during the day. At first we had only one airplane, but later acquired a second. The program was in full swing.

We worked out an agreement with Henderson State University, a four-year college in Arkadelphia that had a good aviation program: Henderson State would accept our students, place them in their junior year, and our students could get their commercial license during their junior year. Then our students could teach during their senior year.

Janet Huckabee, wife of Arkansas Governor Mike Huckabee, came to Newport to publicize the program. She had taken 20 hours of flight instruction in 1993. She flew the Cessna 172 from Newport to Jonesboro as an honorary student of the flight program. It was gracious for her to do this since it brought favorable publicity for our aviation program. There were stories with pictures in the Arkansas *Democrat Gazette*, the Jonesboro *Sun,* and the Newport *Independent* newspapers.

I went to various high schools in the area to recruit seniors for the aviation program. The aviation program offered a two-day event for prospective students to see the program and fly in our plane. We asked for a list of those who wanted to attend but they were screened by the high school guidance counselor to make sure only those qualified to go to college were invited. On average, only about half the interested students were deemed to be college material. One high school I visited did not have any seniors qualified to go to college.

Hijacking Discussion: When I was directing the aviation program, I realized that copilot Billy Johnson, who had been on the longest hijacking in the U.S. up to that point, lived up the road about 15 miles from Newport. I called and asked him to bring down all the memorabilia and newspaper articles he had and give a little discussion to our pilots going through training at ASU. He graciously agreed to do it.

The story he told: Captain William Haas and copilot Billy Johnson were taking off from Detroit on a Southern Airlines flight going down south. Just as they were climbing out, someone kicked in the cockpit door. There was a black guy with a hand grenade with the pin pulled in one hand and a 45 pistol in the other hand. He demanded that the government pay him $8 million and provide a letter from President Nixon that this was for retribution because he was a descendant of slaves.

The Captain told the hijacker, "My company doesn't have $8 million and you can't get money out of my company."

The hijacker said, "You get ahold of the government and tell them." The hijacker had three accomplices back in the cabin and they had the aircraft under their control with guns. The Captain called the company and the company got a wire patch to H. R. Haldeman, Nixon's Chief of Staff, who told the hijackers that he would see what he could work out and call them back.

Haldeman called back and said, "Here's the deal. You fly to Pittsburgh and we'll bring the money to Pittsburgh and when the aircraft lands in Pittsburgh, you can pick up the money."

When the Southern Airlines flight arrived in Pittsburgh, the Learjet with the money had not arrived. The hijackers told the Captain he could not land until the Learjet arrived.

The Captain replied, "We don't have any choice, we have to land and get fuel."

The hijackers said if they didn't get the money, they would take the airplane to Fort Knox and crash it into Fort Knox. The hijackers got the money. I have been told that it was not $8 million; it was $2 million. After the hijackers got the money, the airplane departed from Pittsburgh on its way to Cuba. The hijackers were ecstatic to have the money. They stuffed hundred dollar bills down the Captain's shirt and gave all the passengers hundred dollar bills, they were so elated. When the flight landed in Cuba, the Cuban government would not let them off the airplane.

The hijackers decided they wanted to go to Algiers. They left Cuba and stopped at Homestead Air Force Base in Florida to refuel. The Captain requested charts to get from Florida to Algiers figuring he could go up the East Coast and across. They had to shut down each engine and get oil put in and everything was done satisfactorily. About that time, the FBI shot out the tires on the airplane. At the same time, the hijackers shot copilot Billy Johnson; the bullet went through his arm.

The hijacker turned his gun on the Captain and told him, "If you don't take off now, I'm going to kill you."

The Captain said, "I'll try it but I don't know if we can get off on these flat tires." The Captain thought he would get up to about 100 knots and then stop the airplane on the runway, but he couldn't stop so he rotated up. They were flying – all the original passengers still on board – but had no tires left, just the rims. The only place they could reach with their fuel load was Havana. They returned to Havana and landed on the rims, which ground the wheels right down to the axles. The hijackers opened the escape hatches over the wings, jumped out with their money, and started running. Castro's government rounded them up in pretty short order. Castro put the passengers up in a hotel and had a big banquet for them and the crew. Castro was pretty good to everyone. The next day, Southern Airlines sent a DC-9 to Havana and picked up the passengers. Southern Airlines also sent a maintenance crew and parts to put new wheels on the hijacked airplane. The airplane was ferried back to the states. Castro kept the ransom money and billed Southern Airlines for the hotel accommodations, food, and other things Cuba had done toward securing the hijacked airplane. The bill was about $75,000. At that time, it was one of the longest hijackings in the United States.

And the story, from a pilot involved in the whole affair, left our class spellbound.

New Flight Director: While teaching my semester, we hired Amy Beard, another flight instructor from the college in Arkadelphia. Amy did the primary instruction and I did the instrument instruction. When my semester was over, we ran an ad for someone to come out and run the program. Several people were interested but most did not have any aviation experience. Crop dusters had no instrument time. One guy said I know how to fly under the clouds; they don't need to know how to fly instruments. I said no, these are going to be professional pilots; they are going to learn instrument flying. We couldn't find anyone, so Amy, the flight instructor, got the job by default. She was a good flight instructor but she could not stand up to the bureaucracy at the college.

When I was teaching in the aviation program, I had problems with the director of the college. First, he said you can't fly outside the state of Arkansas and you can't fly after dark. I told him we had to do cross-country and we had to do night flying. I had written a letter to all the student pilots that if they had an incident or an accident, how they were to react to it. The director of the college said I couldn't do that because that had to be handled by College Security. I said the college does not comply with the Federal Aviation Regulations (FARs). We have certain things that have to be done in case of an accident. He said they would take care of that. I said that's not what we are going to do, *this* is what we are going to do. We got into a big confrontation, got the Advisory Board involved and finally got it worked out. In aviation, you must comply with the FARs, and College Security simply did not have the background to handle that type of compliance. It was a continual fight to keep the aviation program going and it eventually died. The director of the college was replaced and the new director who came in cancelled the program.

I was disappointed because – brief as its existence was – several of those students went on to become airline pilots. One is flying a jet for Peabody Hotels, one is in the military flying Blackhawk helicopters. It was a shame to let that program go, especially in a small town like Newport where opportunities to broaden one's horizons are limited.

Mother and I were in Newport for the formal opening of the Aviation Program at the ASU facility in Newport. It was a nice program that introduced the student pilots and faculty to the community, and ended with a speech by Tammy in her America West Captain's uniform:

The first flight I remember flying with my Dad, he put me in the cabin with the flight attendant and let my brother ride in the cockpit. But today I'm a Captain for America West Airlines on the Airbus A-320 and Airbus A-319. I have been with America West Airlines for ten years, but I got my start in a college just like this one. After earning my Private Pilot License in High School, I found a college in Texas that offered degrees in Aviation. I received an Associate of Applied Science Degree and a Bachelor Of Science Degree while obtaining my Commercial & Instrument Rating along with several Flight Instructing ratings and a Multi-Engine Rating.

I began flight instructing at the college trying to build enough flight time to achieve the next rung on the Career Ladder. I bounced from Corporate flying and flight instructing for a while absorbing all the experiences that I could. Both types of flying teach valuable lessons.

Flight instructing teaches you everything that you thought you knew, but soon realize that you only truly know it when you must teach it to another pilot. You learn to communicate quickly, concisely, and correctly. If you don't your student might put you in a situation you didn't expect.

Corporate flying teaches you so much that you didn't learn in flight school. You learn the unpredictability of many situations and dealing with all of them to someone else's satisfaction – The FAA , Air Traffic Control, your Boss, the Passengers, US Customs, etc. You learn that it is all the other stuff that seems to be important. You trained to be a pilot, to safely get your plane and passengers from point A to point B, but now you learn all the other stuff that goes along with the job. You learn to clean the plane, load the bags, make sure the coffee is hot and the ice is cold. You must remember to get the doughnuts for the morning flight along with the paper on the way to the airport. During the flight you keep the passengers informed of the flight conditions, flight times, delays, the weather on arrival, and the scores of the game that they are missing. You coordinate the fuel required; make sure that the plane is fueled before the passengers arrive, order the catering for the flight no matter how short. You learn what to tell Air Traffic Control when you have to circle the airport so the passengers can finish the catered breakfast on that 30 minute flight, burning hundreds of gallons of fuel while they eat.

You realized when you first got hired where you ranked when you saw the bathroom on the plane with its gold plated sink and wall to wall mirror, it was bigger than the cockpit. You thought the cockpit was the most important spot on the plane. You do this all for the experiences and for the love of flying. You would actually pay someone to be able to fly the plane, but you don't dare tell anyone in charge of your paycheck. And you hope that no other pilot will tell them they will do your job for free!

But it's not all hard work. You enjoy the fact that the Boss has a house in Jamaica and likes to go there every month. You get to fly there, stay the week, work on your tan, and get paid the whole time. You don't even mind getting sick of eating lobster.

But you really want to be an airline pilot, so you give it all up to try your hand at flying for the commuter airlines. It is a relief to learn that you don't have to throw bags at your new job.

The coffee pot is not part of your job and you don't have to visit the doughnut shop on the way to work. You get to concentrate on your love, flying. And you get to do a lot of it. Sometimes 8 to 10 hours a day, flying into large airports, learning more than you thought you could. And you want to fly all the time so that you can build up the valuable flight time to get you closer to the major airline job you dream of.

The life of a major airline pilot is a good one. The pay and benefits are the best in the aviation industry. Airlines also have the advantage of free travel for you and your family, discounts on hotels, rent cars, cruises and Federal Express, more time off than most other jobs allow, medical and dental insurance, paid vacation time, paid sick leave, profit sharing, retirement and top of the industry salaries. You may choose the type of airplane you want to fly, where you want to live, and the schedules you want to fly.

The industry today is growing like never before. Record numbers of pilots are being hired and record numbers will be retiring in the next ten years opening up more jobs for the students of today. Flying is a job that is more fun than work. Currently the Government requires airline pilots to retire at age 60. This is not a popular choice for many pilots forced out of the cockpit. It is a job that we all love and hate to give up. I know that my Dad never wanted to leave airline flying.

Tammy then read the poem her Dad had written when he retired. The students knew that an airline captain would speak on this occasion, but they didn't know the captain on the program was Jim's daughter. When that became apparent, the filled auditorium gasped with surprise.

CHAPTER 35

Newport Airport Commission

From January 2000 through April 2007, I was on the Newport Airport Commission (the "Commission"), which included five Commission members and the Airport Manager (the "Manager"). . . The Manager had been there for years. His wife also worked there, and so did his nephew, who was a really good guy.

The Chairman of the Commission, Mr. Albright, had been there since Day 1; he was there when the gentleman who first started the airport got it up and running after the military released it. Albright had been a Navy pilot; he flew off carriers during World War II. He was also a genuinely good guy. He hired the Manager and paid him extremely well, more money than the Mayor of Newport was paid. In addition to his pay, they were paying him bonuses based on how much money he got from grants.

When I joined the Commission, Burton Ford was Chairman. A Commission meeting would start off with the Manager reporting the things he was doing. Next the Financial person reported on the expenditures of the Commission. Sometimes the meetings lasted two to three hours. It was more like a good old boy get-together rather than a business meeting.

I started noticing that some things around the airport were not getting done. After hiring his nephew, the Airport Manager and his wife would be gone on Thursday and Friday each week. The nephew ran the airport alone on those days. It continued to go on that way. I talked to the Mayor about it and he said he really couldn't get involved since it was the responsibility of the Commission.

One of the members left the Commission. I contacted Jim McLarty and told him we really needed him to come back and serve on the Commission. He returned. By then I was Chairman, replacing Burton Ford. As Chairman, I made some changes, the first of which was to alter the meeting agenda to have the Financial guy, who is paid by the hour, first on the agenda; the engineering guy was next; and last was the Manager's report. Joe Taylor, also on the Airport Commission, was supportive of the changes. With Jim McLarty and Joe Taylor, I had enough votes to fire the Manager. The Commission members agreed to fire the Manager. Before doing so, McLarty recommended that we meet with Jim Martin and offer the position to him. We did that and Martin agreed to replace the existing Manager after he was fired and no longer on the property.

The Commission fired the Manager and he and his family members left the property. The Manager was angry about losing his position and made a number of threats against members of the Commission. In his last appearance before the Commission, he demanded to know who voted to fire him – all members of the Commission raised their hands. It had been a unanimous vote.

Jim Martin came on board as the new airport manager immediately. Jim had been an Air Force pilot, and flew in Vietnam. Jim is an excellent manager of the facility. Jim was and still is a member of the school board. A new terminal building is under construction.

Before he was fired, the Commission had cut the Manager's bonus in half. What the Commission didn't know was the Manager wrote a check payable to himself for the other half of the bonus. The unauthorized check was uncovered by the State's annual audit of the Commission's expenditures. The State's auditor reported the unauthorized check to the Commission and told us the State was prepared to prosecute the Manager. McLarty intervened on behalf of the Commission, and told the Manager he must repay the unauthorized amount or face prosecution by the State. The money was repaid.

We obtained a great deal of material for the airport from government surplus. We applied for an airplane for use as a crop duster in a mosquito control program for the City of Newport. Mosquitos were terrible in the area because Newport is in the middle of rice country. About 80 percent of all the rice in the United States is grown in the area of Arkansas where we lived. The City Council raised the sales tax by one-quarter percent for mosquito control at the request of the Commission. We talked to the City of Stuttgart, the center of the rice-growing industry. Stuttgart had a really good mosquito control program, using airplanes and trucks to distribute mosquito repellent. They said we could go to the downtown square of Stuttgart at night and not get a mosquito bite. That impressed us.

We finally got our airplane – a nice twin-engine Navajo that had been confiscated in a drug raid. It was too nice for spraying mosquito repellent, so we decided to use it as a city airplane to promote business for the city. We used it for two or three trips to entice companies to move into Newport. It was an airplane with low time; we maintained the airplane and kept it in good condition. After we owned the airplane for two years, we were free to sell it. We sold the Navajo for $240,000 and put the proceeds into the Airport Commission's budget. We bought a crop duster and one of the residents of Newport offered to fly it for the mosquito control project.

The City of Newport contributes $70,000 per year for the budget to maintain airport operations. The Newport City Council, looking at ways to cut the city's budget, put an item on the agenda to cut the airport budget. When we saw that, the Commission requested permission to speak to the City Council. When we appeared, I was the spokesman for the Commission. I told them we needed the budget and they needed to consider how that cut would impact the City's ability to bring in larger industry. Interested people would not be driving in their Cadillacs and Fords. They will be coming to the airport with their jets. The airport would be their first impression of the environment they are investigating. The Council complied and did not cut the budget.

On November 1, 2010, the City of Newport issued a Proclamation that declared November 1, 2010 as JIM McCARTNEY DAY in recognition of his faithful and dedicated service to the City. The City sent a framed copy of the Proclamation signed by the Mayor of Newport, David Stewart. The Proclamation states in part: "WHEREAS, Jim McCartney served as Chairman of the Newport Airport Commission from 2003 until 2007and under his dedicated leadership long term plans were made and since implemented which formed the foundation of recently completed major runway renovations. . ." He also received a framed aerial photo of the Newport Airport.

His retirement years in Newport were good.

CHAPTER 36

Taylor Made Ambulances, Corporate Pilot

I got pretty tired of flight instructing. I met Joe Taylor while I was on the Airport Commission. His family started a company called Taylor Made Ambulances. They built ambulances from the ground up. They were the primary source of income for the airport because they bought so much fuel. When I first got to know Joe, he had a Cessna 340. When I bought the 340, Joe said to put it in his hangar so I wouldn't have to pay hangar rent. I did that and was most appreciative. Occasionally Joe's pilot would not be available, so I flew a couple of trips for Joe. We became really good friends. He was a good Airport Commissioner. I learned later that he is a great salesman.

Time passed, and I sold the 340. Getting a little antsy, I bought a Mooney. I really liked the Mooney aircraft because it was fuel-efficient and pretty fast. Virginia and I flew it around the country a lot and had a good time in it.

Again, time passed, and Taylor Made Ambulances bought an MU-2. When Joe took delivery on the MU-2, he asked if I would be interested in flying it for him. I told him I was definitely interested in flying it. The MU-2 is a twin-engine turbo prop, fuel-efficient and fast for its day and time. The ambulance company had been using the 340 and the normal operation was in the Sales Department. Joe was head of the Sales Department. He would send the airplane out to places where he had potential customers, pick them up, bring them into the plant, and go over with them the construction of their ambulance.

Taylor had created a niche in the market. Most ambulance companies had a production-line operation and the customer had to choose one or another model. There was no customization. Taylor built the ambulance to the customer's specifications. Want a cabinet in a particular place? That's where Taylor put it. Want it someplace else, Taylor put it there. We brought customers in for pre-construction. Midway through construction, we would pick up those customers again so they and we could be sure everything was being built as specified. When the ambulance was finished, Taylor would pick up the customer and bring them back for final inspection, then fly them home. Taylor's drivers would deliver the ambulance.

I told Joe it would be good for us to hire an Aircraft and Engine (A&E) mechanic to work on the airplane. So Joe hired one to work in the plant. If we had any airplane maintenance work, the A&E mechanic would be available to do that. That worked pretty well.

Quite a bit of flying was involved. Normal business aircraft fly 200 hours per year. We flew much more than that. The airplane was in pretty poor maintenance shape, and we had to do a lot of work on it, and update it with GPS and modern instruments. The airplane had been geared up early in its career, and neither Joe nor I knew about this history. After the first 100 hours, we took the airplane to the Tulsa headquarters and maintenance facility for the MU-2 in the United States. We flew it over to get the 100-hour inspection done and I took our mechanic along with me.

As we started our approach into Tulsa, I put the gear down, but it didn't go down. I pulled up, went around, got the procedure manual out, and we pumped the gear down manually, which takes an ungodly amount of pumps to get it down. A lever had to be pulled to open the doors to the wheel well to pump the handle to ratchet the gear down. We got the gear down and landed. The facility performed the 100-hour inspection, re-rigged the gear, and we took it out to check the work. The bill was tremendous – way beyond what we anticipated it might be. We took it back for the second 100 hours and again the bill was far more than it should have been. So we started to look for another place to have our maintenance work done because we felt we were overcharged.

I contacted the mechanic I used at the Arkansas State University aviation school and asked if he had any experience with an MU-2. He said he didn't have a lot of experience with one but he had been with Boeing for many years, and he had someone working with him that worked at the factory in Kerrville when they were building MU-2s. They were based in Batesville, which was about 15 to 20 miles from Newport, and he agreed to run maintenance for us. They bought the equipment they needed, and from then on they did our 100-hour checks.

It was enjoyable flying and Joe was a great guy to work for. He was more than fair in any situation. My wife, Virginia, was diagnosed with sinus cancer. Our daughter and son-in-law, Connie and Chuck Carney, were living in Bloomington, Indiana. Chuck worked at the Indiana University television station. Chuck had interviewed Dr. Allen Thornton, who was a pioneer in proton radiation. In Little Rock, we saw Dr. James Suen, who was the expert in the treatment of sinus cancer. Dr. Suen kind of patted Virginia on the head and told her they could make her comfortable but she was terminal. Connie and Chuck were there when Dr. Suen said this. Chuck got into their car, drove straight back to Bloomington, and went to see Dr. Thornton. Dr. Thornton said that did not sound reasonable to him and told Chuck to have her come up. I called Joe and told him I wanted to take Virginia to Bloomington, and he told me to take the airplane. We took the MU-2 to Bloomington. On our first visit, Dr. Thornton said he had treated about 400 cases of sinus cancer and had an 86 percent cure rate over five years. Immediately, we began using Dr. Thornton for treatment, Joe kindly let me use the MU-2 to get back and forth to visit Virginia during her cancer treatment. Virginia stayed in Bloomington with Connie and Chuck for the radiation and chemo treatments. It was a great benefit to us – an hour and fifteen minute flight instead of a nine-hour drive.

Joe was one of the best bosses I have ever had. Joe was also a pilot – when he was on board, he would fly one leg and I would fly the next. He is a good aviator with a good feel for the airplane. I flew for Joe until I turned 70. I had an enjoyable time and accumulated about 3,000 hours flying the MU-2

I had two major events flying the MU-2. One was on a return flight from North Carolina with a customer who was also a pilot. I had him in the right seat of the cockpit and as we leveled off and got near Chattanooga, the left engine quit. I feathered the engine and landed in Chattanooga. They had to bring an engine over from Tulsa and put it on. I used it to fly to Tulsa where we put new engines on both sides and put in a new interior – really fixed up the airplane.

The next event was the only time I ever skinned an airplane. We had had two or three gear problems with the airplane, where we had to pump the gear down. There is a shear pin in there when the doors don't properly open. Flying back from North Carolina at 24,000 feet – this time alone, I had just dropped off some customers – coming in for landing I put the gear down and heard a POP! The POP sounded like a 12-gauge shotgun went off in the cabin. I looked, and the gear was not down. I got the gear door handle, pulled it, and the doors would not open. I tried to pump the gear down without the door being open but it didn't work. I called the maintenance people in Newport and told them to call Tulsa. They got Tulsa on the line and they told me to do everything that I had already done. I still couldn't get the gear down.

MU-2 belly landed by Jim McCartney in Newport, Arkansas

The Newport maintenance crew called the Fire Department to come out in case they were needed when I landed. I spotted the fire truck at the opposite end of the runway from where I planned to land and called and requested the fire truck to move to my projected landing site. The Fire Department refused to move the fire truck. I flew around Newport until I had about 20 gallons of gas remaining and landed. It skinned the airplane up, but that was all. The maintenance people came out, jacked it up, put the gear down manually, and locked it down. I flew it back over to Tulsa with the gear down and got it fixed again.

Before I flew the plane to Tulsa, Mitsubishi sent a crew to go over the airplane to determine what happened – a pilot, an engineer and a mechanic. The pilot looked familiar to me and he said I looked familiar to him. He said he had been at Texas International, which rang a bell. I said, "You flew co-pilot with me!" Tommy Bachelor was furloughed from TI due to a cut-back. Later he lost an eye to cancer. He said it was hard to get his medical approved with only one eye. Now he was Chief Pilot for Mitsubishi and had over 15,000 hours in MU-2s. We had a good reunion. Meanwhile, the mechanic and engineer found that the shear pin failed to shear clean and jammed the door so it wouldn't open. It made me feel much better to find out what happened and that it was not something I had done.

After I left Taylor, the gear had to be pumped down several times. Finally two years after I left, Joe called and told me that the plane was again landed on its belly because of the same problem. Joe called a mechanic in Smyrna, Tennessee, who is the expert on MU-2s, and asked him where to take the plane to get the gear and shear pin problem fixed. He gave Joe the name of someone in Tennessee and hopefully it is now fixed. While I was there, I had the shear pin pulled on each 100-hour maintenance check. If it was beginning to wear, I had it replaced. The pin is about an inch and a half long and perhaps a third of an inch in diameter, with a hollow core. The cost for this tiny piece is $250.

When I turned 70, I decided I should probably quit flying. We wanted to move to Bloomington, Indiana, so I told Joe I would be leaving. That was the end of our adventure in Arkansas. We found a house in Bloomington and then sold our house in Arkansas. Joe sent his crew over to load up all our furniture, and they made two trips to Bloomington to deliver our furniture. Joe had two men on the truck for the two trips. He also flew a crew up on the MU-2 to help unload and place the furniture in our house. What kind of guy would be that generous with anyone? It was just great. I enjoyed my time with Joe and he has been a good friend.

Virginia is still cancer-free more than five years after completion of her treatment by Dr. Thornton and Dr. Kaneru in Bloomington.

Living in Bloomington has given me the opportunity to spend more time with our granddaughter, Claire Carney. I taught her to ride a bicycle, which was great fun. I am currently teaching her to drive a car. She is 12 and is a very sweet and beautiful young lady.

Another wonderful event was when Caroline was born and I got to hold her when she was only a few minutes old. It has been great pleasure to watch her growth milestones – learning to walk, talk, etc. She is very charming and I love being Poppy for these two girls!

CHAPTER 37

BMG Aviation – Flight Instructor and Charter Pilot, Bloomington, IN

I became acquainted with BMG Aviation in Bloomington when Virginia had her sinus cancer. We flew the MU-2 to Bloomington on a regular basis in connection with Virginia's cancer treatments. BMG is one of the better fixed-base operations that I have ever encountered. They were always accommodating, always there when we arrived, put fuel in the plane quickly if I needed a quick turnaround, or helped us with bags, etc. It is a helpful operation. I got to know Bob Burke, the owner of BMG Aviation. He has the fuel concession and a maintenance facility.

After we moved to Bloomington, Joe Taylor sent the MU-2 to Bloomington and flew us to Arkansas for a visit. When we returned, Virginia was talking to Bob, who asked her if I had a CFI and CFI-I flight instructor ratings. She told him I did, and he asked her if I would be interested in doing some instruction. She said I probably would, and

I contacted Bob and told him I was interested. So I started working for Bob. It might have been a ploy by Virginia to get me out of the house.

Bob had several airplanes he leased out, and when someone leased an airplane, they would hire me to fly it for them. I was flying a Columbia 400 pretty often and a Cessna 340 quite often. There was also an Aerostar that I flew. It was enjoyable, and Bob was good to me. Along the way, I decided I wanted to get my own airplane again. I started looking around for a Mooney. I asked Bob if he would do a pre-buy on it if we found something. We looked at one in Oklahoma, but when we took the cowling off, it was really not a good airplane. The second one we found was just northwest of Los Angeles. It looked on paper like it was really good. Bob called and made an offer on it for me and they said they would be interested in that price, which was considerably under the asking price. Bob and I left Bloomington one morning at 6:30, drove to Indianapolis, got on the airline, flew to Los Angeles, and rode a bus to a little airport about 30 miles northwest of Los Angeles. We inspected the airplane and it looked in good shape, well maintained, with the equipment on it that I wanted – a good GPS and a good autopilot. It had all the bells and whistles and was well equipped. So we made the deal on the airplane. This was late in the afternoon. We fueled it up with gas and took off heading back to Bloomington. It was not a quick flight. We flew all night, with one stop in Amarillo for fuel, getting back to Bloomington at 6:30 in the morning. I think Bob collapsed on the couch at the airport. I went home and slept all day.

Once, I was flying the Aerostar when the left engine started acting up. I pulled the power back on it and the oil pressure was low. Already on descent into Bloomington, I came in and landed. That was the only major incident I had flying for BMG.

BMG held a biannual training program for private pilots in the area. I presented a paper for this program on how stress and fatigue impact one's flying and decision-making ability in the cockpit. In that paper, I told the group that as a flight instructor it was my goal to have my student become unconsciously competent. Part of that process is continuing education, training, retraining, and developing procedures to ensure the safety of the pilot and his or her passengers.

When a student starts training, he will be unconsciously incompetent. After some training, the student becomes consciously incompetent.

As training progresses, the student becomes consciously competent. At this point, many students feel they are well qualified.

It is my goal, as an instructor, for my students to become unconsciously competent.

That is called pilot reserve capability.

Bob was a really great guy to work for and I really enjoyed my time at BMG. He is one of the better mechanics I have found in the industry – not the kind of guy that just replaces a part, he can repair it. I don't know if his customers realize it or not, but he is such a good mechanic he saves his customers a lot of money that they probably are never aware of.

While working at BMG, Bob invited me as his guest to go to "steak night." I didn't know what it was, but Bob said just be there at five o'clock, and we'd go down to the JB Hangars and have a steak. I didn't know what "JB" meant. On Wednesday night, I met a group of pilots in the area that meets every Wednesday evening for a steak dinner – it is the best steak in the City of Bloomington. There was good camaraderie in which aviation stories are told over and over. The stories improved with each telling. "JB" stood for John Bender. He and another pilot, Tom Boone, had been associated with B-47 aircraft in the Air Force. John was a radar technician on a B-47 based in Wichita, Kansas; I was a crew chief on a B-47 in Lake Charles, Louisiana; and Tom Boone had been an aircraft commander on a B-47. Tom flew B-47s all over and continued his Air Force career until his retirement. He flew everything including DC-10 tankers that dispensed herbicides over the jungles in Vietnam.

John's Air Force career did not keep him occupied full time and that's when he started a little company called Pizza Hut. After Wichita, John was transferred to Abilene, Texas, where he opened his second Pizza Hut. He said he had to teach the Texans what a pizza was because no one had ever heard of pizza. Steak night was always enjoyable; I will miss that group of pilots and the good time we had each Wednesday night. The pilots were a diverse group – several were doctors and others from all aspects of life – all with a shared interest in aviation that keeps the group together.

John has two hangars, one heated and air conditioned with a full kitchen and dishwasher. In one of his hangars, John has a collection of antique cars – all in running condition and John drives all of them. John's family started out in Indiana. His Dad started a lumber business in 1932 – Bender Lumber – that is still thriving today with locations throughout Indiana. His Dad is still alive; the employees of Bender Lumber own a stake in the company; and John now runs the family lumber business. John has a 1932 Ford pickup truck in his collection. It is like the truck his Dad owned when he started Bender Lumber.

I flew one of the 340s on a trip down south. That's when I started having the stomach pains that ended my flying career. The stomach pains turned out to be pancreatic cancer.

* * *

Christmas 2011: In 2010, I barely noticed Christmas. I was so sick that I didn't think I would see another birthday, let alone another Christmas. Christmas in 2011 was much better. I felt better, and I loved watching Claire and Caroline open their gifts. James and Julian arrived for a visit the day after Christmas and I watched Julian open gifts. Virginia had already mailed gifts to California for Julian, but we still had a few for him to open. It was delightful to see the three grandchildren play together. Claire and Julian enjoyed playing "Chicken Foot" a funny game with dominoes.

CHAPTER 38

My Final Chapter

When I started out in this life, I did not imagine all the twists and turns I would meet. Reflecting on my life, I find I would not change a thing because of all the exposure and education I received along the way. The twists and turns led me to meet so many wonderful people in the field of aviation and elsewhere. What little I achieved came primarily because of the support from pilots and ALPA members and staff. My life in flight has been a wonderful ride.

I feel I was able to bring a lot of operational problems at Texas International to the surface where they were resolved. I was proud to have had a hand in negotiating the labor contracts that touched so many pilots and their families. Pilots that flew for Trans Texas and Texas International were in the cellar of the aviation industry when it came to salary and benefits. That situation improved over the years until the Continental acquisition and subsequent strike.

I was proud of the many provisions included in the 1995 America West contract that improved the lifestyle of the pilots with minimal increase in costs to the airline. I know that 1995 contract improved the lifestyle of most pilots at America West today because one of those pilots is my daughter, Tambra McCartney Swan.

As I reflect upon my life, I find I am comfortable with dying, but sad to leave Virginia alone. I am sad that I won't be here to see our grandchildren grow up.

Our children are grown and established in their careers.

Connie has a law degree and a Master's Degree in education. Her husband, Chuck Carney, is working on his PhD and works for Indiana University. Their daughter, Claire, 13, is getting a great education – I would not be surprised if she someday writes a best-selling book. Caroline, almost 4, will undoubtedly take the world by the tail and make it work for her. Claire and Caroline have certainly charmed me! I taught Claire to ride a bicycle and am currently teaching her to drive a car.

James, a senior engineer at Apple, Inc., is responsible for the audio work on Apple products. His wife, Sophie, has a degree in physics from China. In San Francisco, she earned a Master's Degree in Fine Arts at San Francisco Art Institute. She is an accomplished painter of portraits in oils. Their son, Julian, age 6, is fluent in English and Chinese, thanks in no small part to his Chinese grandmother who visits often. Julian reads very well, takes piano lessons, and enjoys the iPhone, the iPad and trains. He has a bright future.

Tammy is still flying for America West as Captain on an A-320. She is helping her lifelong friend, Lisa Menna, with her private foundation that is involved in improving the lives of children in Third World countries. Tammy is Julian's doting aunt who teaches him all the things to do to frustrate his parents.

Virginia and I were fortunate to be members of the Presbyterian Church in Newport with Rev. Allen Ford as the pastor. Allen is the reluctant Presbyterian minister that I coaxed into the cockpit and tried to teach him to fly. He wasn't interested in flying but he is a good person and a wonderful pastor.

God reached down and touched Virginia and me in Newport. That touch moved us to relocate to Bloomington, Indiana, to be near Connie and her family. We discovered many other advantages in Bloomington. We found great medical treatment for Virginia and me, and we are both thankful that she is cancer free after more than five years. That is due to many prayers and the help of many doctors.

We were fortunate to find a wonderful church in Bloomington: United Presbyterian Church, with Rev. David Bremer as the pastor. The congregation is small but close, diverse and loving. We became friends with many in the congregation, including Dr. Souheil Haddad, his wife Alejandra, and his brother, Dr. Fadi Haddad, and his wife Aline. The Drs. Haddad and their families are personifications of the word Christian. My entire church family has been very supportive during my illness. I give special thanks to Bob Burke, John and Colleen Swanson, Irene and Dennis Reedy, Vera and Gerrit Heitink for their gracious support during my illness.

I will miss all my very good lifelong friends: Billy Tate, Bill Baker, J.V. Sclifo, Allen Kelley, Gary Portzline, Burton Ford, Joe Taylor, Mike McDermott, and so many more.

My sister and I have become close during the process of writing this book, remembering our shared childhood, and the character traits we learned while growing up in Arkansas. We both graduated from high school when we were 16 years old, totally unprepared to strike out on our own, but we did it anyway. We learned as much as we could along life's pathway and adapted wherever we landed.

And so I repeat: if I had life to live all over again, I wouldn't want to change a thing. It's been such a good ride. I look forward to the next great adventure when I see what God has planned for me. My thoughts still linger on earth for the people I love here.

Part Six
Pancreatic Cancer Prognosis and Treatment

CHAPTER 39

Diagnosis/Prognosis of Pancreatic Cancer

Jim is my only sibling and I was devastated by his diagnosis of Stage IV pancreatic cancer – adenocarcinoma – with metastases to the liver that had more than 20 lesions or tumors. I searched the internet for treatment options for pancreatic cancer and in general for any information I could find about pancreatic cancer.

The following is my account of Jim's cancer treatment. The first few weeks were so traumatic – I knew I could not remember all the details of how treatment was determined. I kept a diary the first weeks I was in Bloomington. When I returned in November 2010 when Jim was hospitalized, and recovering at home, there was too much to do to continue the diary, so everything else has been written retrospectively. Now I have merged the two – the paragraphs with dates in the beginning came from my diary.

I was desperate for information about how the disease might progress, what drugs were used and why. I wanted to know the specifics of what we may expect to happen. I found only generalities. I read

The Last Lecture by Randy Pausch. His book was about living his life with brief asides on his cancer treatment. Then I found his blog on the internet. The blog was far more detailed but not as specific as I would have liked. I worked for a medical malpractice lawyer once – he defended doctors – so I am familiar with medical terminology. It doesn't scare me – I want to know the specific medical terms. That's why they are used here. I was frustrated by the reference to "chemo" – okay, but what is in the chemo? I wanted to know the exact names of drugs that could be used.

I drove to Bloomington, Indiana, and arrived on August 15, 2010, my 70th birthday. Jim and his wife, Virginia Balch Landrum, my lifelong friend from our childhood together in Arkansas, have been married 16 years and moved from Arkansas to Bloomington a few years earlier to be near Virginia's only daughter, Connie, her husband Chuck Carney, and their only daughter, Claire. Fortunately, Claire became the big sister to Virginia's second granddaughter, Caroline. Claire and Caroline are a joy and delight to both Jim and Virginia. Jim has two children from his first marriage to Mary Jane Lewis: His son, James E. McCartney, lives in Cupertino, California, with his wife, Sophie, and their son, Julian, another joy and delight for Jim and Virginia. James works as a senior engineer for Apple, Inc. Jim's daughter, Tambra McCartney Swan, lives in Chandler, Arizona, with her husband, Dave. She is a Captain for U.S. Airways on an Airbus A-320. James and Tambra also came to Bloomington to help brainstorm on a treatment protocol for Jamie.

Jim had been on a charter flight to Alabama in late July. He started having stomach pain and thought he had food poisoning from something he had eaten on the trip. When he got back to Bloomington, he went to see his internist, Dr. LaFollette, who gave him some anti-acid tablets and asked that he return in two weeks if he was still having a problem. Jim returned in two weeks and Dr. LaFollette ordered an abdominal CT scan on Wednesday. On Thursday, the results were sent to the doctor's office but Dr. LaFollette had the day off. One of his partners saw the report of the CT scan, called Dr. LaFollette, and suggested that someone call Jim immediately to tell him of the diagnosis. Dr. LaFollette agreed and his partner made the call. That was August 12, 2010. Dr. LaFollette scheduled an appointment for Jamie to see

Dr. Spier, a gastroenterologist, to have an endoscopic sonogram and biopsy performed.

In the meantime, Connie called Dr. Souheil Haddad, who was a neurosurgeon, a good friend and a member of Jim and Virginia's church, United Presbyterian. Dr. Haddad was in London on his way to Lebanon, his home country. She left a message and Souheil returned the call quickly. Souheil said they really needed to talk to his brother, Dr. Fadi Haddad, a surgeon specializing in oncology. Fadi, also a good friend and member of their church, was with Souheil on the trip to Lebanon. They would be gone about two weeks. Fadi got on the phone and said he would take care of all details and he would arrange for a needle biopsy of the liver to be performed at Bloomington Hospital. The biopsy was scheduled on Monday afternoon, August 16.

By Monday, August 16, we decided to consult some of the major cancer centers: M.D. Anderson in Houston, Simon Cancer Center in Indianapolis, Moffett Cancer Center in Tampa, Johns Hopkins Hospital in Baltimore, and Northwestern University Hospital in Chicago. We went to the facility that did Jamie's CT scan to get additional disks of the pictures from the CT scan to send to the various cancer centers. We were told it would be tomorrow before they could make the copies. Connie dug in her heels and insisted we get all the disks today so they could be sent via FedEx to cancer centers in Houston, Tampa, St. Louis and Chicago. The staff refused to comply with our request until Connie mentioned she was a lawyer and the refusal to provide the disks would lead to "legal consequences." They decided to copy the disks for us at a cost of $20 each. It took only 20 minutes to give us the copies we requested. The disks were shipped out via FedEx overnight delivery before 11:30 a.m.

Next stop was the appointment with Dr. Spier, gastroenterologist, who could not do a biopsy until next week. He did review the CT scan with us and said he would do an endoscopic ultrasound biopsy, but could not do that today. He also said it was just different from the biopsy scheduled at 3 p.m. with Dr. Wolfer, the radiologist. Dr. Spier said the cancer is advanced but could not suggest a treatment plan without a pathology report from the biopsy. In fact, his only role in the treatment of pancreatic cancer was to make a diagnosis then refer us to an oncologist for a treatment plan. Connie asked if he could make a *referral to M.D. Anderson, and he said he could. Jamie, Virginia and I left to go to Bloomington Hospital for the biopsy at 3 p.m. Connie and her two girls stayed with Dr. Spier to get the M.D. Anderson referral, which didn't happen because we needed the pathology report from the biopsy.*

After checking in at the hospital at 1:30, we were on hold in the radiology lab for blood work before moving to the holding area for the CT scan guided needle biopsy. They finally took him in at 3:10. A little over an hour later we were summoned to meet with Dr. Wolfer and Jamie post-biopsy. Dr. Wolfer was nice but said there was nothing to report until the pathology was processed on the liver specimens obtained in the biopsy. At the earliest, we won't have results for at least 24 hours. Jamie is fine – he was awake for the procedure and experienced no pain. We liked Dr. Wolfer. We also liked Dr. Spier. Neither will be a treating doctor nor a decision maker with respect to any course of treatment.

They kept Jamie in a hospital room for four hours – 4:30 to 8:30 p.m. – to be sure he suffered no ill effects and had no bleeding. They suggested he get the pneumonia vaccine, we agreed, and they gave him that while he was there. So we cooled our jets for the next four hours.

Jamie decided to sell his airplane since he wouldn't be able to pass a flight physical. He was on an emotional roller coaster – up one minute and down the next. We talked of hope, living and doing all that you can. We focused on the positive aspects of living – not dying. We don't get to pick when and how we die – but it is certain we will all die.

The diagnosis did not ensure death – just presented an obstacle. The best course of action appeared to be chemo and the pathology report would help to define the treatment. In the meantime, life goes on. The 3.2 cm mass in the pancreas is in the body and tail and is wrapped around the splenic artery. The splenic artery and liver involvements are the factors that make the cancer unresectable – inoperable. There are more than 20 tumors in the liver. The largest tumor in the liver is 3.0 cm.

Typical symptoms of pancreatic cancer are: back pain, stomach pain, jaundice, loss of appetite, and weight loss. Jamie's only symptom was stomach pain that has now subsided.

Virginia has an 8:30 a.m. appointment tomorrow to see about her eye. Then we had to get ready for Tammy's arrival at 3:30 p.m. James, Sophie and Julian are scheduled to arrive on August 25th.

On Tuesday, August 17, Virginia went to her 8:45 a.m. appointment with an opthamologist to see about a lesion on her left eyelid that may be cancerous. Good News! It's not! He treated her eye for dryness and repaired some scar tissue from cataract surgery with a laser. That afternoon she could see better.

Jamie went to the airport to get some things out of the Mooney so it could be sold. Bob Burke will help Jamie with the sale of the airplane. Bob also has a side business removing snow from driveways and he volunteered to do this for Jim and Virginia. First time it snowed, no one had to call Bob. He was there before we even thought about it. That was such a great thing he did for Jim and Virginia.

Virginia and I went to the grocery store but Jamie called to say Tammy's plane would be 30 minutes early. We called Dr. Haddad's office to tell him to call on Jim's cell phone with news of the pathology report.

We picked up Tammy at 3:30 p.m. and had a nice visit on the drive back to Bloomington. Nice time – except for the undertone and concern about the pancreatic cancer diagnosis and the pending biopsy report.

A one-page report on the CT Abdomen and Pelvis with Contrast states: "IMPRESSION: 1. There is a 3.2 cm pancreatic tail mass, most likely representing pancreatic adenocarcinoma. 2. There are greater than 20 hypodense liver masses, most likely representing metastases. If clinically indicated, one of these liver lesions could be biopsied under ultrasound or CT guidance. 3. Cholecystolithiasis." [The last word means gallstone.]

When we got home, there was a message from Dr. Haddad in Lebanon. He called again and talked to Jamie and Virginia. The news was not good. Jamie and Virginia left immediately to go to Bloomington Hospital to get a copy of the biopsy report. The records office was closed so they went to Pathology to ask about the report. Mark Bauman, M.D., the pathologist, overheard them asking about the report on his way out, immediately turned around, and said he could help them. He printed a copy of the report and talked to them about his findings. He told them this was a fast-growing type of cancer.

Now we have another one page report: NEEDLE ASPIRATION REPORT. "Diagnosis: Malignant cells present from an adenocarcinoma. Comment: The patient has a mass in the body and tail of the pancreas and multiple liver lesions. The cytologic findings are consistent with metastatic pancreatic carcinoma; other sites of origin cannot be definitively excluded. The results have been discussed with Dr. Fadi Haddad on 8/17/2010 at 4:00 p.m. Dr. Haddad was in Lebanon during the telephone conversation."

While Jamie and Virginia were gone, Tammy told me what she had done to research the diagnosis. She talked to Jamie's flight surgeon of 40-plus years and he told her he thinks Jamie's life expectancy is a matter of weeks, three months at the most. We were scheduled to see Dr. Mark Dayton on Thursday at 3:30 p.m. The Drs. Haddad would be back on August 23.

I found an article on the internet presented at a meeting of the American Society of Clinical Oncology (ASCO) in Chicago in June 2010 about a clinical trial conducted in France for the treatment of pancreatic cancer with a combination of drugs called Folfirinox.

Connie will send the biopsy report to the facilities where we sent the CT scan disks yesterday.

Jamie said if the chemo could only extend his life by weeks, he would skip it. If it would give him three to six months, then he would take it. I told him we needed to get input from all sources before making any decisions. Jamie's greatest concerns are for Virginia. He asked her to call their financial advisor in the morning and ask him to come to Bloomington to discuss this change. Jamie started making phone calls. I asked Virginia what he was doing, and she said, "He's making his funeral arrangements, calling people to serve as pall bearers."

Tammy told Jamie and Virginia she believes his life expectancy to be weeks, not months. I have cried more today than I have in the last 10 years. My heart is heavy. This is the last member of my immediate family.

On Wednesday, August 18, Virginia asked James to send an email to Steve Jobs and ask about treatment information. Steve Jobs replied in about 20 minutes and sent the name of his doctor, Dr. George Fisher, at Stanford University Medical Center. Tammy placed a call to Dr. Fisher. I called M.D. Anderson in Houston. Tomorrow, Connie will call the Moffett Cancer Center in Tampa, Florida for an appointment – they have agreed to see him.

Connie scheduled an appointment for tomorrow with Dr. Karen Koneru, Virginia's chemo oncologist. That will be at one p.m., followed by the appointment with Dr. Dayton at 3:30 pm. We are preparing questions.

On Thursday, August 19, Jim, Virginia, Connie, Tammy and I met with Drs. Koneru and Dayton. Both offered similar chemo treatments but Dr. Dayton seemed more positive. Tammy recorded both visits and gave disks to each of us so we can replay the conversations. Jamie felt encouraged and seems to want to go with Dayton but at the same time keeping all options open.

Connie is afraid that we are giving up and failing to consider all treatment options. I don't think that is anyone's intent. We all want what is best for Jamie and definitely want him to develop a more optimistic attitude, but it is really hard to do when you are told the prognosis is 3 months without treatment and 8 months with treatment. No cure. No discussion of remission. Hope is not discussed – except by Dr. Dayton.

On Friday, August 20, Virginia called a family meeting at 11:30 this morning during which she eloquently expressed her feelings to Tammy and me. I cried.

Before the meeting, I told Jamie I thought the treatment plan for him in Bloomington would be more comfortable for him and Virginia and they have a support system in place which is extremely important, but that I think we still need to discuss all options and at least talk to as many health care providers for the treatment of pancreatic cancer that we can.

Later in the day, Jamie called Dr. Dayton's office to schedule his first chemo next week. Virginia was upset that he did that because they planned to wait until Monday, but I think Jamie just wants to set things in motion. We still have the appointment in Indianapolis on Monday about the clinical trial.

I decided we needed to organize the avalanche of information we were acquiring. I purchased two three ring binder notebooks – one for research and one for treatment. I bought index pages and a planning calendar. I began to assemble the material we had, organizing it so it will make more sense, and so we can readily find things.

On Saturday, August 21, I spent the morning setting up both notebooks and both remain a work in progress, but I think they will be helpful.

On Sunday, August 22, Dr. Thornton, who had relocated to a clinic in Virginia, was in Bloomington for the weekend. He stopped by for a short visit. During the long months of treating Virginia's cancer, he had become a good friend of the family. He and Jim also share an interest in aviation. Dr. Thornton has his own airplane and Jim took him for a ride in the MU-2. The financial advisor is scheduled at 2 p.m. on Sunday.

Connie and Caroline came over for a visit. Connie brought more emails to go into the Research notebook and the Fedex receipts for everything that had been sent out. Connie continues to express concern about Dr. Dayton. She looked at his bio and suggested I check on the cancer center he worked for in Minnesota – Parker Hughes Cancer Center. I asked if she had looked it up, and she said I should look it up – so I did. It was closed in 2008 – filed for bankruptcy – amid a whistleblower lawsuit regarding overcharges to Medicare – settled for $150,000. None of the news coverage mentioned Dr. Dayton so it is not clear when he left Parker Hughes CC. I'm not sure that any of this has any impact on Dayton's role as an oncologist.

It is still the plan to seek a second opinion – probably at M.D. Anderson, and perhaps, Stanford's Dr. Fisher. We are undecided about everything, don't want to step on each other's toes so we are doing a dance around each other on the roller coaster ride in the world of cancer and its treatment. Connie continues to campaign for treatment with microspheres and chemical ablation, but that would be in addition to chemo, so I still believe that chemo needs to be started as soon as possible. The chemo regimen recommended is similar among providers. Stanford will not do a telephone consult, would not change any chemo course already in place, but would make changes upon completion of the current course of treatment. M.D. Anderson will see him regardless of whether chemo has been started.

Connie is also concerned about the PET scan scheduled on Tuesday as it is on a mobile unit. We will check to see if that can be done in

Indianapolis. This is important so we know all locations of the cancer so it can be measured following chemo.

Jim, Virginia, Tammy and I went to John and Colleen Swanson's home for dinner and had a delightful evening. We needed the break from the big "C" and time to tell and hear jokes and stories over wonderful food and wine.

Jamie told me late this afternoon that he had been praying that God would give him the strength to face whatever came his way and felt his prayer had been answered because he felt a sense of peace about whatever comes.

I asked him to put the funeral arrangements on hold for a while and he said "okay" but added that he had already completed all that and it made him feel better to have it done. I couldn't argue with that. He is also giving away personal possessions – notably his collection of model airplanes. First, all to Tammy, but he will see what James may want, and he wants Claire to have the MU-2.

This is agonizing.

On Sunday, August 22, Jim, Virginia, Tammy and I went to church this morning at United Presbyterian. The pastor, Rev. David Bremer, prepared his sermon with Jim in mind. He acknowledged Jim at the beginning of the service and Jim told the congregation that his prayer that he will have the strength to face the challenges ahead had been answered and that he is at peace with whatever the outcome may be. I was proud but I think I better start making the same prayer for all of us who watch over the battle against pancreatic cancer.

Jamie mentioned he wants to write a book about his flight experiences and asked me to help him with it. I said I would be delighted. I think this will be a fun project and will give us something to think about other than the hated cancer.

Dr. Thornton arrived shortly after 1 p.m. First, he reviewed Virginia's recent CT scan and pronounced her sinus cancer cured! He looked at the spot on the lid of her left eye and said it was nothing! Virginia then told him she put a warm compress on her eye, then pricked it with a sterilized needle and drained the spot. Dr. Thornton said that was NOT a good idea but probably did relieve the problem, but don't do it again! He reviewed her scan in detail and declared there is no evidence of cancer and why.

Dr. Thornton started his discussion of the elephant in the room: Jim's diagnosis of Stage IV pancreatic cancer with metastases to the liver. He quickly shot down the applicability of the use of microspheres or chemoembolization because the liver tumors are spread over too large an area of the liver. He said Dayton's chemo protocol is good – he likes him – and thinks Jim should keep the Thursday, August 26, appointment for the first chemo treatment. However, he said we should request that CT scans be performed after two cycles of chemo – not three – and request Dayton to send the scans to Thornton so he can track the progress of the chemo for an opportunity to hit the pancreas with proton radiation therapy.

We asked about the PET scan scheduled on Tuesday on the mobile unit in view of his insistence that Virginia have her PET scans in St. Louis. Dr. Thornton thinks the PET scan is unnecessary – just Dayton being diligent – but mobile unit would be fine. Virginia's cancer was a very different and difficult type of cancer to scan and she also needed to be monitored by an ENT specialist – Dr. Vavares.

I asked if we should make appointments with various cancer centers and he said not really – but call and get additional information before deciding, but he believes the most important thing is to get the chemo started. He asked how we would feel about the issue two years down the road.

Connie still wants to investigate the microsphere delivery options and I promised I would make the calls tomorrow to determine what needed to be provided to get opinions from Northwestern University Hospital in Chicago and Johns Hopkins University Hospital in Baltimore.

Dr. Thornton was reassuring. Jamie still asks if he should take the chemo. I keep insisting yes he should, if not for himself then for Virginia and Connie. If he takes chemo, he has a chance; if he doesn't, then there is no chance. He can always stop.

If the post-chemo scans indicate a decrease in the size of the tumor in the pancreas, Dr. Thornton has a surgeon who will insert a breast implant between the pancreas and the bowel to protect the bowel from the proton treatment. Then Dr. Thornton can deliver proton radiation to the tumor in the pancreas. If the systemic chemo (or microspheres) eliminates the liver tumors, more will develop as long as the pancreatic tumor remains.

Jim and Virginia left the room to meet with Brent Perry, their financial advisor. Dr. Thornton said while Jim looks healthy today, his appearance would decline rapidly over the next two to three months. Dr. Thornton agreed with the prognosis that Jim would likely not last much more than three months. I pray that Dr. Thornton and the other doctors are wrong.

Tammy noticed that Jim had a spot on his forehead that looks like the squamous cell carcinoma Tammy recently had removed. Jim called his pilot/dermatologist friend who said to call his office at 7a.m. tomorrow to schedule an appointment to take care of this before Thursday. We may have to cancel the 2 p.m. appointment in Indianapolis about the clinical trial of Abraxane. Tammy researched that drug and determined that it has been used for several years for breast cancer. It is available outside the clinical trial if we choose to do so. We agree that it is preferable to keep the appointment for the sole purpose of education. Each time we talk to someone, we learn more. Tomorrow will be a heavy telephone day.

On Monday, August 23, Jamie went to the dermatologist who removed the spot on his forehead – diagnosis seborrhic keratosis – benign. No problem.

Jamie has had several skin cancers removed from his face and head. It seems that pilots are particularly susceptible for such skin cancers due to the time spent in the cockpit at high altitudes and increased exposure to the rays of the sun. It is well documented. These skin cancers could be prevented by the installation of a sun shield to block the UVA rays, but Boeing deemed the $1,500 cost to be too expensive to implement. Perhaps they should check that cost against the costs for removal of multiple skin cancers.

SIRA Center called to schedule the PET scan for 8:45 a.m. tomorrow.

I called Johns Hopkins in Baltimore for Dr. Geschwind, but the operator could not locate him in their directory. I told her to check the Department of Interventional Radiology – again she said there was no one there by that name. Finally, she gave me the name and phone numbers of three doctors who are pancreatic cancer specialists. I called the first on the list and left a message.

I sent an email to Dr. Abruzzese at M.D. Anderson to request that he look at the disk of the CT scan that we sent previously to Dr. Vauthey,

Professor of Oncology Surgery. Dr. Abruzzese replied to say he would locate the disk and take a look at it.

Then we left at 11:30 am to go to the Simon Cancer Center Pavilion in Indianapolis to find out more about their clinical trial of the drug Abraxane. Dr. Gabrielle Elena Chiorean met with us – Jim, Virginia, Tammy and me. Dr. Chiorean talked at length about the clinical trial. Jamie decided to go with the clinical trial even though he may not get Abraxane because it is a randomized computer selection.

On the way home, we tried to call and cancel the PET scan in the morning but decided to go ahead since we couldn't reach anyone to cancel. They will do another PET scan in Indy at no cost. The GEMZAR drug will also be free.

We also discussed other treatment options and Dr. Chiorean summarily dismissed the use of microspheres – very expensive – $180,000 for a single treatment – and not helpful. Much in the same vein as Dr. Dayton dismissed the efficacy of the Indianapolis clinical trial.

She also discouraged the use of proton therapy on the pancreas until we convinced her that it was only an option to be considered after the chemo had reduced the size of the pancreatic tumor.

Tammy asked whether pancreatic cancer is hereditary and Dr. Chiorean said frequently there are a number of cases of pancreatic cancer within a family. It is not always hereditary but there is a clear indication that you may be more susceptible than the general population if a close relative has been diagnosed with pancreatic cancer. Tammy asked what steps she and James should take to catch this earlier when there would be more treatment options. Dr. Chiorean said it might be a good idea to get a CT scan as a baseline. She added that in any event, if either of them should have stomach pain as experienced by their father, they should insist that their doctor order a CT scan to rule out pancreatic cancer.

Cancer is very big business...

Dr. Chiorean gave us stacks of papers on the clinical trial and Tammy read it on the return trip to Bloomington. Jamie told Dr. Chiorean he would call her tomorrow to confirm whether he will join the clinical trial. Tammy expressed concern about the increased toxicity of one of the chemo regimes to be used if he does not get Abraxane or if that does not work and the cancer gets worse. That alternative treatment is *Folfirinox*, a combination of several drugs as reported at the June 2010 ASCO meeting in Chicago. The clinical trial in France of 345 patients – found an average survival rate of 11.1 months vs. survival of 3 months with Gemcitabine alone. It was suggested that Folfirinox be the new standard of care for treatment of pancreatic cancer, but others objected and feel more study is required.

It is overwhelming but ultimately is Jamie's decision. He still considers doing nothing and I told him doing nothing ensures that he has no chance, and he must do something to have any chance. The only success offered in any treatment plan is to extend his life by months – from three months to six months – perhaps 12 months or more. I also told him he needs to be at peace with whatever he elects to do and I support any decision he makes.

Around the kitchen table, Jamie again told us – Tammy, Virginia, Connie, Claire and me – that he prayed God would give him the strength he would need to face whatever came his way and that he had experienced a profound sense of peace and calm on Friday that continued through the weekend. He has decided to enter the clinical trial in Indy and felt good about the decision. It is time to move forward and let the treatment begin.

It is such a roller coaster ride and the amount of complex information on treatment protocols is daunting. For example, in Indy, chemo will be infused over a 30-minute period of time; in Bloomington, it is infused over 100 minutes. So the question is: Is the chemo dose the same or different? Does the infusion time determine the strength of the dose? How does the infusion time affect the efficacy of the treatment? The more answers we get, the greater the number of questions that arise.

At the end of the day, I'm sure Jamie will be fine no matter what – but I'm not so sure about the rest of us.

Yesterday we ended the day on top of the roller coaster with the decision to enter the clinical trial in Indy. Today, Tuesday, August 24, we started the free fall down upon learning that chemo will not start until September 7. The PET scan in Indianapolis cannot be scheduled until September 2.

Jamie received a call from Joe Taylor in Newport and then received a call from Dr. Istvan Molnar who now lives in New Jersey. Dr. Molnar *is in cancer research at Bayer. He plans to come visit weekend after next. Jamie taught him how to fly when he lived in Newport.*

Connie called Dr. Dayton to see if he could administer the drug Abraxane that is the subject of the clinical trial in Indy. He says he can but it would not be covered by insurance and the cost is $20,000 per month. Minimum treatment would be two months.

Connie sent an email to Dr. Thornton to get his take on the change in circumstances. Once again, we will see what tomorrow brings and whether we end on top of the roller coaster again or if we are once again in a free fall.

Wednesday, August 25, was a good day. Connie called IU and pleaded with them to move Jamie up in the schedule. She told IU we had found another place that would give him the trial drug, Abraxane, and we would do that unless IU could get him into their clinical trial earlier! They re-scheduled him for tomorrow for his lab work, consents and PET scan. Then the first chemo will be scheduled.

On Thursday, August 26, we arrived at the Simon Cancer Center Pavilion at 10:30 am for the 11a.m. appointment. The RN in charge of the clinical trial, Jan Flynn, greeted us before 11a.m. and went over all the consents. Blood was drawn for lab work for Jim and an ekg was performed. Next Jan took us on a tour of the infusion area – plush compared to the facilities at Baylor in Dallas or the facility in Bloomington. Simon Cancer Center is a new facility. Next Jan took us to the Radiology Dept. for the PET scan that was completed at 1p.m. We ate lunch in the hospital cafeteria so we could get copies of the disk of the PET scan. After lunch we picked up the disks and headed back to Bloomington.

We got partial results of the lab work before we left. When we got home, there was an email from Jan Flynn prefaced by the comment, "As I discussed with you over the telephone . . ." but no one had talked to her. Bottom line, bilirubin is elevated along with other values related to Jim's liver function. Tammy pulled up info on the clinical trial and the way I read it, it does not exclude him from the clinical trial. However, the final decision is made by the lab in New York. Those results are due Friday afternoon. New lab work will be done on Monday at the Simon Cancer Center when we go in for the first chemo treatment. At that time it will be determined whether he gets GEMZAR alone or combined with Abraxane.

Tomorrow we will pick up the lab and the PET scan reports in Bloomington. So the day ends in turmoil that was soothed by the presence of Julian, James and Sophie. It will be a long weekend before Monday and hopefully the first chemo treatment.

On Friday, August 27, Jan Flynn called and burst my bubble. The elevated bilirubin does exclude him from the clinical trial. She said that the PET scan was being reviewed by their GI Department and they might want to do an endoscopic exam if they think there is an obstruction of the bile duct. However, a later call said there was no dilatation of the bile duct so no obstruction and no need for a stent to open the bile duct. They are still awaiting results on the lab work from New York. If it does not get back before 5 p.m., we won't know anything further until Monday when we go back for the chemo and another set of blood work. Did not get the New York lab results.

Regular value of bilirubin is 1.0; Jamie's bilirubin is 2.0

I offered to go home so they would have more space for the children but Jamie wants me to stay and go to Indy with them on Monday. I will start home on Tuesday.

On Saturday, August 28, Virginia and I went to the Farmers Market in Bloomington. I cried on the way over and for the first 20 minutes or so of shopping. Virginia bought organic vegetables. I bought a bunch of zinnias and white cheddar cheese made with unpasteurized milk. Expensive but good.

On Sunday, August 29, I went to church with Jamie and Virginia and made a spectacle of myself. I started crying in the car on the way to church, continued throughout the church service, and afterward during the social time. I couldn't stop the tears running down my face. As I write this, the tears are welling up again. James and his family have gone home.

On Monday, August 30, we drove to Indianapolis for Jim's first chemo treatment. As expected, he was excluded from participating in the clinical trial of the drug Abraxane. The New York lab read his bilirubin as 1.7 but the cut-off point is any value above 1.5 and that is final.

Lab results today indicate that Jim's liver function is declining. Dr. Chiorean believes if they go with Gemzar alone it may not be enough to stop the cancer from growing. She suggested using Folfirinox before the liver is further weakened in which case they would be unable to add *secondary drugs such as Folfirinox, Tarceva, etc. However, cannot do chemo today because Folfirinox must be administered through a port. Dr. Chiorean scheduled installation of the port tomorrow. Dr. Chiorean said chemo could be administered immediately after the port is installed, but the chemo takes six hours and must be complete before 5 p.m., so we will return on Wednesday for the first chemo. One of the drugs, 5-FU, must be infused over a two-day period. Home Health care will come to the chemo infusion facility to install the portable pump to administer the drug and will come to the house after 46 hours to remove the pump.*

Folfirinox is a combination of drugs that include 5-fluorouracil (5-FU), leucovorin, irinotecan, and oxaliplatin, along with a number of premeds to prevent nausea and a follow-up dose of steroids. It was recommended that the combination be used only in patients with normal or near normal levels of bilirubin and good performance status. It is more toxic than gemcitabine alone, but overall was deemed to be manageable toxicity. It is recommended for patients with adequate health and strength to withstand the toxicity. At that point in time Jim did not have any symptoms since the initial stomach pain had subsided. We counted on Jim's lifelong good health to withstand the daunting treatment regimen. Jim said he did not feel sick – just felt like he does usually and can't believe he is so sick.

I think Jamie is apprehensive about the chemo.

This chemo is administered every two weeks. After two months, they will do a CT scan to determine the efficacy of the chemo.

Dr. Chiorean suggested that future chemo could be administered in Bloomington by Dr. Koneru (Dr. Chiorean knows Dr. Koneru). I'm glad for that convenience so they won't have to make the one-hour drive each way to Indy.

When we got back to Bloomington, we met with Dr. Lois Lambrecht, Virginia's primary care physician. She reviewed her holistic approach to medicine. We gave her the information we have on the chemo, prescriptions, OTC meds, etc. She will review, contact the oncologist, and make recommendations regarding any supplements, such as green tea extract, she thinks may be helpful. She also mentioned the use of imagery to visualize the destruction of cancer cells.

I feel much more hopeful given the broad-spectrum approach that is being taken.

Jamie asked me to stay another few days until he completes his first round of chemo.

Jamie has had many calls from his friends in aviation – J.V. Sclifo, Allen Kelley, Mike McDermott, Joe Taylor, Dr. Molnar, Burton Ford, Bill Baker, etc. Several are planning to visit Jim in Bloomington.

Jamie asked Dr. Chiorean about scheduling trips – for fun – and she said, "We will hope." So we hope! I hope not only for extension of life, but survival. Jamie asked if I thought he could make it a year and I said, "Certainly, expect it."

On Tuesday, August 31, the port was installed. Dr. David M. Agarwal at Indiana University Hospital installed "8 French CT Injectable AngioDynamic Smart Port" into Jamie's chest to administer his chemo treatments. This port is also known as a "power port." Everything went fine except Jamie was hungry! We drove all the way back to Bloomington before we ate. We went to Chili's for baby back ribs. They were so good.

When we got back to the house, one of the neighbors, Irene Reedy, had left a bowl of potato soup and a plate of brownies. Both refrigerators are packed with food. People are good.

Yesterday, Jamie again asked if I thought he could make it a year and I told him I was sure he could but he needs to plan on it. We talked more today about future plans. Jamie says if he comes through this, then we will go to Hawaii and just lay on the beach for a while. That would really be something!

We talked more about positive imaging. Virginia used that in her battle against sinus cancer. We also talked about the many, many prayers being offered on his behalf. I told Jamie that my daughter, Susan, is part of a Buddhist group in Denton, Texas, and they are saying chants for him. There are many avenues to heaven and God, and I believe all are valid.

On Wednesday, September 1, we left at 6 a.m. to go to Indianapolis for Jamie's first chemo treatment. Linda Kay, R.N., handled his chemo; she was wonderful. She was diligent in explaining each step for the various drugs administered through his port that comprise the Folfirinox regimen.

The only hitch with the first chemo concerned the pump that would infuse the 5-FU drug over a 46-hour period. Other drugs were completed by 1:30 p.m., but the nurse with the pump – Pam – couldn't find the order. When she found the order, Jamie's birthday was wrong. Pam, *correctly, refused to administer the drug until the order was corrected. It took two hours to get that little problem resolved.*

Thursday, September 2, was my last day in Bloomington. I was in a somber mood. Jamie is nervous about the infusion pump. He will finish with it about 2 tomorrow afternoon.

Tammy came in about 2:15 am and Jamie was waiting up for her. He had trouble sleeping because of the pump.

The pastor came to visit at 2 p.m. – Rev. David Bremer. He told us he had been diagnosed with terminal cancer of the blood six years ago. He is taking thalidomide and so far it is working. He said for us not to be afraid – specifically to me, probably because I cried so much in church on Sunday. I am not afraid for Jamie; I just realize how much I will miss him. And I grieve over the thought that the third member of our four person family unit may die from cancer.

At 2:15 p.m. I drove Tammy to Indianapolis and dropped her at her hotel at 2:50 pm. Made pretty good time! We left early because there are two football games tonight, one in Bloomington (IU) and one in Indianapolis (Colts), so we successfully avoided the football traffic.

Bob Burke, the airport manager, stopped by to bring three-dozen eggs Jamie bought from the sons of Bill Oliver of Oliver Wineries – Jim had flown with Bill Oliver.

Bob said someone called to fly with Jim on Saturday, and Bob said Jim would not be available, but just couldn't tell him about the cancer. Bob will wait and tell him in person when he gets to the airport on Saturday.

Virginia and I talked about the "Illness" and what lies ahead. Virginia has a scan scheduled in St. Louis in October and wants to move it up or cancel it altogether. I told her she must NOT cancel and needs to be sure to take care of herself.

On Friday, September 3, I left at 7:30 a.m. on my drive home and drove all the way to Texarkana, arriving at 6:30 p.m. Flying is definitely cheaper. I don't know what possessed me to drive from Dallas to Bloomington; I think I just needed the time alone in the car to think. Future trips will be by air.

I didn't sleep much last night so I need to catch up tonight.

CHAPTER 40

✦

Cancer Crisis

In October, Jim really started to feel the effects of the Folfirinox chemo treatment. He was nauseated to the point that even the smell of food cooking triggered nausea and vomiting. He started losing weight. On one visit to the oncologist, Jim told Dr. Dayton he simply couldn't keep any food down. Dr. Dayton admonished him to eat more and to eat smaller amounts more frequently. Virginia called and told me he was getting really sick from the chemo and he couldn't eat anything. He was getting weaker and rapidly losing weight. Soon he would simply throw up every time he ate. Then he developed diarrhea and Lomotil did little to control it.

On November 8, 2010, Virginia insisted on taking him to the hospital emergency room. Jim was so weak that he could not walk to the car without assistance. Virginia didn't call anyone for help but called me when they got to the hospital. She hoped he would be admitted. Fortunately, Dr. Karen Kaneru (the doctor who handled Virginia's chemo) was on call and she gave the order to admit him. I flew to Indianapolis the next day. Connie picked me up at the airport in Indianapolis and took me to the hospital. I have never seen Jamie that sick in my life.

Jamie's platelets, red and white cells were extremely low. They wanted to do an endoscopic exam of his stomach and lower digestive tract but couldn't without giving him blood transfusions to get his platelet level up to 55,000. They administered packed cells instead of whole blood. After the blood transfusions, Jim's platelet count reached 55,000 and the endoscopic exam by Dr. Ghosh, a gastroenterologist, was scheduled immediately. When they took Jamie down for the exam, he was not wearing a hospital gown, just pajama pants. He was covered with a blanket. Seeing Jim's bare shoulders, Dr. Ghosh's nurse asked Jim if he had any clothes on under the blanket.

Jim said, "Not a stitch."

Aghast, the nurse said, "Nothing?"

Jamie reached for the blanket and yanked it back to show her.

The nurse flinched, shocked that this man was going to expose himself, then started laughing when she realized he was wearing pajama pants! We all cracked up laughing. His sense of humor was intact; he couldn't resist pulling a joke on the nurse. The endoscopic exam revealed jejunitis, inflammation of the jejunum, the juncture between the duodenum and the small bowel. The biopsy did not find any cancer cells.

The treatment was to allow the inflammation to heal by restricting all food by mouth. Dr. Dayton and Dr. Ghosh prescribed Total Parenteral Nutrition (TPN), administered through a Peripherally Inserted Central Catheter (PICC line). This was separate from the Smart Port in his chest that was used for administration of his chemo. The Smart Port could be used for all things: drugs, chemo, blood draw, etc. The PICC line is put into a vein in the arm and guided into a larger vein in the chest. Jim's PICC line had two lumens (tubes outside the body) with caps on the ends. That way Jim could have more than one IV at a time while the chemo was administered through the Smart Port. The PICC line can stay in place longer than a regular IV line. While hospitalized, Jamie received IV antibiotics, fluids, blood, anti-nausea meds, and was scheduled for chemo the following week. Frequently, all three lines were in use at the same time.

After a few days on the TPN, Jamie started to recover. He was still extremely weak but the debilitating episodes of nausea, vomiting and diarrhea abated. Jim started walking around the floor in the hospital to build his strength. Virginia and I had to walk fast to keep up with him. Patients, nurses and doctors commented about how fast he walked. He pushed his IV pole and I named it Matilda. After a few days of improvement, Dr. Dayton was ready to send him home. Virginia would administer the TPN at home under the supervision of home healthcare. However, Medicare refused to approve TPN at home.

Medicare insisted that the doctors put in a stomach tube (PEG) to feed Jamie. The doctors treating Jamie said it was nothing but torture since they knew that even a sip of water caused nausea, vomiting and diarrhea. Each doctor suggested we write to our Senators and Congressman. There was no time to do that to change the course of treatment. The PEG was inserted; he was given food through the tube. The nausea, vomiting and diarrhea returned with vengeance. Jim stopped walking and we were back to Square One. This was reported to Medicare after a few days. Then Medicare approved TPN at home. Again, Jamie had to recover sufficiently to be able to go home. During this critical illness, Jamie lost about 30 pounds. The nursing care he received on the oncology floor of Bloomington Hospital was both caring and professional. Procedures and meds were carefully documented. Some meds required a second nurse to validate the orders to ensure Jim was getting the medicine and dose as ordered. I thought their attention to detail was extraordinary.

This is the only serious illness Jamie has had in his life. He has had medical checkups every six months since age 40. Other than overnight stays in the hospital from bicycle and motorcycle accidents, he has never been hospitalized

Virginia and I took turns staying with Jim at the hospital, alternating days and nights. Tammy came for a few days and stayed with him long enough to see how sick he was. It was a sobering experience, but we got through it. Dr. Fadi Haddad and Dr. Souheil Haddad came by to see Jamie every day he was in the hospital. The Drs. Haddad each gave Jamie a surgical cap to wear on his walks around the hospital floor. When you have no hair, your head gets cold! Fadi gave him one with airplanes and Souheil gave him the Sponge Bob Square Pants cap. Fadi and Souheil continue to be unfailingly cheerful, optimistic and comforting. The Drs. Haddad and their wives have been bright lights, close and caring friends, in helping Jim and Virginia through his cancer treatment.

Three weeks and three days after admission Jamie was discharged on November 29, 2010. The discharge summary, dictated by Dr. Dayton, stated:

> *I would note that his hospitalization was prolonged by 11 days due to Medicare's insistence that we torture him with tube feedings to prove that his severe jejunitis would indeed be exacerbated by this therapy as predicted by all of the doctors who had seen the patient and been involved in his care. I would point out that this cost more money than the TPN for 3 months would have cost in the first place and resulted in total frustration and depression of the patient and his wife.*

I plan to draft letters to the appropriate congressional representatives for Indiana from Jim and Virginia and for Texas from me.
The discharge summary listed the following discharge medications:
(1) 5-FU, leucovorin, irinotecan, oxaliplatin and Sandostatin as ordered by chemotherapy;
(2) Clinimix 5/29 – 2200 mL IV once daily for 12 hours starting at 8 p.m. (TPN);
(3) Intralipid 20% fat emulsion IV once daily starting at 10 p.m. [added to the TPN];
(4) Diflucan 200 mg p.o. daily x 7 days (for Thrush);
(5) Lomotil 1 to 2 tablets p.o. after each loose stool as directed for diarrhea;
(6) Imodium 4 mg p.o. every 6 hours scheduled, as needed for constipation;
(7) Levemir 10 units subcu q.h.s. (insulin was given by the Levemir pen and also added to the TPN mixture);
(8) Probiotics 2 capsules p.o. b.i.d.;
(9) Prilosec 20 mg p.o. q.h.s.; to reduce stomach acid
(10) Zofran ODT 4 mg p.o. every 6 hours p.r.n. nausea and vomiting;
(11) Phenergan 12.5 to 25 mg p.o. every 4 hours p.r.n nausea and vomiting;

(12) Phenergan suppositories 25 mg PR every 6 hours p.r.n. nausea and vomiting;
(13) Saliva substitute 5 mL as directed; to relieve dryness in mouth
(14) Simethicone 80 mg p.o. q.i.d. a.c. and h.s. p.r.n for gas buildup;
(15) Zocor 20 mg p.o. q.h.s., currently optional; and
(16) Saline nasal spray each nostril as directed p.r.n. nasal congestion.

Taking the meds, frequency taken, TPN, recording blood pressure (BP), pulse, temperature and blood sugar was daunting, so I prepared a checklist. This listed all meds to be taken throughout a 24-hour period. We noted the time taken and the time and values of blood sugar levels, temperature, BP, pulse and number of loose stools.

Bloomington Hospital Home Health care came out to train us on connecting and disconnecting the TPN. Colleen and John Swanson and Irene and Dennis Reedy are both neighbors and close friends of Virginia and Jim. Irene is a retired Registered Nurse. Colleen and Irene are cancer survivors and both came over for the TPN training. Virginia and I were both nervous and apprehensive about this responsibility. It was a great comfort to have Irene and Colleen with us to catch whatever we might not understand or hear.

Virginia and I took turns connecting the TPN each evening and disconnecting each morning. There were such detailed procedures to follow and hooking up the TPN was not easy! Because it was so complicated, I prepared a checklist for us to follow to make sure we remembered each step. We had to take his temperature, blood pressure, pulse and check his blood sugar. The TPN was delivered in weekly batches by home health care. Before hooking it up, we had to clip the line and add a dark yellow substance (lipids) to the bag and mix it in thoroughly. Next we added a shot of insulin. Then we had to hang the bag on an IV pole, attach the line to the PICC line, unclip the line and turn on the computer to monitor the drip for the next 12 hours. Each morning and evening we checked his temperature, blood sugar and blood pressure. I prepared sheets to record this information and listed all the medicines Jamie had to take throughout each day – a separate sheet for each day. In the evening we gave him a shot of insulin with an insulin pen. The next morning many of the same procedures were repeated, but this time after the TPN bag was removed, we had to flush the PICC line *with saline and cap it off with a new sterile cap. The saline always gave Jamie a bad taste in his mouth, so he countered that by putting an Altoid in his mouth to disguise the taste. He had tried lollipops but found the Altoids to be far more effective. Kim, the home health nurse, came every Monday to see how Jim was doing. The pharmacist who mixed the TPN was also helpful in making whatever adjustments were required and frequently delivered the TPN himself. The home health service was valuable, supportive and comforting in this journey.*

After a few weeks, Jamie developed an increase in weakness. They gave him IVs of fluid when he had chemo and that seemed to help. So the extra fluid was added to the TPN but that increased the time for the overnight IV from 12 hours to 18 hours. That continued for a few weeks before the fluid was discontinued and dropped back to 12 hours every night.

I returned to Dallas January 15, 2011. TPN was discontinued on March 11, 2011.

CHAPTER 41

∽

Treatment with Theraspheres

*B*y January 2011, Jamie developed neuropathy – numbness and tingling in his hands and feet. This symptom of toxicity indicated the need to find an alternative cancer treatment.

In September, Virginia sent Jim's medical records and CT scans, pathology report on the biopsy and slides to Johns Hopkins Medicine International with a request for a remote second opinion, a review of the records only without actually examining the patient. The second opinion, dated September 30, 2010, was prepared by Dr. Daniel Laheru. It contained Dr. Laheru's biography, a review of Jim's medical information, and Dr. Laheru's recommendations. The second opinion agreed with the use of Folfirinox as first-line chemotherapy and suggested a number of different therapies to consider if the Folfirinox became too toxic. That was encouraging.

Through her research, Connie discovered that the liver tumors could be treated with microspheres – tiny glass beads filled with radioactive material are put into either the right or left lobe of the liver *through the artery that feeds the liver. When we approached each of the oncologists we consulted in Indiana, all advised us to forget that procedure. Jamie's tumors were too diffuse across the liver; the treatment was not proven to be effective; the infusion of microspheres was too expensive.*

Since none of us is too good at taking "No" for an answer, we pursued the microsphere treatment. Through one of her friends in Germany, Connie was connected to a doctor in Italy, Dr. Riccardo Lencioni of the University of Pisa in Italy. Connie exchanged emails with Dr. Lencioni who gave her the names of two doctors in the U.S. who use microspheres in the treatment of metastatic liver cancer: Dr. Said Salem at Northwestern University Hospital in Chicago and Dr. Jeff Geschwind at Johns Hopkins University Hospital in Baltimore.

I called Dr. Salem in September to discuss treatment with microspheres just as Jamie started chemo with Folfirinox. I talked to his Physician's Assistant, Karen Marshall, and she was helpful in providing information. She said it is too early to think about microspheres – he must take chemo first and then consider this treatment option after the cancer is under control. She gave my message to Dr. Salem and he immediately called me back to make sure Jamie had started chemo treatment. I told him yes, Jim was taking Folfirinox. Dr. Salem said when he could no longer take chemo would be the time to consider treatment with the microspheres, but emphasized the importance of taking chemo first. I was impressed that out of concern for the patient that the doctor had quickly called to make sure that Jamie was being treated with chemo.

In late January 2011, Connie sent emails to Dr. Geschwind and Dr. Salem. Jim and Virginia opted to go to Johns Hopkins Hospital and scheduled an appointment to meet with the multidisciplinary group that treats pancreatic cancer. I returned to Bloomington to go with them to Baltimore. The first appointment was Tuesday, February 1, 2011. We met with three different doctors:

Dr. Kenzo Hirose, liver surgeon
Dr. David Cosgrove, medical oncologist
Dr. J. F. Geschwind and the Interventional Radiology Team

Before we arrived, the multidisciplinary group met and reviewed Jim's medical records and CT scans. When we met with each doctor separately, we were advised that: (1) Dr. Hirose said the tumors were inoperable (that was a short meeting); (2) Dr. Cosgrove indicated the group had decided on treatment with microspheres and chemo must be discontinued for the infusion of the microspheres; and (3) Dr. Geschwind and his team confirmed they agreed that at this point, the best treatment would be to treat the liver tumors with microspheres. Dr. Geschwind said the first step would be to make an appointment to do an angiogram to map the blood flow in the liver. If that looked okay, they would put the TheraSpheres (brand name) into the right lobe of the liver since 90% of the tumors were located in the right lobe of the liver. If that proved to be successful, they would do the same procedure in the left lobe of the liver.

Upon our arrival in Baltimore, a snowstorm closed the airport. We were scheduled to return the next day, Wednesday. Since we were snowed in, we asked Dr. Geschwind if he could do the mapping angiogram since we had to stay over anyway. He checked schedules, scheduled an MRI on Wednesday and scheduled the procedure on Friday. We scheduled our return flight on Saturday.

When we left Bloomington, we expected to be gone overnight and Home Health said it would be okay to skip the TPN for one night. When it turned out we would be there all week, we called and Home Health sent the TPN to our hotel via FedEx overnight delivery. However, something was left out of the package and Jamie didn't get the TPN that entire week, but did not appear to have any ill effects. He could eat small amounts of real food. We were buoyed by the promise of this new treatment. After the MRI and liver mapping was complete, the treatment was declared a GO!

The treatment was scheduled for February 25, 2011. On February 18, 2011, Virginia was scheduled to go to St. Louis to have a small cancerous spot removed from her left eyelid – the spot that had previously been declared "Okay" was actually a small cancer caused by radiation from her sinus cancer treatment. Connie took her mother to St. Louis and I stayed in Bloomington with Jim. Virginia and Connie returned on Saturday, February 19, 2011. The surgery was successful but she had to return for follow-up treatment on February 22 and back home the next day. Leaving Virginia at home to rest, Jamie and I went to Baltimore on February 24 for the infusion of TheraSpheres in the right lobe of his liver on February 25. We returned to Bloomington on Saturday, February 26.

I returned to Dallas some time the next week. Jim and Virginia went back to Baltimore on March 21 for a consultation with Dr. Cosgrove and an MRI on March 22. The MRI indicated the liver tumors were either dead or dying. That was good news.

Jim and Virginia returned to Baltimore and met with Dr. Geschwind on April 10. Dr. Geschwind said with the success of the first treatment he thought it would be appropriate to treat the left lobe of the liver. That treatment was scheduled and performed on May 25, 2011. Jim's PICC line was removed April 18, 2011. James and Tammy visited their Dad in late April.

During the time of the treatment with TheraSpheres, from February 4 to May 31, 2011, Jim did not receive chemotherapy. He started feeling better and his hair started growing back. But that was short lived.

Chemotherapy was started again.

CHAPTER 42

More Chemo

*D*r. Dayton felt it was time to resume chemotherapy and recommended the use of Gemcitabine and Abraxane. Abraxane was the drug being tested in the clinical trial at Indiana University Hospital by Dr. Chiorean. While Jamie didn't get into the clinical trial, now he was getting the chance to see what he missed.

The first new chemo was on May 31, 2011. The second chemo was scheduled for June 14, 2011 but was cancelled because his blood count was too low. It was rescheduled for June 17. The blood counts were:

	06/14/11	06/17/11	Normal Range
Platelets	124	185	150 – 450
RBC	3.69	3.76	4.0 – 6.0
WBC	1.4	2.1	4.5 – 10.5

Jim had a total of six treatments with Gemcitabine and Abraxane. The hair was the first to go. Next to go was his appetite. He started losing weight and his weight dropped below 150. Jim continued walking but no longer went to the YMCA. He walked 30 minutes twice a day inside the house. Sometimes he would walk in 10-minute increments until he completed one hour. He was too weak to go outside. Finally, Virginia and Jim told Dr. Dayton that after each chemo treatment he felt so badly that it just knocked him down for 12 of the 14 days between treatments.

Dr. Dayton ordered another CT scan and changed the chemo to Gemcitabine and Tarceva. Tarceva is a tablet taken by mouth daily. The cost of the first prescription for 30 pills was over $2,000. On the second prescription, the price was dropped to $375 because the CVS pharmacist argued about it. On the third prescription, CVS said the prescription had to be sent to a specialty pharmacy by mail and that prescription was a little over $200. Apparently, Medicare made this decision. As of November 8, 2011, he had completed six treatments with Gemcitabine and Tarceva.

Jim felt better with the new chemo. However, he worried that it is not working since he feels better. Cancer is pervasive and all health care providers continue to tell us that there is no hope for cure with pancreatic cancer. It is difficult not to worry. Dr. Dayton ordered a CT scan to see if it is working because Jamie had been worried about the rising level of CA 19-9 markers – up to 1231 on October 25, 2011. It is working. All tumors are smaller. Jamie feels good. Now he just needs to learn to enjoy feeling good on the days that it happens.

On October 15th I returned to Bloomington to work on the book with Jamie. I returned to Dallas on November 15th. We made significant progress on the book.

CHAPTER 43

Unrelated Hiccup

The Sunday before November 15th, Jamie got sick at church and we left before the social hour was over. He was extremely nauseated all the way home and developed pain in his back on the right side that radiated around to the front. When we got home he went straight to bed and threw up. Pain did not subside so Virginia called Dr. Fadi Haddad. He said he would be there in about 30 minutes, but he arrived much sooner. After looking him over, he said we could either wait to see what happens or go to the emergency room. Fadi thinks it may be a kidney stone or it may be that one of the liver tumors has started bleeding. Jamie wanted to go on to the ER and not wait because the pain was getting progressively worse.

We headed to the ER and first thing they did was to give him shots for nausea and pain. Then they sent him off to get a CT scan. When we got the results, they didn't see any reason for the pain and nausea. The ER doctor admitted him to the hospital. Dr. Dayton was out of town on vacation and we hoped that Dr. Koneru would be on call. The next *morning Dr. Koneru came by to see Jamie and discussed his symptoms. She decided to go talk to the radiologist who did the CT scan. When she returned, she reported that the cause of the problem was a kidney stone and she called on a nephrologist to handle the treatment. The nephologist came by later and said he wanted to keep Jim in the hospital for a few days to see if the kidney stone would pass without intervention, and if not, the doctor would remove it. By Friday, the kidney stone had moved down a little, and the doctor removed it. In the meantime, they put an IV pump of pain medicine so Jamie could push a button to manage the pain. They continued to give him meds for the nausea.*

Dr. Dayton returned from his European cruise on Friday. He told Jamie that he looked at his CT scan and the chemo was not working. He was going to think about it over the weekend, and when Jamie returned to his office for chemo, they would decide what to do next.

When Jamie went in for his chemo, Dr. Dayton said he misread the CT scan – the chemo was working and everything was fine. Jim, still concerned about the CA 19-9 count, asked Dr. Dayton about the fact they were still rising.

Dr. Dayton replied, "I don't treat the numbers."

I returned to Dallas on November 15th as planned. Jamie was released from the hospital on Saturday after I left.

CHAPTER 44

⚜

Continuing Chemo and Problems

While I was in Bloomington, I consolidated a lot of the material we had gathered, got rid of duplicates and decided what needed to be saved and what could be discarded. Then I prepared spreadsheets on his treatment: one for chemo treatments, scans and other procedures; one for lab work to track Alkaline Phosphatase values, Glucose values, Platelet counts, RBC and WBC counts all compared to normal values for each; and one for the worrisome CA 19-9 tumor markers. [See Appendix F: Jim McCartney, Treatment for Pancreatic Cancer]

Jamie had two more chemo treatments of Gemcitabine and Tarceva on November 22nd and December 7th. His hair started growing back and the tumor marker count continued to increase. Jamie worries that he does not feel as bad as he did when he was on Folfirinox and Abraxane. He just instinctively feels that things are not going right.

In December, Jamie watched as the tumor marker counts increased. He looked at the spreadsheet. He started out in August 2010 with a tumor marker count of 22,635. The first chemo treatment with Folfirinox was

September 1. The tumor marker count has progressed as follows on the various chemo regimens:

Folfirinox: 09/01/10 – 01/26/11	22,635 to 224
Theraspheres: 02/25/11 – 05/25/11	224 to 972
Gemzar & Abraxane: 05/31/11 – 08/12/11	972 to 474
Gemzar & Tarceva: 08/30/11 to 12/07/11	474 to 8,394
Gemzar & Xeloda: 12/21/11 to 01/12/11	8,394 to 3,927

Xeloda appears to be working!
On December 20, 2011, Dr. Dayton ordered a PT scan that states:

"IMPRESSION: 1. Since 08/24/10, the liver has shrunken and has multiple scars and there is now a significant amount of ascites (fluid) and increased linear and nodular markings in the mesenteric and omental fat. It is difficult to determine how much of the ascites is due to liver disease versus peritoneal carcinomatosis. There are several implants in the abdomen (antrum of stomach, omentum, pouch of Douglas, and left side of rectum). 2. The liver had a mixed response. Some of the large lesions seen on 08/24/10 have responded favorably. There are multiple liver lesions however, at least some of which have increased in size since 08/24/10. The distortion of the liver makes it difficult to compare all of the liver lesions. 3. No pulmonary parenchymal nodules are seen. There are multiple coarse linear opacities in the basilar segments of the lower lobes consistent with foci of subsegmental atelectasis or scarring developing since 08/24/10. ADDENDUM Impression: Compared with 11/03/11 CT scan, the amount of ascites has increased and the implants on the anterior antrum of the stomach and in the omentum appear larger by CT than on 11/03/11. Bibasilar focal atelectatic changes have progressed."

Following are recent scans that show the changes following treatments:

03/22/11 MRI	Increased number of necrotic (dead) lesions in right lobe of liver
03/28/11 CT	Most hepatic metastases are either unchanged or slightly smaller than they were on 01/03/11. One new lesion in left lobe of liver
05/10/11 MRI	Index lesions stable in size and enhancement. Non-index lesions increased in size.
08/29/11 CT	Size and number of liver metastases have not significantly changed. Significant increase in amount of ascites and now infiltrative changes involve the root of the mesentery and omentum consistent with progression of peritoneal carcinomatosis.
11/03/11 CT	Decrease in size of some of the hepatic metastases and no change in number. Moderate to large amount of ascites, slightly less than on 08/29/11.
12/20/11 PT	See Impression cited in previous paragraph.

It appears to me that since the original diagnosis in August 2010, there has been no increase in the size of the tumor in the pancreas. Isn't that good? The liver is further compromised but some of the tumors have gone and others have grown – that appears to be a net effect of keeping the level of disease in the liver stable but so much appears to be happening that I don't understand. What does the word "implant" mean in the context of the last PT scan report? What is the effect of "peritoneal carcinomatosis?" What is it? What is the effect and meaning of the increased ascites other than making him miserable? What does "foci of subsegmental atelectasis or scarring developing since 08/24/10" mean with respect to his lungs? Translation, please? How can he be comforted at this stage?

There is always the question that no one will answer: How much longer can he live?

Xeloda appears to be working! The CA 19-9 tumor markers took a dive; the test on January 12, 2012, revealed a drop of more than 50%, from 8,394 to 3,927.

The ascites (buildup of abdominal fluid) increased and the paracentesis procedure (removal of abdominal fluid by x-ray guided needle) was performed on January 10, 2012, for the second time. Four liters of fluid was removed from Jim's abdomen. Dr. Wolfer, who performed the procedure, suggested that Jim get a standing order from Dr. Dayton to have the fluid removed in the future. It had been four months since it was removed. Jim has experienced extreme pain and discomfort. Removal of the fluid gave him relief from pain and discomfort. But the fluid returned almost immediately. Dr. Dayton does not think it should be removed; other doctors don't see why not. Jim got the standing order for paracentesis, so Dr. Dayton has changed his mind and now agrees.

Jim had the paracentesis procedure on Monday, January 23, 2012. They removed 6.5 liters of fluid from his abdomen. Dr. Wolfer scheduled Jim to come in each Monday for paracentesis. The procedure makes him weak but relieves the pain caused by the pressure of the fluid in his abdomen.

Jim went for chemo January 20, 2012, but they could not give it; he was incorrectly given a Neulasta shot the day after his last chemo, one week earlier, when it should have been scheduled for after the chemo scheduled today. Chemo was postponed to January 27. Will they give him another Neulasta shot?

Jim, Virginia and I met in Houston on January 24 to have dinner at Bill and Kate Baker's home with J.V. Sclifo, Gary Portzline and their wives on January 25. Allen Kelley had to be at M.D. Anderson that day for several tests in connection with his battle with prostate cancer. Jim, Bill and I visited with Allen and Sue at M.D. Anderson for about an hour and a half between tests. It was a good meeting but very emotional for Jim and Allen.

CHAPTER 45

Hospice

During the week of February 6, 2012, Virginia took Jamie to the ER twice. He has rapidly gotten weaker and cannot hold down any food. The doctor said it was time to call his children and me to come see him for perhaps the last time. I arrived Sunday, February 12, at 2:00 pm. James and Tambra both arrived about mid-afternoon.

Jamie wanted to go to the ER as soon as we all arrived. However, he felt better (because we were there, I think) and decided to wait until Monday morning. Sunday night was rough. Monday morning we got Jim to the ER about 9:00 am. The ER was full of people and Jim was at the end of the line. Since he had an appointment at 11:00 am for paracentesis, Virginia went to advise that doctor that he was in the ER and probably could not withstand the procedure. I told the admitting nurse that Jim needed to lie down immediately because he was feeling faint. They quickly brought in a bed and put him into an intake room. Dr. Wolfer's office intervened with the ER staff to get him quickly admitted to the hospital. He was critically ill. James, Jim's son, stayed in the hospital with his Dad on Monday night.

Dr. Dayton came in on Tuesday morning and said the trips to the ER were counterproductive. He said Jim has reached the point where the chemo was no longer effective. Paracentesis had resulted in his wasting away. Dr. Dayton said he could tell because of the hollowness of his temples. He recommended hospice and said he would have them come by to discuss this within the hour. For some reason I went home. I think the hospital room was crowded. Virginia met with hospice and they convinced her to admit Jim to a new hospice facility. First, the paracentesis procedure was performed and six liters removed from his abdomen. Then he was transferred by ambulance to Indiana University Health Hospice House on February 14, 2012.

As soon as Virginia called that he was transferred, I went over and found the facility ideal for their needs. Jim did not want to be in a hospice facility, but at the same time he didn't want to be in the living room at home, as our Mother had been in October 2009 when she died of lymphoma. Virginia and Connie spent the night with Jim. Connie took care of Jim and Virginia got a reasonable amount of sleep. I also got a good night's sleep at the house and did not wake until 7:00 am.

After 8:00 am I arrived at hospice and Virginia went home and slept all day until someone called and woke her up. Dr. Bomba, Medical Director for the hospice, came by and examined Jim about mid-day and said Jim would probably get worse over the next couple of days. On the other hand, he said his lungs are clear and he still had a strong heartbeat. I said he was having trouble getting water through the straw and Dr. Bomba said he really didn't need to drink water and it would be better to swab his mouth with water to keep it moist. Dr. Bomba said the main thing now is to keep him comfortable and all efforts will go to that end. The nursing staff was very attentive by turning him every couple of hours, giving him pain medication, and checking to see how he was doing and if he needed anything.

Dr. Fadi Haddad stopped by this evening. Virginia asked about the swelling in Jim's hands and he said that was because he has no albumin (protein). He added that his liver is completely gone. Fadi said Jim has really put up a good fight and now must let go and put it in

God's hands. Jim is pretty much sleeping around the clock but he seems peaceful. I am sure he knows that he is dearly loved.

The final vigil; we awaited the end of Jim's life on earth as he approached his new life in the hands of God.

Jim died peacefully just before 11:00 am EST on Friday, February 17, 2012. He did not make a sound; he simply stopped breathing and his heart stopped beating.

CHAPTER 46

Facts About Pancreatic Cancer

After learning about my brother's diagnosis of Stage IV Pancreatic Cancer with metastases to the liver, I searched for as much information as I could find about the disease. While I knew it was the really bad boy among cancers, I had no idea so little research had been done when compared to lung, breast, colon and prostate cancers. According to the Pancreatic Cancer Action Network, of all cancers tracked by both the American Cancer Society and the National Cancer Institute, pancreatic cancer is the only one with a relative five-year survival rate in the single digits.

Pancreatic cancer is the 10th most commonly diagnosed cancer, but the 4th leading cause of cancer deaths in the United States. More than 80% of pancreatic cancer patients present with advanced, unresectable (inoperable) disease. Even in patients who undergo "curative" resection (surgery), approximately 20% percent will reach the five year survival rate.

The statistics have remained virtually unchanged for the last 40 years!
Research dedicated to pancreatic cancer receives just approximately 2 percent of the federal dollars distributed by the National Cancer Institute (NCI).

There is no long-term and comprehensive strategy in place to improve survival. The Pancreatic Cancer Research & Education Act (S. 362/H.R. 733) will ensure that the NCI develops a long-term comprehensive strategic plan for developing early diagnostic tools and treatment options that will increase the survival rate for pancreatic cancer patients. <u>Please urge your senators and congressman to support this legislation.</u>

For further information about pancreatic cancer, please go to:

www.pancan.org – **The Pancreatic Cancer Action Network**
Mission: The Pancreatic Cancer Action Network is a nationwide network of people dedicated to working together to advance research, support patients and create hope for those affected by pancreatic cancer.

www.lustgarten.org – **The Lustgarten Foundation**
Mission: To advance the science related to the diagnosis, treatment, cure and prevention of pancreatic cancer.

Both of these organizations are dedicated to raising awareness of pancreatic cancer and advancing pancreatic cancer research.
A portion of the proceeds from this book will be donated to pancreatic cancer research.

Glossary

Term	Definition
ADF	Automatic Directional Finder – Navigational Aid instrument.
Aileron	Moveable part of wing at outer trailing edge – roll control.
ALEA	Air Line Employee Association, union for ground employees in the airline industry.
ALPA	Air Line Pilots Association, union for commercial airline pilots.
ATC	Air Traffic Control.
ATR rating	Air Transport Rating, highest rating for a pilot; FAA Line.
CAB	Civil Aviation Board.
Cam shaft	Device to open or close intake and exhaust value in piston engine.
CFI	Certified Flight Instructor rating issued by FAA.
CFI-I	Certified Flight Instructor-Instruments rating issued by FAA.
Check Airman	Pilot designated by the FAA to administer check rides for other pilots to ensure that their skills in the Cockpit are efficient and meet the parameters set by the FAA.
Check Ride	FAA requirement for testing pilots to ensure that their cockpit skills are efficient and meet the parameters established by the FAA.
CRM	Cockpit Resource Management, a program for the effective use of resources in the cockpit.
CVR	Cockpit Voice Recorder, one of two so-called "black" boxes that are painted neon orange; 30 minute loop

	tape that records the last thirty minutes of conversation in the cockpit.
ECM	Electronic Counter Measure pod to record radar frequencies.
Elevator	The elevators are located on the trailing part of the horizontal stabilizers on the tail of the airplane. The elevators move up and down to control the pitch (angle) of the airplane.
FAA	Federal Aviation Administration.
FDR	Flight Data Recorder, one of two so-called "black" boxes that are painted neon orange; records all flight data from beginning to end of each flight.
FSS	Flight Service Station manned by FAA personnel.
Heading bug	Movable arrow on the directional gyro compass to show the desired heading (direction of the flight).
HIMS	Human Intervention Motivation Study, formal program for pilots who may require treatment for alcohol and/or drug abuse.
IFR	Instrument Flight Rules; weather determines the requirement for use of IFR.
ILS Approach	Instrument Landing System – gives vertical and horizontal information; gives guidance to land.
LEC	Local Executive Council, captain's rep and co-pilot's rep for each crew base
MEC	Master Executive Council: Two LECs, when they meet, are the MEC
MEC Chairman	Member elected as MEC Chairman by all of the LEC.
NTSB	National Transportation and Safety Board.
OEW	Operating Empty Weight of each aircraft.
Rudder	The rudder is the vertical part of the trailing edge of the tail of the airplane. The rudder is a movable part that moves left and right to control the direction of the nose of the aircraft.
Scud running	Flying below the clouds very close to the ground.
Spoilers	Panels that come up when landing to put weight on the wheels for better braking.

GLOSSARY

Sterile Cockpit No conversation allowed about anything other than the flight at hand.
Trip Pairings   Pairings of Individual Flights put together. For example, a trip pairing may consist of three flights that originate in Houston, goes to Phoenix, then to Los Angeles, with three separate flight numbers.
VFR   Visual Flight Rules, weather is not a factor, clear visibility.
VOR Station   Visual Orientation Range, a ground navigation aid.

Appendix

Appendix A

Chronology of Jim McCartney's Aviation Career

Date	Event
Aviation Licenses and Ratings	
12/27/1958	Solo in C172
08/10/1959	Private Pilot License in C150
08/25/1960	Commercial Pilot License in C150
11/01/1960	Instrument Rating in C180
11/06/1960	Multi-Engine Rating in Lockheed L-12
01/06/1966	Air Transport Rating (ATR) in Twin Beechcraft
11/15/1997	Flight Instructor and Instrument Instructor ratings (CFII)
Aviation Employment	
01/15/1960 – 07/12/1960	Madrid Oil & Gas, Houston, Texas
07/13/1960 – 07/02/1963	Pan American Sulphur, Houston, Texas
07/03/1963 – 09/11/1963	Eastern Airlines (EAL), Washington, DC
09/12/1963 – 01/06/1967	Pan American Sulphur, Houston, Texas
01/07/1967 – 05/13/1967	Trans Texas Airlines (TTA), Houston, Texas – *furloughed*
05/16/1967 – 12/01/1967	Pan American Sulphur – *recalled to TTA*
12/02/1967 – 12/30/1981	Trans Texas Airlines, n/k/a Continental Airlines
01/01/1982 – 12/16/1986	Continental Airlines Bankruptcy followed by Pilot Strike
12/17/1986 – 10/01/1987	Trans Star Airlines, Houston, Texas
11/10/1987 – 07/08/1989	Evergreen Airline, hauled military cargo, check airman, various AFBs
08/02/1989 – 10/31/1997	America West Airlines, Phoenix – check airman – *retired at age 60*
11/01/1997 – 06/04/1999	Flight Instructor in my C150, Newport, Arkansas
06/05/1999 – 08/06/2001	Director of the Arkansas State College Aviation Program, Newport
January 2000 – April 2007	Member and Chairman, Newport Airport Commission
08/06/2001 – 10/31/2007	Taylor Made Ambulance, Newport – corporate pilot
11/01/2007 – 08/12/2010	BMG Aviation-flight instructor and charter pilot, Bloomington, Indiana

Appendix B-1

AIRCRAFT ACCIDENT REPORT

TEXAS INTERNATIONAL AIRLINES, INC.
CONVAIR 600, N94230
MENA, ARKANSAS
SEPTEMBER 27, 1973

ADOPTED APRIL 11, 1974

NATIONAL TRANSPORTATION SAFETY BOARD
Washington, D.C. 20591
REPORT NUMBER: NTSB-AAR-74-4

APPENDIX

Appendix B-2

TECHNICAL REPORT STANDARD TITLE PAGE

1. Report No. NTSB-AAR-74-4	2. Government Accession No.	3. Recipient's Catalog No.
4. Title and Subtitle Aircraft Accident Report: "Texas International Airlines, Inc., CV-600, N94230, Mena, Arkansas, September 27, 1973		5. Report Date April 11, 1974
		6. Performing Organization Code
7. Author(s)		8. Performing Organization Report No.
9. Performing Organization Name and Address National Transportation Safety Board Bureau of Aviation Safety Washington, D. C. 20591		10. Work Unit No. 1267
		11. Contract or Grant No.
		13. Type of Report and Period Covered Aircraft Accident Report September 27, 1973
12. Sponsoring Agency Name and Address NATIONAL TRANSPORTATION SAFETY BOARD Washington, D. C. 20591		
		14. Sponsoring Agency Code

15. Supplementary Notes
This report does not contain aviation Safety Recommendations.

16. Abstract At 2052, September 27, 1973, a Texas International Airlines, Inc.; CV-600, N94230, crashed in the Ouachita Mountain Range, Arkansas. The accident occurred 80 nautical miles north-northwest of Texarkana and 8.5 nautical miles north-northwest of Mena, Arkansas. Eight passengers and three crewmembers were killed, and the aircraft was destroyed. The aircraft was making a round trip flight from Dallas, Texas, to Memphis, Tennessee, with intermediate stops at Texarkana, El Dorado, and Pine Bluff, Arkansas. The accident occurred during the westbound flight from El Dorado to Texarkana. The flight was conducted at night under visual flight rules. A cold front with associated thunderstorms and instrument meteorological conditions existed between El Dorado and Texarkana. The crew deviated about 100 nautical miles north of the direct course to their destination and attempted to operate the aircraft visually after instrument meteorological conditions. No radio transmissions were made by the crew after the aircraft was found at 1730 c.d.t., on September 30, 1973.
The National Transportation Safety Board determines that the probable cause of the accident was the captain's attempt to operate the flight under visual flight rules in night and instrument meteorological conditions, without using all the navigational aids and information available to him; and his deviation from the preplanned route, without adequate position information. The carrier did not monitor and control adequately the actions of the flightcrew or the progress of the flight.

17. Key Words
VFR Flight Plan, Instrument Meteorological Flight Conditions, Visual Navigation, Thunderstorms, Search and Rescue, Night Flight, Dispatcher/Pilot Coordination, CV-600

18. Distribution Statement
This report is available to the public through the National Technical Information Service, Springfield, Virginia 22151

19. Security Classification (of this report) UNCLASSIFIED	20. Security Classification (of this page) UNCLASSIFIED	21. No. of Pages 37	22. Price

NTSB Form 1765.2 (11/70)

11

303

Appendix C-1

ALPA Code of Ethics

An Air Line Pilot will keep uppermost in his mind that the safety, comfort, and well-being of the passengers who entrust their lives to him are his first and greatest responsibility.

• He will never permit external pressures or personal desires to influence his judgment, nor will he knowingly do anything that could jeopardize flight safety.

• He will remember that an act of omission can be as hazardous as a deliberate act of commission, and he will not neglect any detail that contributes to the safety of his flight, or perform any operation in a negligent or careless manner.

• Consistent with flight safety, he will at all times operate his aircraft in a manner that will contribute to the comfort, peace of mind, and well-being of his passengers, instilling in them trust in him and the airline he represents.

• Once he has discharged his primary responsibility for the safety and comfort of his passengers, he will remember that they depend upon him to do all possible to deliver them to their destination at the scheduled time.

• If disaster should strike, he will take whatever action he deems necessary to protect the lives of his passengers and crew.

An Air Line Pilot will faithfully discharge the duty he owes the airline that employs him and whose salary makes possible his way of life.

• He will do all within his powers to operate his aircraft efficiently and on schedule in a manner that will not cause damage or unnecessary maintenance.

• He will respect the officers, directors, and supervisors of his airline, remembering that respect does not entail subservience.

• He will faithfully obey all lawful directives given by his supervisors, but will insist and, if necessary, refuse to obey any directives that, in his considered judgment, are not lawful or will adversely affect flight safety. He will remember that in the final analysis the responsibility for safe completion of the flight rests upon his shoulders.

• He will not knowingly falsify any log or record, nor will he condone such action by other crew members.

• He will remember that a full month's salary demands a full and fair month's work. On his days off, he will not engage in any occupation or activity that will diminish his efficiency or bring discredit to his profession.

• He will realize that he represents the airline to all who meet him and will at all times keep his personal appearance and conduct above reproach.

APPENDIX

Appendix C-2

- He will give his airline, its officers, directors, and supervisors the full loyalty that is their due, and will refrain from speaking ill of them. If he feels it necessary to reveal and correct conditions that are not conducive to safe operations and harmonious relations, he will direct his criticism to the proper authorities within ALPA.

- He will hold his airline's business secrets in confidence, and will take care that they are not improperly revealed.

An Air Line Pilot will accept the responsibilities as well as the rewards of command and will at all times so conduct himself both on duty and off as to instill and merit the confidence and respect of his crew, his fellow employees, and his associates within the profession.

- He will know and understand the duties of each member of his crew. If in command, he will be firm but fair, explicit yet tolerant of deviations that do not affect the safe and orderly completion of the flight. He will be efficient yet relaxed, so that the duties of the crew may be carried out in a harmonious manner.

- If in command, he will expect efficient performance of each crew member's duties, yet he will overlook small discrepancies and refrain from unnecessary and destructive criticism, so that the crew member will retain his self-respect and cooperative attitude. A frank discussion of minor matters of technique and performance after the flight will create goodwill and a desire to be helpful, whereas sharp criticism and peremptory orders at the moment will result only in the breakdown of morale and an inefficient, halting performance of future duties.

- An Air Line Pilot will remember that his is a profession heavily dependent on training during regular operations and, if in command, will afford his flight crew members every reasonable opportunity, consistent with safety and efficiency, to learn and practice. He will endeavor to instill in his crew a sense of pride and responsibility. In making reports on the work and conduct of his crew members, he will avoid personal prejudices, make his reports factual and his criticisms constructive so that actions taken as a result of his reports will improve the knowledge and skill of his crew members, rather than bring discredit, endanger their livelihood, and threaten their standing in the profession.

- While in command, the Air Line Pilot will be mindful of the welfare of his crew. He will see to it that his crew are properly lodged and cared for, particularly during unusual operating conditions. When cancellations result in deadheading, he will ensure that proper arrangements are made for the transportation of his crew before he takes care of himself.

An Air Line Pilot will conduct his affairs with other members of the profession and with ALPA in such a manner as to bring credit to the profession and ALPA as well as to himself.

- He will not falsely or maliciously injure the professional reputation, prospects, or job security of another pilot, yet if he knows of professional incompetence or conduct detrimental to the profession or to ALPA, he will not shrink from revealing this to the proper authorities within ALPA, so that the weak member may be brought up to the standards demanded, or ALPA and the profession alike may be rid of one unworthy to share its rewards.

- He will conduct his affairs with ALPA and its members in accordance with the rules laid down in the Constitution and By-Laws of ALPA and with the policies and interpretations promulgated therefrom. Whenever possible, he will attend all meetings of ALPA open to him and will take an active part in its

305

Appendix C-3

activities and in meetings of other groups calculated to improve air safety and the standing of the profession.

• An Air Line Pilot shall refrain from any action whereby, for his personal benefit or gain, he take advantage of the confidence reposed in him by his fellow members. If he is called upon to represent ALPA in any dispute, he will do so to the best of his ability, fairly and fearlessly, relying on the influence and power of ALPA to protect him.

• He will regard himself as a debtor to his profession and ALPA, and will dedicate himself to their advancement. He will cooperate in the upholding of the profession by exchanging information and experience with his fellow pilots and by actively contributing to the work of professional groups and the technical press.

An Air Line Pilot the honor of his profession is dear, and he will remember that his own character and conduct reflect honor or dishonor upon the profession.

• He will be a good citizen of his country, state, and community, taking an active part in their affairs, especially those dealing with the improvement of aviation facilities and the enhancement of air safety.

• He will conduct all his affairs in a manner that reflects credit on himself and his profession.

• He will remember that to his neighbors, friends, and acquaintances he represents both the profession and ALPA, and that his actions represent to them the conduct and character of all members of the profession and ALPA.

• He will realize that nothing more certainly fosters prejudices against and deprives the profession of its high public esteem and confidence than do breaches in the use of alcohol.

• He will not publish articles, give interviews, or permit his name to be used in any manner likely to bring discredit to another pilot, the airline industry, the profession, or ALPA.

• He will continue to keep abreast of aviation developments so that his skill and judgment, which heavily depend on such knowledge, may be of the highest order.

Having Endeavored to his utmost to faithfully fulfill the obligations of the ALPA Code of Ethics and Canons for the Guidance of Air Line Pilots, a pilot may consider himself worthy to be called... an AIRLINE PILOT.

APPENDIX

Appendix D-1

October 26, 1978

THE STRAIGHT BULL SHEET
A PUBLICATION OF THE TXI MEC

FROM THE CHAIRMAN:

Gentlemen:

Since we sent the following letter to the company the MEC has attended two weight and balance meetings. We are encouraged by what we have seen so far. We think for the first time the company has abandoned it's bandaid approach to the weight and balance and is willing to make the necessary corrections to resolve the problems.

The following letter is one that was sent to Mr. Cathell in September concerning the weight and balance problems that continue to occur.

September 21, 1978

Mr. E. J. Cathell, Jr.
Texas International Airlines Inc.

Dear Ed:

It is encouraging that the company has again stated it is going to correct the weight and balance problems; however, it's very hard for the pilot group to believe the company is sincere in this understanding for the following reasons.

This commitment by the MEcompany came only after the FAA became involved in a weight and balance incident at LFT. The MEcompany had brought an almost identical incident at LFT to the company's attention a few days earlier. Apparently there was no action taken to eliminate the problem until the FAA became involved. We must wonder to what extent the company's commitment is directed at placating the FAA.

We have seen the company go through an extensive weight and balance training program for the agents. We are surprised this training has not been done from our standpoint. Another weight and balance reliability in the field. The change in the weight and balance format has not eliminated many consideration amount of the errors. We suggest a change in the weight and balance format for operational balance forms - but will insure the crew is not receiving proper information from the weight and balance forms. We will bring this to the attention of the proposed weight and balance committee.

We are disappointed that we have not received an answer to our letter of July 18. We still think the suggestions presented in that letter should be implemented. In that letter, we still company to make a strong policy statement on weight and balance. We suggest that this statement be promulgated immediately. The other suggestion is to be taken seriously. In this endeavor, such policy flight department. We also suggest that you place a moratorium on the weight and balance meetings by the an acceptable components until the company establishes that the weight and balance reliability is at half weights and head wind components, the potential for company errors in effect the elimination of

Ed; when the company approached the pilot group about overspeed takeoffs and increased takeoff weight, it committed to correct the weight and balance problems. The company has not delivered are convinced that, therefore the MEC will discourage the use of overspeed takeoffs until we agent loading the baggage bins to sign stating how many bags are on board. This could put a temporary fix on our transfer baggage problems.

The MEC feels we have exhausted every avenue to solve this problem in-house. We hope this last effort will prove fruitful in a short period of time. If not, we will be forced to take additional steps to resolve this problem.

s/ J. F. McCartney

307

Appendix D-2

PAGE 2

The scheduled start-up date of the L.O.F.T. program is set for November 1, 1978. We have been in communication with NWA concerning this program as well as with the FAA. The NWA line pilots as well as the check pilots have told us that they are very much in favor of this program. They have had one bust in the two year history of their LOFT program.

The MEC has talked to Mr. McCabe and advised him that we felt as long as the FAA considered the LOFT program as a check it could never reach its full potential. The LOFT program cannot be changed by the check pilot. The failures that are programmed into the trip series are the same for all.

We have asked the company to furnish the pilots with a study guide and an outline of what would constitute a bust. At this time the best we can determine the only thing that would cause a bust would be breaking an FAR or exceeding structural limitations of the aircraft.

Remember crew concept! Please call ALPA and report on your impressions of the LOFT program after you ride.

The merger hearings will begin October 31, 1978. With a decision from the bull board due the first of April.

The Mexican controllers are still on strike. Crews flying into Mexico please be very cautious of your clearances. The MEC has asked the company to debrief every crew returning from Mexico. We hope that the information provided by the crew will be evaluated before the next flight is dispatched.

The following are highlights of the deregulation bill.

Free entry and exit at the end of 1981.

Until the end of 1981 the following conditions will exist:

Carriers will be able to protect one route per year.

Carriers will be able to make one entry per year.

The most immediate effect we will see is in the dormant route authority rules. A route where only one is operating and another carrier has authority but is not operating under the deregulation bill the give the route to the first carrier that applies.

Where two or more carriers are operating a route and another carrier had the route authority but is not operating under this rule the company that is a willing applicant it is consistent with public necessity requirements. Our IAH-DFW route falls under this rule. Braniff has this route authority that they are not operating.

J. F. McCartney

N O T I C E !

The MEC will be in MIA for the ALPA Board of Directors Meeting the first two weeks of November. In our absence if you have a problem, call one of the following pilots. They will be able to get in touch with us.

Al Kelly   358 6184
Gary Konzine   443 6256
Ray Hornsley   293 6254
Ray Priest   367 0353

APPENDIX

Appendix D-3

THE SCHEDULING COMMITTEE:

Pilots with regular bids may now listen to the charter tape recording, then call scheduling and bid for a charter. In the past, charter bid holders and reserve pilots could use the tape recorder system but regular bid holders had to go to the crew room to bid.

Eventually all charter information and bidding will be done by phone, but for now, until the company can install better taping equipment, all pilots can bid for charters by phone or use the bid sheets in the crew room.

Some pilots on the short board for the month of August and September, 1978, were paid for trips they could have flown but did not due to scheduling problems. Those who feel they are not being called when on the short board, please submit to the committee the information in writing.

The company has ruled that anytime a crew waves a legal rest break to operate a trip on schedule it will be paid as one four hour average day instead of two. It is up to you whether you elect to do this or not if you will be more than 15 hours on duty. If you do wave your legal rest, go ahead and file for two 4:00 average days on the yellow forms and if the company should choose to deny the claim then we will file a grievance.

L. A. Lowe
Mike Wood

FROM THE SECRETARY-TREASURER:

Gentlemen, I know that many of you have questions concerning the merger assessment and how the money is being handled. I enclose the following figures in the hope that they will answer most of your questions.

At the time the company announced its acquisition plans there was $8,121.09 in the old merger fund. $5,000 of that was paid to Needham and Associates in the form of a retainer. The law firm bills us monthly and is reimbursed from the retainer. When the retainer is used, another retainer is sent. We have had legal expenses to date of $10,000 through Oct. 1 and an additional $1,089.39 into the current fund. The old merger... and has been used and we are at $1,089.39 into the current fund.

So far we have collected $36,625.00 of the current assessment which represents 71% of the pilot group that has paid. I would like to request that those of you who have not paid please do so.

The money is in a savings account and is drawing interest. That portion that is not used will be returned with interest.

Through the end of August, we have had expenditures amounting to $28,269.53 from the MEC Controllable Budget which leaves $12,087.47 remaining in the budget for operations through the remainder of the year which amounts to a monthly budget of $3,021.87.

Through the first of October, we have all moved into a different office in the same building. It is on the same floor and the new number is but suite 2025. The phone number and mailing address are unchanged.

I trust that those who have a phone received the new address and phone list which the MEC put out in October. Please check that your address and phone number are correct and advise us if not so that we can make the appropriate changes.

We are leaving for the Board of Directors meeting the 1st part of November and when we return we will be contacting those who have not paid the assessment to determine when they can pay.

Respectfully,

F. D. Self

309

Appendix E

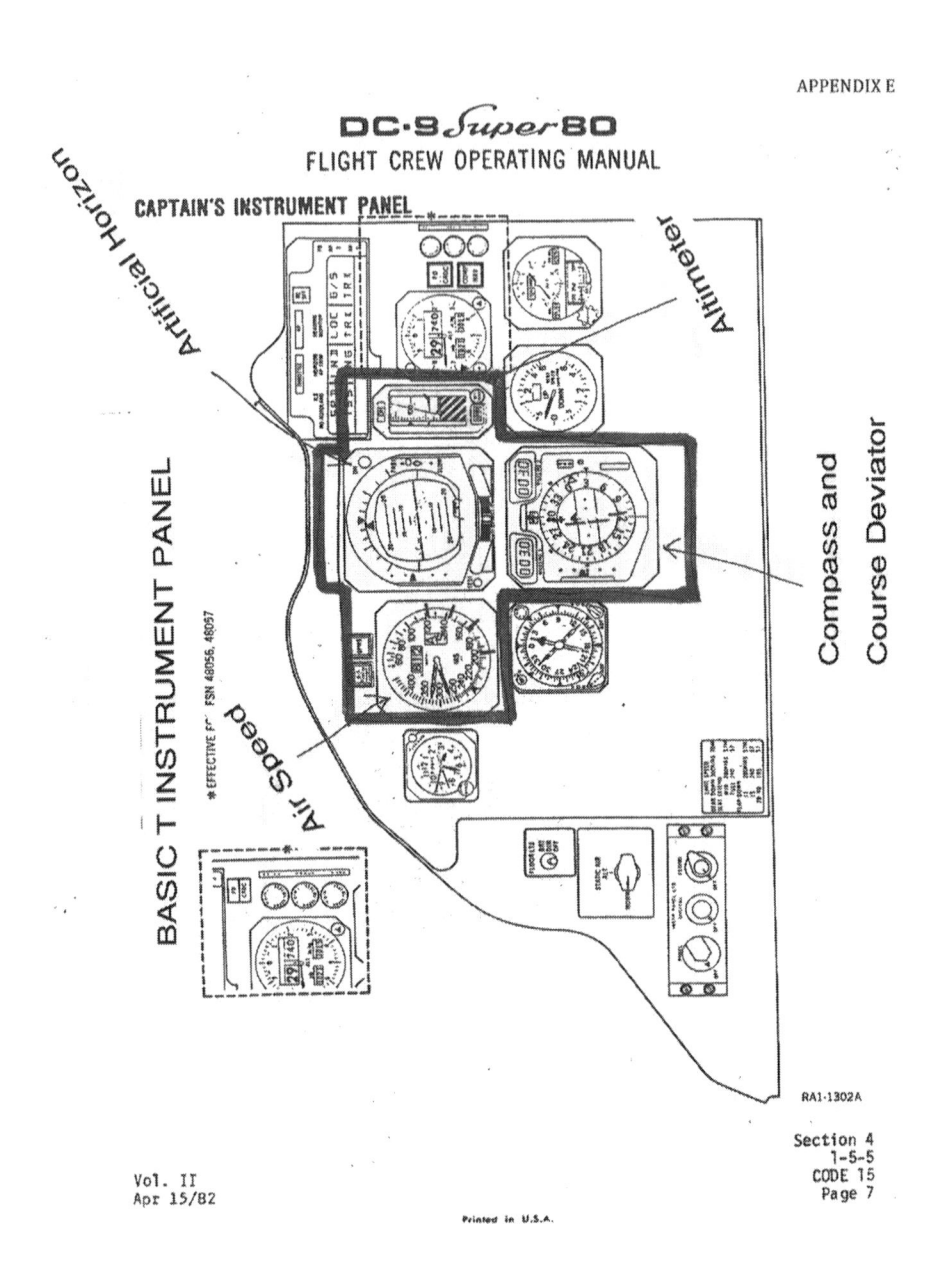

APPENDIX

Appendix F-1

Jim McCartney
Treatment for Pancreatic Cancer
CA 19-9 Tumor Markers

No.	Date	Tumor Marker	Test Value	Regular Range	Abnormal	Where	Chemo
1	08/30/10	Cancer Antigen 19-9	22,635	0-35	H	Indianapolis	
2	09/13/10	Cancer Antigen 19-9	16,918	0-35	H	Indianapolis*	FOLFIRINOX
3	10/04/10	Cancer Antigen 19-9	4,494	0-35	H	IMA Bloomington	09/01/10 - 01/26/11
4	11/01/10	Cancer Antigen 19-9	773	0-35	H	IMA Bloomington	
5	12/01/10	Cancer Antigen 19-9	329	0-35	H	IMA Bloomington	
6	12/22/10	Cancer Antigen 19-9	292	0-35	H	IMA Bloomington	
7	01/10/11	Cancer Antigen 19-9	224	0-35	H	IMA Bloomington	
8	03/16/11	Cancer Antigen 19-9	337	0-35	H	Premier Health Bloomington	THERASPHERE INFUSIONS
9	03/31/11	Cancer Antigen 19-9	344	0-35	H	IMA Bloomington	02/25/11 - 05/25/11
10	04/14/11	Cancer Antigen 19-9	541	0-35	H	IMA Bloomington	
*	05/10/11	Cancer Antigen 19-9	972	0-36	H	Johns Hopkins Hospital*	
11	05/31/11	Cancer Antigen 19-9	3,385	0-35	H	IMA Bloomington	GEMZAR & Abraxane
*	06/22/11	Cancer Antigen 19-9	1,217	0-36	H	Johns Hopkins Hospital*	05/31/11 - 08/12/11
13	07/01/11	Cancer Antigen 19-9	1,324	0-35	H	IMA Bloomington	
14	07/15/11	Cancer Antigen 19-9	685	0-35	H	IMA Bloomington	
15	07/29/11	Cancer Antigen 19-9	474	0-35	H	IMA Bloomington	
16	08/30/11	Cancer Antigen 19-9	272	0-35	H	IMA Bloomington	GEMZAR & Tarceva
17	09/27/11	Cancer Antigen 19-9	425	0-35	H	IMA Bloomington	08/30/11 to Present
18	10/25/11	Cancer Antigen 19-9	1,231	0-35	H	IMA Bloomington	
19	11/08/11	Cancer Antigen 19-9	2,238	0-35	H	IMA Bloomington	
20	12/07/11	Cancer Antigen 19-9	7,425	0-35	H	IMA Bloomington	
21	12/21/11	Cancer Antigen 19-9	8,394	0-35	H	IMA Bloomington	GEMZAR & Xeloda
22	01/12/12	Cancer Antigen 19-9	3,927	0-35	H	IMA Bloomington	
						*In Tests Section	

Appendix F-2

Jim McCartney
Treatment for Pancreatic Cancer
Chemo Treatment and Diagnostic Tests

No.	Date	Treatment	Where	Comment
1	08/12/10	CT Abd, Pelvis	SIRA Imaging Center	3.2 cm pancreatic tail mass; more than 20 liver masses; Cholecystolithlasis (gallstone).
2	08/16/10	Biopsy of Liver	Bloomington Hospital	Fine needle aspiration: malignant cells present from adenocarcinoma.
3	08/24/10	CT PET	SIRA Imaging Center	Impression: abnormal increased metabolic activity involves multiple liver metastases and mass in body of pancreas, extending posteriorly into pancreatic fat, consistent with clinical history of pancreatic carcinoma.
4	08/26/10	CT PET, Skull-Thigh	Indianapolis	Impression: 1. 3.4 x 3.1 cm ill-defined pancreatic mass at the junction of the body and tail. Abuts the superior mesenteric artery without encasement. There is encasement of the splenic vein with partial thrombosis. Mass extends posteromedially with loss of normal fat plane of the adjacent left adrenal gland. 2/ Multiple (greater than 20) hypoattenuating hypermetabolic lesions in right and left hepatic lobes. Findings compatible with hepatic metastatic disease. 3. There is no hypermetabolic retroperitoneal or peripancreatic lymphadenopathy. There is a 1.5 x 2.6 cm non-FDG-avid celiac axis lymph node. Test prior to blind clinical trial of gemcitabine with Abraxane. Excluded because of increase in bilirubin count.
5	08/29/10	CT Thorax, Abd, Pelvis	SIRA Imaging Center	Impression: 1. No evidence of metastatic disease in the thorax. Focal atelectasis involved the lower aspect of the right middle lobe and basilar segments of the right lower lbe. 2. CT of abdomen shows there has been a significant increase in the amount of ascites and now infiltrative changes involve the root of the mesentery and omentum consistent with progression of peritoneal carcinomatosis. 3. The size and number of liver metastases and the size of the primary tumor in the body of the pancreas have not significantly changed.
5A	08/31/10	Chest Port Placement	Indianapolis	Impression: Successful right internal jugular vein 8 French CT-injectable AngioDynamics Smart Port chest port placement. Accessed with a Huber needle for immediate use. Follow-up in Interventional Radiology Clinic or with referring physician for incision check in -10 days. Dr. David M. Agarwal, ordered by Dr. Chiorean.
6	09/01/10	FOLFIRINOX - 1	Indianapolis	CHEMO: Recommended by Dr. Chiorean, M.D. Anderson Hospital, Johns Hopkins Hospital. Includes: Oxaliplatin IV 165 mg over 2 hours concurrent with Leucovorin IV 776 mg over 2 hours; Irinotecan IV 349 mg over 90 minutes; 5FU IV 776 mg in IVpush, 5FU IV pump over 46 hours. Pre-meds include Aloxi 0.25 mg with Decadron 10 mg IV and Atropine 0.4 mg IV. Neulasta shot given day after chemo. Weight: 192 pounds.
6	09/13/10	FOLFIRINOX	Indianapolis	*CHEMO CANCELLED DUE TO WBC COUNT AT 400.* Shot of Neupogen and IV of Vancomycin.
6	09/20/10	FOLFIRINOX - 2	Bloomington	CHEMO
6	10/04/10	FOLFIRINOX - 3	Bloomington	CHEMO
6	10/18/10	FOLFIRINOX - 4	Bloomington	CHEMO

APPENDIX

Appendix F-3

Jim McCartney
Treatment for Pancreatic Cancer
ChemoTreatment and Diagnostic Tests

No.	Date	Treatment	Where	Comment
7	10/25/10	CT Chest, Abd, Pelvis	SIRA Imaging Center	Impression: 1. Interval decrease in size of mass in pancreatic tail as well as decrease in size of multiple hepatic metastases, decrease in adenopathy in gastrohepatic ligament region, findings consistent with response to therapy. 2. Chronic invasion of the splenic vein by the patient's pancreatic tail mass. 3. Stable left renal cysts. 4. Cholelithiasis.
8	10/27/10	Chest AP bedside	Bloomington Hospital	Impression: No active intrathoracic process.
6	11/01/10	FOLFIRINOX - 5	Bloomington Hospital	CHEMO - weight loss of 20 pounds.
8	11/07/10	Chest x-ray	Bloomington Hospital	Impression: No acute cardiopulmonary process.
8	11/08/10	Comparison: CTs Thorax, Abd, Pelvis on 8/12/10 and 8/24/10	Bloomington Hospital	Comparison by John Alexander MD of CTs on 8/12/10 and 8/24/10. Impression: 1. Interval decrease in the size of the patient's mass within the pancreatic tail, as well as decrease in the size of multiple hepatic metastases. There has also been a decrease in the adenopathy in the gastrohepatic ligament region. The findings are consistent with a response to therapy. 2. Chronic invasion of the splenic vein by the patient's pancreatic tail mass. 3. Stable left renal cysts. 4. Cholelithiasis (gallstone).
8	11/08/10	Hospital Admission	Bloomington Hospital	Admitted for extreme weakness, nausea, vomiting, diarrhea.
8	11/11/10	Operative Report on Esophagogastroduodenoscopy with biopsy.	Bloomington Hospital	Impression: 1. Enteritis. This would certainly explain his dysmotility which would result in vomiting as well as diarrhea. 2. Etiology undertain at this point, status post biopsy. I do not believe a GJ tube would be the right thing here as all it would end up doing would be just giving him lots of diarrhea. If support is needed, he would be better off using hyperalimentation. Dr. Ghosh
8	11/11/10	Pathology Report from endoscopic exam by Dr. Ghosh	Bloomington Hospital	Diagnosis: Small intestine biopsy: Ulceration with marked acute and chronic inflammation and reactive changes of intestinal epithelium. Negative for evidence of Cytomegalic Virus (CMV) infection. Negative for malignancy.
8	11/13/10	Chest x-ray & arm	Bloomington Hospital	Impression: PICC line appears to be in good position.
6	11/15/10	FOLFIRINOX - 6	Bloomington Hospital	CHEMO
8	11/15/10	Chest x-ray bedside	Bloomington Hospital	Impression: PICC line in place and venous port in place. Otherwise negative chest.
8	11/13/10	PICC line placement	Bloomington Hospital	Venous port with two lumens with caps.
8	11/18/10	Fluoroscopy	Bloomington Hospital	Admitted 11/08/10; fluoro of digestive system. Dx: Jejunitis
8	11/20/10	Esophagogastroduodenoscopy with percutaneous endoscopic gastrojejunostomy placed.	Bloomington Hospital	Impression: Percutaneous endoscopic gastrojejunostomy tube (PEG) placement with removal of the nasojejunal tube. Dr. Ghosh was requested to facilitate a G-tube since Medicare had denied his intravenous hyperalimentation (TPN) at home.

313

Appendix F-4

Jim McCartney
Treatment for Pancreatic Cancer
ChemoTreatment and Diagnostic Tests

No.	Date	Treatment	Where	Comment
8	11/29/10	Discharge Summary	Bloomington Hospital	Hospital course: Admitted to hospital with severe diarrhea, anorexia and weight loss. He was placed on bowel rest. His electrolyte abnormalities were corrected. He was started on total parenteral nutrition (TPN). He had an EGD that showed severe distal duodenum and proximal jejunum inflammation. Despite this, Medicare denied home TPN and the patient had to undergo a nasal jejunostomy tube placement, followed by PEG tube placement and enteral feedings. He had severe diarrhea on Osmolite which continued on an elemental formula resulting in up to 15 to 20 diarrheal episodes a day. Under the circumstances, his tube feedings were stopped and the patient resumed TPN. Diarrhea continued unabated for several days, presumably due to the recurrent inflammation of the bowel, predominantly thought to be due to the tube feedings but potentially exacerbated by his chemotherapy as well. The patient did get FOLFIRINOX chemotherapy during this hospitalization. There was actual improvement in the jejunitis on TPN despite the administration of the chemotherapy. He was due for chemo on the day of discharge but continued to have thrombocytopenia so it was delayed. The hospitalization was prolonged by 11 days due to Medicare's insistence that we torture him with tube feedings to prove that his severe jejunitis would be exacerbated by this therapy as predicted by all of the doctors who had seen this patient and been involved in his care. I would point out that this cost more money than the TPN for 3 months would have cost in the first place and resulted in total frustration and depression of the patient and his wife.
6	12/01/10	FOLFIRINOX - 7	Bloomington	CHEMO: Dosage adjusted to weight.
8	12/06/10	Dehydration, fainting	Bloomington	Pt to Infusion Center for Neupogen, did not want IVF, was feeling "fine." When walking to exit, he felt lightheaded and sat down against the wall. He was assisted by Dr. Trueblood and seen by her in the WIC. He was pale, BP 106/64, taken to bedroom in Infusion Center, blood drawn, gave IV and pt felt better.
6	12/13/10	FOLFIRINOX	Bloomington	CHEMO: Cancelled because platelets too low.
6	12/27/10	FOLFIRINOX - 8	Bloomington	CHEMO
9	12/30/10	Transthoracic Echocardiogram	Bloomington	Impression: Normal left and right ventricular systolic function. Initial mild regurgitation; mildly sclerotic aortic valve with mild aortic regurgitation; no aortic stenosis. Trivial tricuspid regurgitation with minimal pulmonary hypertension. No pericardial effusion.
10	01/03/11	CT Thorax, Abd. Pelvis	SIRA Imaging Center	Impression: Decrease in size and number of hepatic metastases since 10/25/10. Small amount of ascites in abdomen and pelvis is new. CT findings suspicious for a diffuse colitis.
6	01/10/11	FOLFIRINOX	Bloomington	CHEMO: Cancelled because platelets too low.
6	01/12/11	FOLFIRINOX - 9	Bloomington	CHEMO
8	01/19/11	ER - weakness, unable to tolerate p.o. liquids	Bloomington Hospital	Short Stay Summary: Patient admitted for severe weakness and to initiate IV fluid hydration and patient will followup with Dr. Dayton early next week. Dr. Koneru.

APPENDIX

Appendix F-5

Jim McCartney
Treatment for Pancreatic Cancer
Chemo Treatment and Diagnostic Tests

No.	Date	Treatment	Where	Comment
	01/21/11	PEG removed	Bloomington Hospital	From notes on Virginia's calendar
6	01/26/11	FOLFIRINOX - 10	Bloomington	CHEMO - Added Sandostatin in R. hip.
6A	02/02/11	MRI Abdomen	John Hopkins Hospital	Findings: Spiculated mass in tail of pancreas 1.9 x 3.4 cm in size ... Segment of splenic artery is encased by the pancreatic mass, with associated luminal narrowing of the artery. Numerous (at least 15) intermediate T2 hyperintense lesions scattered in both the right and left hepatic lobes, more numerous in the right hepatic lobe, hypovascular relative to the surrounding hepatic parenchyma, compatible with hepatic metastases ... Largest measures 2.1 x 1.8 cm at the hepatic dome. Second largest lesion measures 1.6 x 1.3 cm ... Other lesions are small in size while others are bigger when compared to the ... [Page 2 of report is missing]
11	02/25/11	Radioembolization	John Hopkins Hospital	TheraSpheres infused into right lobe of liver by Dr. Geschwind. TheraSpheres consist of million sof tiny glass beads containing radioactive yttrium-90. They are injected into the hepatic artery of the liver through a small flexible tube known as a catheter. The tiny radioactive glass beads flow directly into the liver tumor via its own blood vessels and become permanently lodged in the small blood vessels of the tumor. The radiation destroys the tumor cells from within the tumor, with minimal impact to the surrounding healthy liver tissue. The radioactive microspheres will continue to emit radiation over the course of several weeks after TheraSphere treatment and radiation levels will decrease to insignificant levels. TheraSphere treatment is referred to as radioembolization or selective internal radiation therapy (SIRT).

Appendix F-6

Jim McCartney
Treatment for Pancreatic Cancer
Chemo Treatment and Diagnostic Tests

No.	Date	Treatment	Where	Comment
11	03/21/11	Consultation	John Hopkins Hospital	Dr. Cosgrove discussed further systemic therapy options after recent radioembolization. Problems/Diagnoses: Pancreatic cancer. As discusssed with Mr. McCartney in some detail at our Liver Cancer Multidisciplinary visit, he underwent very aggressive up-front therapy with FOLFIRINOX chemotherapy, which has been proven the most effective first-line regimen in pancreas cancer based on a most recent research. He has developed signifcant neuropathy symptoms, which has ot really impacted his daily activities, but are somewhat troubling and had significant jejunities and diarrhea with this regimen. He is now mostly recovered from his acute symptoms, but his neuropathy remains bothersome. Standrd approaches for a second-line chemotherapy in patients in whom we want to avoid oxaliplatin would be mostly based on gemcitabine. The only phase III data is for gemcitabine with Tarceva, both of which have moderate response rates and impacts. There is some earlier phase data for more aggressive gemcitabine-based combinations including the combination of gemcitabine, Taxotere, and Xeloda, which was developed at Columbia by Dr. Fine. This would certainly be a feasible option for him, although there is some risk of progressive neuropathy with the taxane. There is not really a standard approach in this case and I stressed to Mr. McCartney that he is under no obligation to get systemic therapy resumed in short order. He has no symptoms from his tumor His performance status is actually improving and we will wait and see how his scan looks tomorrow. I would not base treatment decision solely on a CA 19-9 tumor marker, and overall my advice would be to hold tight for the time being and see what kind of duration of response he gets from the radioembolization. If he does need to initiate therapy again, but I believe before he becomes particularly symptomatic or has a deteriorating performance status related to his tumor and the options would be obviously single-agent gemcitabine, gemcitabine with Tarceva, or gemcitabine, Taxotere, and Xeloda, which would be my preference if his performance status remains good. He will discuss further local therapy options with the Interventional Radiology team tomorrow (he may require further radioembolization depending on the area treated with his initial therapy) and will follow up with th elocal medical oncologist at home in Indiana. I have provided him with my contact details should further questions arise. I would be happy to touch base with him as clinical trials open throughout the year for which he may be eligible.
12	03/22/11	MRI Abdomen	John Hopkins Hospital	Impression: Increased number of necrotic appearing lesions in right lobe, more apparent in the portal venous phase. Stable size of two index lesions. Decreased size of pancreatic mass. Small perihepatic ascites along the right hepatic lobe. Followup of radioembolization of right lobe of liver on 2/25/11. Splenic vein is thrombosed. The pancreatic duct is dilated. Pancreatic mass measures 3.1 cm in largest dimension.

APPENDIX

Appendix F-7

Jim McCartney
Treatment for Pancreatic Cancer
Chemo Treatment and Diagnostic Tests

No.	Date	Treatment	Where	Comment
12A	03/28/11	CT Thorax, Abd, Pelvis	SIRA Imaging Center	Impression: 1. No evidence of metastatic disease in the chest. 2. NO change in size of pancreatic mass. 3. Most of the hepatic metastases are either unchanged or slightly smaller than they were on 1/3/11. There appears to be one new lesion in the left lobe of the liver, which cannot be identified retrospectively on the prior study, and it measures 1.0 cm. 4. Slight increase in the amount of ascites. 5. There is a single gallstone in the neck of the gallbladder with thickening of the gallbladder wall. The thickening represents a change as does the location of the gallstone. **This should be correlated with any clinical signs of acute or chronic cholecystitis.** 6. There has been a change in the appearance of the right lobe of the liver with the posterior segment becoming lower in attenuation and somewhat atrophic. The low-attenuation may represent some focal fatty infiltration.
13	05/10/11	MRI Abdomen	John Hopkins Hospital	Impression: 1. Index lesions: (stable) in size and (stable) in enhancement. 2. Non-index lesions: (increase) in size. 3. Other Findings: Pancreatic tail mass with splenic vein thrombosis. Small volume perihepatic ascites. Cholelithiasis (gall stone).
14	05/12/11	Ultrasound Abdomen Upper	SIRA Imaging Center	Impression: 1. Diffuse parenchymal abnormality in the right lobe of the liver compatible with the patient's treated metastatic disease. The appearance is grossly stable compared to the more recent previous CT on 4/25/11. 2. Scattered additional low density lesion seen in the liver on the recent CT are much less distinct on ultrasound. This may reflect isoechoic echotexture to the hepatic parenchyma or interval improvement. 3. Stable cholelithiasis or stable chronic gallbladder wall thickening. There is no new pericolecystic fluid to suggest acute cholecystitis. 4. Stable 3.1 cm pancreatic mass compatible with the patient's known pancreatic carcinoma. 5. Stable 3.9 cm left renal cyst.
15	05/25/11	Radioembolization	John Hopkins Hospital	TheraSpheres infused into left lobe of liver by Dr. Gesclwind
16	05/31/11	GEMZAR, ABRAXANE-1	Bloomington	CHEMO: Gemzar IV 1910mg over 100 minutes; Abraxane IV 239mg over 30 minutes. Premeds: Zofran 8mg and Decadron 10mg. Neulasta shot day after chemo.
16	06/17/11	GEMZAR, ABRAXANE-2	Bloomington	CHEMO
17	06/21/11	MRI Abdomen	John Hopkins Hospital	Impression: Overall increase in size and number of lesions in both lobes of liver compared to prior study. Striated Nephrogram right kidney which can be seen in setting of infection, correlate clinically. **[WAS ANYTHING DONE?]**
16	07/01/11	GEMZAR, ABRAXANE-3	Bloomington	CHEMO
16	07/15/11	GEMZAR, ABRAXANE-4	Bloomington	CHEMO
16	07/29/11	GEMZAR, ABRAXANE-5	Bloomington	CHEMO
16	08/12/11	GEMZAR, ABRAXANE-6	Bloomington	CHEMO
18	08/15/11	Ultrasound Abdomen	SIRA Imaging Center	Impression: Ascites has increased since 07/22/11.

Appendix F-8

Jim McCartney
Treatment for Pancreatic Cancer
Chemo Treatment and Diagnostic Tests

No.	Date	Treatment	Where	Comment
	08/29/11	CT Thorax, Abd, Pelvis	SIRA Imaging Center	Impression: No evidence of metastatic disease in the thorax. Focal atelectasis involves the lower aspect of the right middle lobe and basilar segments of the right lower lobe. CT of abd shows significant increase in the amount of ascites and now infiltrative changes involve the root of the mesentery and omentum consistent with progression of peritoneal carcinomatosis. The size and number of liver metastases and the size of the primary tumor in the body of the pancreas have not significantly changed.
16	08/30/11	GEMZAR & Tarceva - 1	Bloomington	CHEMO: Stopped Abraxane, Dr. Dayton prescribed Tarceva, 100 mg tablets, take one daily by mouth without food.
16	09/13/11	GEMZAR & Tarceva - 2	Bloomington	CHEMO
16	09/27/11	GEMZAR & Tarceva - 3	Bloomington	CHEMO
16	10/11/11	GEMZAR & Tarceva - 4	Bloomington	CHEMO
16	10/25/11	GEMZAR & Tarceva - 5	Bloomington	CHEMO
19	11/03/11	CT Chest, Abd, Pelvis	SIRA Imaging Center	Impression: 1. No evidence of metastatic disease in the chest. 2. Although there is a moderate to large amount of ascites in the abdomen and pelvis, it is slightly less than that seen on 08/29/2011. 3. No significant change in size of the residual soft tissue mass in the body of the pancreas. 4. Decrease in size of some of the hepatic metastases and no change in number. 5. There is some nodular soft tissue stranding in the mesenteric fat which may be a manifestation of peritoneal metastases, and this finding is stable.
20	11/08/11	GEMZAR & Tarceva - 6	Bloomington	CHEMO
	11/09/11	Neulasta Shot	Bloomington	Post-CHEMO shot
	11/22/11	GEMZAR & Tarceva - 7	Bloomington	CHEMO
	11/21/11	Neulasta Shot	Bloomington	Post-CHEMO shot
	12/07/11	GEMZAR & Tarceva - 8	Bloomington	CHEMO
	12/08/11	Neulasta Shot	Bloomington	Post-CHEMO shot

APPENDIX

Appendix F-9

Jim McCartney
Treatment for Pancreatic Cancer
Chemo Treatment and Diagnostic Tests

No.	Date	Treatment	Where	Comment
21	12/20/11	PT scan	Bloomington	Impression: 1. Since 08/24/10, the liver has shrunken and has multiple scars and there is now a significant amount of ascites and increased linear and nodular markings in the mesenteric and omental fat. It is difficult to determine how much of the ascites is due to liver disease versus peritoneal carcinomatosis. There are several implants in the abdomen (antrum of stomach, omentum, pouch of Douglas, and left side of rectum). 2. The liver had a mixed response. Some of the large lesions seen on 08/24/10 have responded favorably. There are multiple liver lesions however, at least some of which have increased in size since 08/24/10 as described above. The distortion of the liver makes it difficult to compare all of the liver lesions. 3. No pulmonary parenchymal nodules are seen. There are multiple coarse linear opacities in the basilar segments of the lower lobes consistent with foci of subsegmental atelectasis or scarring developing since 08/24/10. ADDENDUM Impression: Compared with 11/03/11 CT scan, the amount of ascites has increased and the implants on the anterior antrum of the stomach and in the omentum appear larger by CT than on 11/03/11. Bibasilar focal atelectatic changes have progressed.
22	12/21/11	GEMZAR & Xeloda - 1	Bloomington	CHEMO: GEMZAR & Xeloda Note: Xeloda started by mouth on Dec.24th
	12/22/11	Neulasta Shot	Bloomington	Post-CHEMO shot
	01/10/12	Paracentesis -2	Bloomington Hospital	Removed 4 liters of fluid from abdomen. One and a half liter remains in abdomen. Doctor suggests standing order for paracentesis so Jim or Virginia may call when he becomes uncomfortable. Second time for this procedure. Last time was four months ago.
	01/12/12	GEMZAR & Xeloda - 2	Bloomington	CHEMO: GEMZAR & Xeloda.
	01/13/12	Neulasta Shot	Bloomington	Post-CHEMO shot
	01/19/12	Chemo cancelled	Bloomington	Cancelled because Jim had the Neulasta shot after the previous chemo and it should have been scheduled after the second chemo in the two-week treatment period.
	01/23/12	Paracentesis -3	Bloomington Hospital	Removed 6.5 liters of fluid from abdomen. Set up schedule to repeat every Monday.
	01/27/12	GEMZAR & Xeloda - 3	Bloomington	CHEMO: GEMZAR & Xeloda.
	01/30/12	Paracentesis - 4	Bloomington Hospital	Removed 4 liters of fluid from abdomen.

Appendix F-10

Jim McCartney
Treatment for Pancreatic Cancer
Blood Tests for Chemo

No.	Date	Test Name	Test Value	Regular Range	Abnormal	Where	Comment
2	08/26/10	Alkaline Phosphatase	187		H	Indianapolis	For clinical trial of Abraxane
3	08/27/10	Alkaline Phosphatase	182	37 - 145	H	New York Lab/Indy	For clinical trial of Abraxane
2	08/30/10	Alkaline Phosphatase	183		H	Indianapolis	For clinical trial of Abraxane
4	09/13/10	Alkaline Phosphatase	222		H	Indianapolis	CHEMO: FOLFIRINOX 09/01/10 - 01/26/11
5	09/20/10	Alkaline Phosphatase	242	38 - 126	H	Bloomington	
7	10/04/10	Alkaline Phosphatase	246	38 - 126	H	Bloomington	
8	10/18/10	Alkaline Phosphatase	202	38 - 126	H	Bloomington	
11	11/01/10	Alkaline Phosphatase	164	38 - 126	H	Bloomington	
12	11/29/10	Alkaline Phosphatase	267	32 - 120	H	Bloomington Hospital	
13	12/01/10	Alkaline Phosphatase	372	38 - 126	H	Bloomington	
8*	12/06/10	Alkaline Phosphatase	725	32 - 120	H	Bloomington Hospital	
14	12/08/10	Alkaline Phosphatase	650	38 - 126	H	Bloomington	
15	12/09/10	Alkaline Phosphatase	539	38 - 126	H	Bloomington	
17	12/13/10	Alkaline Phosphatase	493	32 - 120	H	Bloomington Hospital	
20	12/27/10	Alkaline Phosphatase	220	38 - 126	H	Bloomington	
21	01/03/11	Alkaline Phosphatase	219	32 - 120	H	Bloomington Hospital	
23	01/10/11	Alkaline Phosphatase	206	32 - 120	H	Bloomington Hospital	
25	01/17/11	Alkaline Phosphatase	236	32 - 120	H	Bloomington Hospital	
26	01/24/11	Alkaline Phosphatase	185	32 - 120	H	Bloomington Hospital	
28	02/08/11	Alkaline Phosphatase	279	38 - 126	H	Bloomington	
29	02/14/11	Alkaline Phosphatase	314	38 - 126	H	Bloomington	
30	02/21/11	Alkaline Phosphatase	315	32 - 120	H	Bloomington Hospital	
31	02/28/11	Alkaline Phosphatase	438	32 - 120	H	Bloomington Hospital	
32	03/07/11	Alkaline Phosphatase	607	32 - 120	H	Bloomington Hospital	Dayton thinks increase due to procedure at Johns Hopkins
33	03/14/11	Alkaline Phosphatase	592	32 - 120	H	Bloomington Hospital	
35	03/22/11	Alkaline Phosphatase	589	30 - 120	H	Johns Hopkins Hospital	
36	05/10/11	Alkaline Phosphatase	402	30 - 120	H	Johns Hopkins Hospital	
37	05/31/11	Alkaline Phosphatase	296	38 - 126	H	Bloomington	CHEMO: GEMZAR & Abraxane 05/31/11 - 08/12/11
41	06/21/11	Alkaline Phosphatase	356	30 - 120	H	Johns Hopkins Hospital	
46	08/12/11	Alkaline Phosphatase	277	38 - 126	H	Bloomington	
47	08/15/11	Alkaline Phosphatase	251	38 - 126	H	Bloomington	CHEMO: GEMZAR & Tarceva 08/30/11 - 12/07/11
54	12/07/11	Alkaline Phosphatase	189	38 - 126	H	Bloomington	
55	12/21/11	Alkaline Phosphatase	200	38 - 126	H	Bloomington	CHEMO: GEMZAR & Xeloda 12/21/11 to Present
2	08/26/10	Glucose	95	70 - 99		Indianapolis	For clinical trial of Abraxane
3	08/27/10	Glucose	90	56 - 115		New York Lab/Indy	For clinical trial of Abraxane
2	08/30/10	Glucose	101	70 - 99	H	Indianapolis	For clinical trial of Abraxane
4	09/13/10	Glucose	96	51 - 99		Indianapolis	CHEMO: FOLFIRINOX 09/01/10 - 01/26/11
5	09/20/10	Glucose	111	51 - 99	H	Bloomington	
7	10/04/10	Glucose	127	51 - 99	H	Bloomington	
8*	10/18/10	Glucose	140	51 - 99	H	Bloomington	
9	10/27/10	Glucose	119	70 - 139		Bloomington Hospital	
11	11/01/10	Glucose	105	51 - 99	H	Bloomington	
12	11/29/10	Glucose	214	70 - 139	H	Bloomington Hospital	
8	12/06/10	Glucose	110	70 - 139		Bloomington Hospital	

APPENDIX

Appendix F-12

Jim McCartney
Treatment for Pancreatic Cancer
Blood Tests for Chemo

No.	Date	Test Name	Test Value	Regular Range	Abnormal	Where	Comment
20	12/27/10	Platelets	196	150 - 450		Bloomington	
21	01/03/11	Platelets	68	130 - 430	L	Bloomington Hospital	
22	01/05/11	Platelets	27	150 - 450	L	Bloomington	
23	01/10/11	Platelets	67	150 - 450	L	Bloomington	
24	01/12/11	Platelets	114	150 - 450	L	Bloomington	
25	01/17/11	Platelets	59	130 - 430	L	Bloomington Hospital	
26	01/24/11	Platelets	47	130 - 430	L	Bloomington Hospital	
27	01/26/11	Platelets	116	150 - 450	L	Bloomington	
28	02/08/11	Platelets	135	130 - 430		Bloomington Hospital	
29	02/14/11	Platelets	44	130 - 430	L	Bloomington Hospital	
30	02/21/11	Platelets	49	130 - 430	L	Bloomington Hospital	
31	02/28/11	Platelets	141	130 - 430		Bloomington Hospital	THERASPHERE INFUSIONS:
32	03/07/11	Platelets	172	130 - 430		Bloomington Hospital	02/25/11 right lobe
33	03/14/11	Platelets	150	130 - 430		Bloomington Hospital	03/25/11 left lobe
34	03/16/11	Platelets	123	140 - 440	L	Bloomington	
35	03/22/11	Platelets	106	150 - 350	L	Johns Hopkins Hospital	
35A	03/28/11	Platelets	84	130 - 430	L	Bloomington Hospital	
36	05/10/11	Platelets	165	150 - 350		Johns Hopkins Hospital	
37	05/31/11	Platelets	131	150 - 450	L	Bloomington	CHEMO: GEMZAR & Abraxane 05/31/11 - 08/12/11
38	06/07/11	Platelets	65	150 - 450	L	Bloomington	
39	06/14/11	Platelets	124	150 - 450	L	Bloomington	
40	06/17/11	Platelets	185	150 - 450		Bloomington	
41	06/21/11	Platelets	147	150 - 350	L	Johns Hopkins Hospital	
42	07/01/11	Platelets	133	150 - 450	L	Bloomington	
43	07/15/11	Platelets	164	150 - 450		Bloomington	
44	07/21/11	Platelets	54	150 - 450	L	Bloomington	
45	07/29/11	Platelets	140	150 - 450	L	Bloomington	
46	08/12/11	Platelets	148	150 - 450	L	Bloomington	
48	08/30/11	Platelets	192	150 - 450		Bloomington	CHEMO: GEMZAR & Tarceva 08/30/11 to 12/07/11
49	09/13/11	Platelets	123	150 - 450	L	Bloomington	
50	09/27/11	Platelets	187	150 - 450		Bloomington	
51	10/11/11	Platelets	150	150 - 450		Bloomington	
52	10/25/11	Platelets	141	150 - 450		Bloomington	
53	11/08/11	Platelets	152	150 - 450		Bloomington	
	11/22/11	Platelets		150 - 450		Bloomington	
54	12/07/11	Platelets	233	150 - 450		Bloomington	
55	12/21/11	Platelets	183	150 - 450		Bloomington	CHEMO: GEMZAR & Xeloda 12/21/11 to Present
56	12/28/11	Platelets	120	150 - 450	L	Bloomington	
57	01/12/12	Platelets	289	150 - 450		Bloomington	
1	07/30/10	RBC	4.95	4.00 - 6.10		Bloomington	Dr. LaFollette
2	08/26/10	RBC	5.01	4.6 - 6		Indianapolis	For clinical trial of Abraxane
3	08/27/10	RBC	5.14	4.50 - 5.90		New York Lab/Indv	For clinical trial of Abraxane
2	08/30/10	RBC	5.17	4.6 - 6		Indianapolis	For clinical trial of Abraxane
4	09/13/10	RBC	4.77	4.6 - 6		Indianapolis	CHEMO: FOLFIRINOX 09/01/11 - 01/26/11

Appendix F-13

Jim McCartney
Treatment for Pancreatic Cancer
Blood Tests for Chemo

No.	Date	Test Name	Test Value	Regular Range	Abnormal	Where	Comment
5	09/20/10	RBC	4.85	4.00 - 6.00		Bloomington	
6	09/24/10	RBC	4.92	4.00 - 6.00		Bloomington	
7	10/04/10	RBC	4.4	4.00 - 6.00		Bloomington	
8	10/18/10	RBC	4.53	4.00 - 6.00		Bloomington	
9	10/27/10	RBC	4.25	4.20 - 5.40		Bloomington Hospital	IV of saline and antibiotics. Atypical lymphocytes.
10	10/29/10	RBC	4.36	4.00 - 6.00		Bloomington	IV of saline at Infusion Center
11	11/01/10	RBC	4.29	4.00 - 6.00		Bloomington	CHEMO: FOLFIRINOX 09/01/11 - 01/26/11
12	11/29/10	RBC	2.89	4.20 - 5.40	L	Bloomington Hospital	
13	12/01/10	RBC	3.48	4.00 - 6.00	L	Bloomington	
8*	12/06/10	RBC	3.17	4.20 - 5.40	L	Bloomington	
14	12/08/10	RBC	2.89	4.00 - 6.00	L	Bloomington	
15	12/09/10	RBC	2.83	4.00 - 6.00	L	Bloomington	
16	12/10/10	RBC	2.7	4.00 - 6.00	L	Bloomington	
17	12/13/10	RBC	2.29	4.20 - 5.40	L	Bloomington Hospital	
18	12/15/10	RBC	2.67	4.00 - 6.00	L	Bloomington	
19	12/22/10	RBC	3.28	4.00 - 6.00	L	Bloomington	
20	12/27/10	RBC	3.2	4.00 - 5.00	L	Bloomington	
21	01/03/11	RBC	2.92	4.20 - 5.40	L	Bloomington Hospital	
22	01/05/11	RBC	2.43	4.00 - 6.00	L	Bloomington	
23	01/10/11	RBC	3.17	4.00 - 6.00	L	Bloomington	
24	01/12/11	RBC	3.24	4.00 - 6.00	L	Bloomington	
25	01/17/11	RBC	2.77	4.20 - 5.40	L	Bloomington Hospital	
26	01/24/11	RBC	2.83	4.20 - 5.40	L	Bloomington Hospital	
27	01/26/11	RBC	2.94	4.00 - 6.00	L	Bloomington	
28	02/08/11	RBC	2.88	4.20 - 5.40	L	Bloomington Hospital	
29	02/14/11	RBC	2.77	4.20 - 5.40	L	Bloomington Hospital	
30	02/21/11	RBC	2.69	4.20 - 5.40	L	Bloomington Hospital	
31	02/28/11	RBC	2.66	4.20 - 5.40	L	Bloomington Hospital	THERASPHERE INFUSIONS:
32	03/07/11	RBC	2.81	4.20 - 5.40	L	Bloomington Hospital	02/25/11 right lobe of liver
33	03/14/11	RBC	3.06	4.20 - 5.40	L	Bloomington Hospital	03/25/11 left lobe of liver
34	03/16/11	RBC	3.03	4.00 - 6.10	L	Bloomington	
35	03/22/11	RBC	3.2	4.50 - 5.90	L	Johns Hopkins Hospital	
35A	03/28/11	RBC	3.06	4.20 - 5.40	L	Bloomington Hospital	
36	05/10/11	RBC	3.95	4.50 - 5.90	L	Johns Hopkins Hospital	
37	05/31/11	RBC	3.74	4.00 - 6.00	L	Bloomington	CHEMO: GEMZAR & Abraxane 05/31/11 - 08/12/11
38	06/07/11	RBC	3.72	4.00 - 6.00	L	Bloomington	
39	06/14/11	RBC	3.69	4.00 - 6.00	L	Bloomington	
40	06/17/11	RBC	3.76	4.00 - 6.00	L	Bloomington	
41	06/21/11	RBC	3.84	4.50 - 5.90	L	Johns Hopkins Hospital	
42	07/01/11	RBC	3.43	4.00 - 6.00	L	Bloomington	
43	07/15/11	RBC	3.34	4.00 - 6.00	L	Bloomington	
44	07/21/11	RBC	3.11	4.00 - 6.00	L	Bloomington	
45	07/29/11	RBC	3.25	4.00 - 6.00	L	Bloomington	
46	08/12/11	RBC	3.21	4.00 - 6.00	L	Bloomington	
48	08/30/11	RBC	3.23	4.00 - 6.00	L	Bloomington	CHEMO: GEMZAR & Tarceva 08/30/11 to 12/07/11

APPENDIX

Appendix F-14

Jim McCartney
Treatment for Pancreatic Cancer
Blood Tests for Chemo

No.	Date	Test Name	Test Value	Regular Range	Abnormal	Where	Comment
49	09/13/11	RBC	3.29	4.00 - 6.00	L	Bloomington	
50	09/27/11	RBC	3.26	4.00 - 6.00	L	Bloomington	
51	10/11/11	RBC	3.19	4.00 - 6.00	L	Bloomington	
52	10/25/11	RBC	3.19	4.00 - 6.00	L	Bloomington	
53	11/08/11	RBC	3.16	4.00 - 6.00	L	Bloomington	
	11/22/11	RBC		4.00 - 6.00		Bloomington	
54	12/07/11	RBC	3.34	4.00 - 6.00	L	Bloomington	
55	12/21/11	RBC	3.35	4.00 - 6.00	L	Bloomington	CHEMO: GEMZAR & Xeloda 12/21/11 to Present
56	12/29/11	RBC	2.96	4.00 - 6.00	L	Bloomington	
57	01/12/12	RBC	3.36	4.00 - 6.00	L	Bloomington	
1	08/03/10	WBC	7.3	4.8 - 10.8		Bloomington	Dr. LaFollette
2	08/26/10	WBC	6.6	4.5 - 11.5		Indianapolis	For clinical trial of Abraxane
3	08/27/10	WBC	6.9	4.5 - 11.0		New York Lab/Indy	For clinical trial of Abraxane
2	08/30/10	WBC	6.9	4.5 - 11.5		Indianapolis	For clinical trial of Abraxane
4	09/13/10	WBC	1.8	4.5 - 11.5	L	Indianapolis	CHEMO: FOLFIRINOX 09/01/10 - 01/26/11
5	09/20/10	WBC	7.9	4.5 - 10.5		Bloomington	
6	09/24/10	WBC	53.4	4.5 - 10.5	H	Bloomington	
7	10/04/10	WBC	13.7	4.5 - 10.5	H	Bloomington	
8	10/18/10	WBC	10.7	4.5 - 10.5	H	Bloomington	
9	10/27/10	WBC	3.1	3.6 - 9.4		Bloomington Hospital	IV of saline and antibiotics. Atypical lymphocytes.
10	10/29/10	WBC	6.2	4.5 - 10.5		Bloomington	IV of saline at Infusion Center
11	11/01/10	WBC	11.9	4.5 - 10.4	H	Bloomington	CHEMO: FOLFIRINOX 09/01/10 - 01/26/11
12	11/29/10	WBC	5.2	3.6 - 9.4		Bloomington Hospital	
13	12/01/10	WBC	19.5	4.5 - 10.5	H	Bloomington	
8*	12/06/10	WBC	2.7	3.6 - 9.4	L	Bloomington	
14	12/08/10	WBC	5.4	4.5 - 10.5		Bloomington	
15	12/09/10	WBC	2	4.5 - 10.5	L	Bloomington	
16	12/10/10	WBC	1.6	4.5 - 10.5	L	Bloomington	
17	12/13/10	WBC	11	3.6 - 9.4	H	Bloomington Hospital	
18	12/15/10	WBC	9.5	4.5 - 10.5		Bloomington	
19	12/22/10	WBC	4.7	4.5 - 10.5		Bloomington	
20	12/27/10	WBC	4.2	4.5 - 10.5	L	Bloomington	
21	01/03/11	WBC	7.9	3.6 - 9.4		Bloomington Hospital	
22	01/05/11	WBC	6.2	4.5 - 10.5		Bloomington	
23	01/10/11	WBC	5.1	4.5 - 10.5		Bloomington	
24	01/12/11	WBC	5.4	4.5 - 10.5		Bloomington	
25	01/17/11	WBC	14.7	3.6 - 9.4	H	Bloomington Hospital	Schistocytes indicate possibility of a micro-angiopathic hemolytic process. Clinical correlation is suggested.
26	01/24/11	WBC	6.1	3.6 - 9.4		Bloomington Hospital	CHEMO: FOLFIRINOX 09/01/10 - 01/26/11
27	01/26/11	WBC	8.5	4.5 - 10.5		Bloomington	
28	02/08/11	WBC	12.8	3.6 - 9.4	H	Bloomington Hospital	
29	02/14/11	WBC	23.5	3.6 - 9.4	H	Bloomington Hospital	
30	02/21/11	WBC	8.5	3.6 - 9.4		Bloomington Hospital	Schistocytes. Clinical correlation is suggested.
31	02/28/11	WBC	6	3.6 - 9.4		Bloomington Hospital	THERASPHERE INFUSIONS 02/25/11 - 05/25/11

Appendix F-15

Jim McCartney
Treatment for Pancreatic Cancer
Blood Tests for Chemo

No.	Date	Test Name	Test Value	Regular Range	Abnormal	Where	Comment
32	03/07/11	WBC	4.1	3.6 - 9.4		Bloomington Hospital	Rare giant platelet seen. Schistocytes. Clinical correlation is suggested.
33	03/14/11	WBC	3.8	3.6 - 9.4		Bloomington Hospital	THERASPHERE INFUSIONS 02/25/11 - 05/25/11
34	03/16/11	WBC	3.3	4.8 - 10.8	L	Bloomington	02/25/11 left lobe of liver
35	03/22/11	WBC	3180	4500 - 11000	L	Johns Hopkins Hospital	05/25/11 right lobe of liver
35A	03/28/11	WBC	5	3.6 - 9.4		Bloomington Hospital	
26	05/10/11	WBC	3750	4500 - 11000	L	Johns Hopkins Hospital	
37	05/31/11	WBC	3.2	9.0 - 10.5	L	Bloomington	CHEMO: GEMZAR & Abraxane 05/31/11 - 08/12/11
38	06/07/11	WBC	1.2	4.5 - 10.5	L	Bloomington	
39	06/14/11	WBC	1.4	4.5 - 10.5	L	Bloomington	
40	06/17/11	WBC	2.1	4.5 - 10.5	L	Bloomington	
41	06/21/11	WBC	9420	4500 - 11000		Johns Hopkins Hospital	
42	07/01/11	WBC	7.7	4.5 - 10.5		Bloomington	
43	07/15/11	WBC	7.8	4.5 - 10.5		Bloomington	
44	07/21/11	WBC	6	4.5 - 10.5		Bloomington	
45	07/29/11	WBC	8.6	4.5 - 10.5		Bloomington	
46	08/12/11	WBC	9.4	4.5 - 10.5		Bloomington	
48	08/30/11	WBC	7.3	4.5 - 10.5		Bloomington	CHEMO: GEMZAR & Tarceva 08/30/11 to 12/07/11
49	09/13/11	WBC	8.2	4.5 - 10.5		Bloomington	
50	09/27/11	WBC	7.4	4.5 - 10.5		Bloomington	
51	10/11/11	WBC	9.1	4.5 - 10.5		Bloomington	
52	10/25/11	WBC	8	4.5 - 10.5		Bloomington	
53	11/08/11	WBC	7.9	4.5 - 10.5		Bloomington	
	11/22/11	WBC		4.5 - 10.5		Bloomington	
54	12/07/11	WBC	8.6	4.5 - 10.5		Bloomington	
55	12/21/11	WBC	8.7	4.5 - 10.5		Bloomington	CHEMO: GEMZAR & Xeloda 12/21/11 to Present
56	12/29/11	WBC	3	4.5 - 10.5	L	Bloomington	
57	01/12/12	WBC	10.4	4.5 - 10.5		Bloomington	

8* - In Chemo documents

Made in the USA
Charleston, SC
27 April 2012